Elements of Literature
Fourth Course

Holt Multicultural Reader

- Respond to and Analyze Texts
- Apply Reading Skills
- Develop Vocabulary and Practice Fluency

HOLT, RINEHART AND WINSTON
A Harcourt Education Company
Orlando • Austin • New York • San Diego • London

Copyright © by Holt, Rinehart and Winston

All rights reserved. No part of this publication may be reproduced or transmitted in any form or by any means, electronic or mechanical, including photocopy, recording, or any information storage and retrieval system, without permission in writing from the publisher.

Requests for permission to make copies of any part of the work should be mailed to the following address: Permissions Department, Holt, Rinehart and Winston, 10801 N. MoPac Expressway, Building 3, Austin, Texas 78759.

COVER
Front cover (inset): *Kit Carson Street* (detail), early twentieth century, by Victor Higgins (1884–1949). Oil on linen. (17 x 27 in.)
Museum of the Southwest, Midland, TX. Gift of Fred T. and Novadean Hogan

ELEMENTS OF LITERATURE, HOLT, and the **"Owl Design"** are trademarks licensed to Holt, Rinehart and Winston, registered in the United States of America and/or other jurisdictions.

Printed in the United States of America

If you have received these materials as examination copies free of charge, Holt, Rinehart and Winston retains title to the materials and they may not be resold. Resale of examination copies is strictly prohibited.

Possession of this publication in print format does not entitle users to convert this publication, or any portion of it, into electronic format.

ISBN 0-03-078596-0   2 3 4 5 179 09 08

Contents

To the Student xi
A Walk Through the Book xiii

• PART ONE •
READING LITERATURE 1

COLLECTION 1 Plot and Setting 2

Academic Vocabulary for Collection 1 3

Before You Read: Tony Went to the Bodega
but He Didn't Buy Anything 4
Literary Focus: Plot and Setting 4
Reading Skills: Reading a Narrative Poem 4

Martín Espada   Tony Went to the Bodega but He Didn't
Buy Anything .... POEM 5
Skills Practice: Plot Chart 9
Skills Review: Reading Comprehension 10

Before You Read: For My Sister Molly Who in the Fifties 11
Literary Focus: Conflict 11
Reading Skills: Making Inferences 11

Alice Walker   For My Sister Molly Who in the Fifties .... POEM 12
Skills Practice: Conflict Chart 17
Skills Review: Reading Comprehension 18

Before You Read: A Real-Live Blond Cherokee and
His Equally Annoyed Soul Mate 19
Literary Focus: Plot 19
Reading Skills: Cause and Effect 19
Vocabulary Development 20

Cynthia Leitich Smith   A Real-Live Blond Cherokee and
His Equally Annoyed Soul Mate .... SHORT STORY 21
Skills Practice: Story Map 30
Skills Review: Vocabulary and Comprehension 31

Contents   iii

COLLECTION 2 — Character ... 32

Academic Vocabulary for Collection 2 ... 33

Before You Read: Museum Indians ... 34
Literary Focus: Character—Describing a Person ... 34
Reading Skills: Making Inferences About Characters ... 34
Vocabulary Development ... 35

Susan Power — **Museum Indians** ... ESSAY ... 36
Skills Practice: Inference and Character Chart ... 41
Skills Review: Vocabulary and Comprehension ... 42

Before You Read: Super Unleaded ... 43
Literary Focus: Character and Motivation ... 43
Reading Skills: Reading Graphic Stories ... 43

Derek Kirk Kim — **Super Unleaded** ... GRAPHIC STORY ... 44
Skills Practice: Character Motivation Chart ... 50
Skills Review: Reading Comprehension ... 51

COLLECTION 3 — Narrator and Voice ... 52

Academic Vocabulary for Collection 3 ... 53

Before You Read: Sweet Potato Pie ... 54
Literary Focus: First-Person Point of View and Voice ... 54
Reading Skills: Identifying Cause and Effect ... 54
Vocabulary Development ... 55

Eugenia Collier — **Sweet Potato Pie** ... SHORT STORY ... 56
Skills Practice: Voice Chart ... 70
Skills Review: Vocabulary and Comprehension ... 71

Before You Read: Golden Glass ... 72
Literary Focus: Point of View and Setting ... 72
Reading Skills: Making Inferences ... 72
Vocabulary Development ... 73

Alma Luz Villanueva — **Golden Glass** ... SHORT STORY ... 74
Skills Practice: Point of View and Setting Chart ... 80
Skills Review: Vocabulary and Comprehension ... 81

COLLECTION 4 **Comparing Themes** 82

Academic Vocabulary for Collection 4 83

       Before You Read: Learning to Read and Write 84
       Literary Focus: Theme and Conflict 84
       Reading Skills: Paraphrase and Summarize 84
       Vocabulary Development 85

Frederick Douglass   **Learning to Read and Write** .... AUTOBIOGRAPHY 86

       Before You Read: *from* **The Autobiography of Malcolm X** 94
       Literary Focus: Universal Themes 94
       Reading Skills: Comparing and Contrasting 94
       Vocabulary Development 95

Malcolm X   *from* **The Autobiography of Malcolm X** .... AUTOBIOGRAPHY 96
       Skills Practice: Comparison-and-Contrast Chart 100
       Skills Review: Vocabulary and Comprehension 101

       Before You Read: Superman and Me 102
       Literary Focus: Theme and Character 102
       Reading Skills: Making Generalizations 102
       Vocabulary Development 103

Sherman Alexie   **Superman and Me** .... ESSAY 104
       Skills Practice: Character and Theme Chart 110
       Skills Review: Vocabulary and Comprehension 111

COLLECTION 5 **Irony and Ambiguity** 112

Academic Vocabulary for Collection 5 113

       Before You Read: Van Gogh's Ear 114
       Literary Focus: Situational Irony 114
       Reading Skills: Cause and Effect 114
       Vocabulary Development 115

Moacyr Scliar   **Van Gogh's Ear** .... SHORT STORY ... 116
       Skills Practice: Irony Chart 120
       Skills Review: Vocabulary and Comprehension 121

	Before You Read: The Third Bank of the River	122
	Literary Focus: Ambiguity	122
	Reading Skills: Making Inferences	122
	Vocabulary Development	123
João Guimarães Rosa	**The Third Bank of the River** SHORT STORY	124
	Skills Practice: Ambiguity Chart	132
	Skills Review: Vocabulary and Comprehension	133

COLLECTION 6 — Symbolism and Allegory 134

Academic Vocabulary for Collection 6 135

	Before You Read: My Wonder Horse	136
	Literary Focus: Symbolic Meaning	136
	Reading Skills: Visualizing the Story	136
	Vocabulary Development	137
Sabine R. Ulibarrí	**My Wonder Horse** SHORT STORY	138
	Skills Practice: Symbolism Chart	146
	Skills Review: Vocabulary and Comprehension	147
	Before You Read: The Alligator War	148
	Literary Focus: Allegory	148
	Reading Skills: Identifying Relationships	148
	Vocabulary and Development	149
Horacio Quiroga	**The Alligator War** SHORT STORY	150
	Skills Practice: Allegory Chart	164
	Skills Review: Vocabulary and Comprehension	165

COLLECTION 7 — Poetry 166

Academic Vocabulary for Collection 7 167

	Before You Read: Magic Island	169
	Literary Focus: Sound Devices in Free-Verse Poetry	169
	Reading Skills: Reading a Poem	169
Cathy Song	**Magic Island** POEM	170
	Skills Practice: Sound Devices Chart	173
	Skills Review: Reading Comprehension	173

vi   Contents

Before You Read: Legal Alien; Child of the Americas **174**
    Literary Focus: Rhythm in Free-Verse Poetry 174
    Reading Skills: Comparison and Contrast 174

Pat Mora   **Legal Alien** . . . . POEM . . . **175**

Aurora Levins Morales   **Child of the Americas** . . . . POEM . . . **177**
    Skills Practice: Comparison-and-Contrast Chart 179
    Skills Review: Reading Comprehension 180

Before You Read: Without Title **181**
    Literary Focus: Figurative Language 181

Diane Glancy   **Without Title** . . . . POEM . . . **182**
    Skills Practice: Figurative Language Chart 184
    Skills Review: Reading Comprehension 185

Before You Read: Offspring **186**
    Literary Focus: Extended Metaphor 186
    Reading Skills: Summarizing 186

Naomi Long Madgett   **Offspring** . . . . POEM . . . **187**
    Skills Practice: Summary Chart 189
    Skills Review: Reading Comprehension 189

Before You Read: There Is No Word for Goodbye **190**
    Literary Focus: Imagery and Figurative Language
    in Lyric Poetry 190

Mary TallMountain   **There Is No Word for Goodbye** . . . . POEM . . . **191**
    Skills Practice: Imagery and Figurative Language Chart 194
    Skills Review: Reading Comprehension 195

COLLECTION 8   **Literary Criticism: Evaluating Style** **196**
Academic Vocabulary for Collection 8 197

Before You Read: Late-Night Chitlins with Momma **198**
    Literary Focus: Style, Diction, and Tone 198
    Reading Skills: Drawing Conclusions 198
    Vocabulary Development 199

Audrey Petty   **Late-Night Chitlins with Momma** . . . . ESSAY . . . **200**
    Skills Practice: Style Chart 207
    Skills Review: Vocabulary and Comprehension 208

	Before You Read: My Two Lives	209
	Literary Focus: Style	209
	Reading Skills: Cause and Effect	209
	Vocabulary Development	210
Jhumpa Lahiri	**My Two Lives** .... ESSAY	**211**
	Skills Practice: Cause-and-Effect Chart	216
	Skills Review: Vocabulary and Comprehension	217

COLLECTION 9 — Literary Criticism: Biographical and Historical Approach ... 218

Academic Vocabulary for Collection 9 ... 219

	Before You Read: Theme for English B	220
	Literary Focus: Biographical Approach	220
	Reading Skills: Making Inferences About Biographical Details	220
Langston Hughes	**Theme for English B** .... POEM	**221**
	Skills Practice: Biographical Details Chart	224
	Skills Review: Reading Comprehension	224
	Before You Read: The Disappearances	225
	Literary Focus: Historical Context	225
	Reading Skills: Re-Reading	225
Vijay Seshadri	**The Disappearances** .... POEM	**226**
	Skills Practice: Historical Context Chart	229
	Skills Review: Reading Comprehension	229
	Before You Read: How It Feels to Be Colored Me	230
	Literary Focus: Biographical and Historical Approach	230
	Reading Skills: Compare and Contrast	230
	Vocabulary Development	231
Zora Neale Hurston	**How It Feels to Be Colored Me** .... ESSAY	**232**
	Skills Practice: Historical Context Chart	238
	Skills Review: Vocabulary and Comprehension	239

viii   Contents

COLLECTION 10 **Drama** **240**

    Academic Vocabulary for Collection 10 241

        Before You Read: *from* **A Raisin in the Sun** 242
        Literary Focus: Drama 242
        Reading Skills: Causes and Effects 242
        Vocabulary Development 243

Lorraine Hansberry   *from* **A Raisin in the Sun** .... DRAMA ... **244**
        Skills Practice: Cause-and-Effect Chart 268
        Skills Review: Vocabulary and Comprehension 269

• PART TWO •

READING INFORMATIONAL TEXTS 270

    Academic Vocabulary: Informational Articles 271

        Before You Read: Reign of the Reader 272
        Informational Focus: How to Generate Questions 272
        Reading Skills: Make a KWL Chart 272
        Vocabulary Development 273

M. Freeman   **Reign of the Reader** .... ARTICLE ... **274**
        Skills Practice: *5w-How?* Chart 278
        Skills Review: Vocabulary and Comprehension 279

        Before You Read: Matthew Henson's Polar Travails;
        National Geographic Society Honors Arctic Explorer;
        Matthew Henson 280
        Informational Focus: Synthesizing Sources 280
        Reading Skills: Informational Articles 280
        Vocabulary Development 281

        Matthew Henson's Polar Travails .... ARTICLE ... **282**

Jennifer Mapes   **National Geographic Society Honors**
        Arctic Explorer .... ARTICLE ... **284**
        Matthew Henson .... WEB PAGE ... **287**
        Skills Practice: Synthesizing Sources 289
        Skills Review: Vocabulary and Comprehension 290

        Before You Read: Islam in America;
        Proud to Wear My Hijab 291
        Informational Focus: Primary and Secondary Sources 291
        Reading Skills: Identify and Elaborate on Main Ideas 291
        Vocabulary Development 292

Patricia Smith	Islam in America .... ARTICLE ... 293
Syeda Rezwana Nodi	Proud to Wear My Hijab .... ESSAY ... 299
	Skills Practice: Elaboration Chart 302
	Skills Review: Vocabulary and Comprehension 303

Before You Read: Appearances Are Destructive 304
Informational Focus: Author's Argument 304
Reading Skills: Identifying Author's Purpose and Tone ... 304
Vocabulary Development 305

Mark Mathabane	Appearances Are Destructive .... ARTICLE ... 306
	Skills Practice: Argument Chart 309
	Skills Review: Vocabulary and Comprehension 310

Academic Vocabulary: Consumer, Workplace, and Public Documents 311

Before You Read: The 411 on Your Job Rights;
Youth@Work 312
Informational Focus: Workplace Document 312

The 411 on Your Job Rights .... WORKPLACE DOCUMENT ... 313
Youth@Work .... WORKPLACE DOCUMENT ... 315
Skills Practice: Workplace Documents Organizer 318
Skills Review: Reading Comprehension 319

Before You Read: The Basics of Downloading a Podcast 320
Informational Focus: Technical Document 320

The Basics of Downloading
a Podcast .... TECHNICAL DOCUMENT ... 321
Skills Practice: Structure and Format Chart 324
Skills Review: Reading Comprehension 325

Before You Read: Audio Help 326
Informational Focus: Functional Document 326

Audio Help .... FUNCTIONAL DOCUMENT ... 327
Skills Practice: Form Fields Chart 329
Skills Review: Reading Comprehension 330

Before You Read: Citing Internet Sources: Podcasts 331
Informational Focus: Documentation 331

Citing Internet Sources: Podcasts .... BIBLIOGRAPHY ... 332
Skills Review: Reading Comprehension 334

Index of Authors and Titles 335

Vocabulary Development 336

To the Student

A Book for You

Teachers open the door, but you must enter by yourself.
—Chinese Proverb

Reading is an interactive process. The more you put into it, the more you get out of it. This book is designed to do just that—help you interact with the selections you read by marking them up, asking your own questions, taking notes, recording your own ideas, and responding to the questions of others.

A Book Designed for Your Success

The *Holt Multicultural Reader* goes hand-in-hand with *Elements of Literature.* It is designed to help you interact with the selections and master the language arts skills.

To do this, the book has two parts that each follow a simple format:

Part 1   Reading Literature

To help you master how to respond to, analyze, evaluate, and interpret literature, the *Holt Multicultural Reader* provides—

For each collection:
- The academic vocabulary you need to know to master literature skills for the collection, defined for ready reference and use.
- Selections printed in an interactive format to support and guide your reading. As you read and respond to these selections, you will apply and extend your skills and build toward independence.

For each selection:
- A Before You Read page that preteaches the literary focus and provides a reading skill to help you comprehend the selection.
- A Vocabulary Development page that preteaches selection vocabulary and provides a vocabulary skill to use while reading the prose selections.
- Literature printed in an interactive format to guide your reading and help you respond to text.
- A Skills Practice graphic organizer that helps you understand the literary focus of the selection.
- A Skills Review page that helps you practice vocabulary and assess your understanding of the selection you've read.

Part 2   Reading Informational Texts

To help you master how to read informational texts, this book contains—

For Informational Articles:
- The academic vocabulary you need to know to master informational skills, defined for ready reference and use.
- A Before You Read page that preteaches the informational focus and provides a reading skill to help you comprehend the selection.
- A Vocabulary Development page that preteaches selection vocabulary and provides a vocabulary skill to use while reading the selection.
- Informational selections in an interactive format to guide your reading and help you respond to the text.
- A Skills Practice graphic organizer that helps you understand the informational focus of the selection.
- A Skills Review page that helps you practice vocabulary and assess your understanding of the selection you've read.

For Consumer, Workplace, and Public Documents:
- The academic vocabulary you need to know to master the skills, defined for ready reference and use.
- A Before You Read page that preteaches the document focus and defines specialized terms.
- New documents in an interactive format to guide your reading and help you respond to the text.
- A Skills Practice page that helps you understand the focus of the selection.
- A Skills Review page that assesses your understanding of the selection you read.

A Book for Your Own Thoughts and Feelings

Reading is about *you*. It is about connecting your thoughts and feelings to the thoughts and feelings of the writer. Make this book your own. The more you give of yourself to your reading, the more you will get out of it. We encourage you to write in it. Jot down how you feel about the selection. Question the text. Note details you think need to be cleared up or topics you would like to learn more about.

A Walk Through the Book

Academic Vocabulary
Academic vocabulary refers to the language of books, tests, and formal writing. Each collection begins with the terms, or academic language, you need to know to master the skills for that collection.

Before You Read
Previewing what you will learn builds success. This page tells you what the selection is about and prepares you to read it.

Literary Focus
This feature introduces the literary focus for the selection.

Reading Skills
This feature provides a reading skill for you to apply to the selection. It ties into and supports the literary focus.

Language Arts Skills
The skills covered with the selection are listed here.

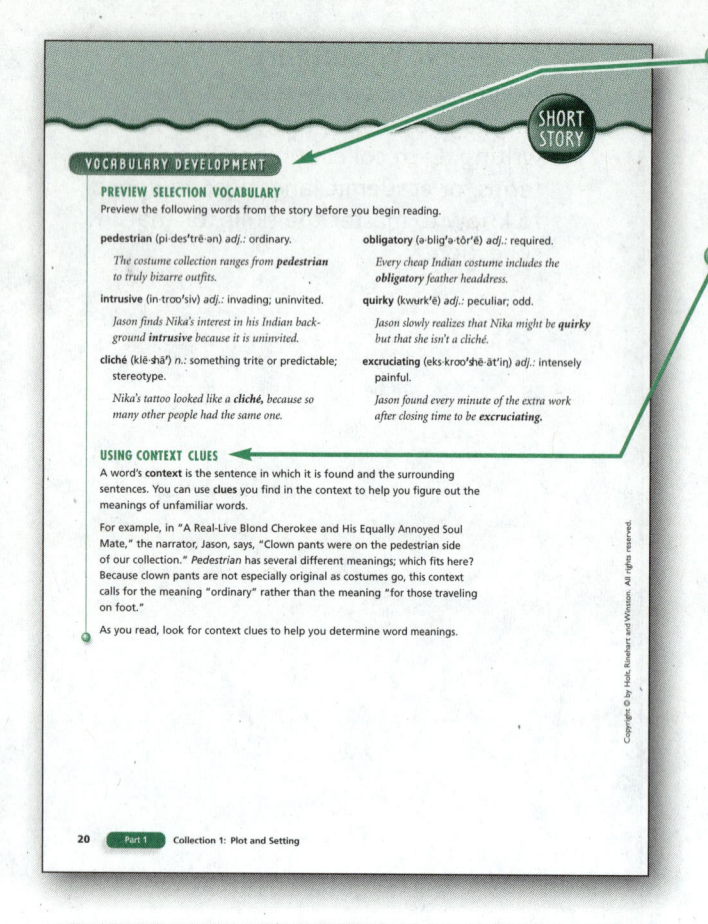

Vocabulary Development
Vocabulary words for the selection are pretaught. Each entry gives the pronunciation and definition of the word as well as a context sentence.

Vocabulary Skills
When you read, you not only have to recognize words but also decode them and determine meaning. This feature introduces a vocabulary skill to use to understand words in the selection.

Side-Column Notes
Each selection is accompanied by notes in the side column that guide your interaction with the selection. Many notes ask you to underline or circle in the text itself. Others provide lines on which you can write your responses to questions.

Types of Notes
The different types of notes throughout the selection help you—
- Focus on literary elements
- Apply the reading skill
- Apply the vocabulary skill
- Think critically about the selection
- Develop word knowledge
- Build vocabulary
- Build fluency

VOCABULARY DEVELOPMENT

PREVIEW SELECTION VOCABULARY
Preview the following words from the story before you begin reading.

pedestrian (pi-des′trē-ən) *adj.*: ordinary.

The costume collection ranges from pedestrian to truly bizarre outfits.

intrusive (in-trōō′siv) *adj.*: invading; uninvited.

Jason finds Nika's interest in his Indian background intrusive because it is uninvited.

cliché (klē-shā′) *n.*: something trite or predictable; stereotype.

Nika's tattoo looked like a cliché, because so many other people had the same one.

obligatory (ə-blig′ə-tôr′ē) *adj.*: required.

Every cheap Indian costume includes the obligatory feather headdress.

quirky (kwurk′ē) *adj.*: peculiar; odd.

Jason slowly realizes that Nika might be quirky but that she isn't a cliché.

excruciating (eks-krōō′shē-āt′iŋ) *adj.*: intensely painful.

Jason found every minute of the extra work after closing time to be excruciating.

USING CONTEXT CLUES

A word's **context** is the sentence in which it is found and the surrounding sentences. You can use **clues** you find in the context to help you figure out the meanings of unfamiliar words.

For example, in "A Real-Live Blond Cherokee and His Equally Annoyed Soul Mate," the narrator, Jason, says, "Clown pants were on the pedestrian side of our collection." *Pedestrian* has several different meanings; which fits here? Because clown pants are not especially original as costumes go, this context calls for the meaning "ordinary" rather than the meaning "for those traveling on foot."

As you read, look for context clues to help you determine word meanings.

A Real-Live Blond Cherokee and His Equally Annoyed Soul Mate

Cynthia Leitich Smith

I'm a card-carrying, respectably thick-blood Oklahoma Cherokee. That's right, I said "Cherokee." And yeah, my hair is blond. Sandy blond.

Sure, I know every "take-me-to-your-sweat-lodge" wannabe claims he's a Cherokee. Yeah, Mama's mama is the full blood. No, I didn't call her a "princess," and don't make fun of my gramma. So what if I'm not dark like her or a redhead like Dad's mama? I took after my grandpas, the Swedes.

Really. Check out this picture in my wallet. It's from my cousin Robbie's wedding last spring. Here's my tribal ID. And if you're wondering how my family got to Austin, Texas—well, we drove a U-Haul truck south down I-35.

That's all right, nothing personal. But now, you understand.

Looks aside, I'm a real-live Indian, and I felt like one when Little Miss Gentrification[1] tapped my shoulder at work and said in this whooshy breath, "Mickey tells me that you're part Native American. My American history teacher, Mr. Cavazos, he says that we have to use primary sources because if you want to find out about a people's history, you have to hear their side. As it turns out, I'm getting a C minus in history, and I was wondering if I could interview you about—"

---

1. **gentrification** (jen′tri-fi-kā′shən) *n.*: conversion of a deteriorating area into a more affluent one.

INFER
In lines 1–12, the narrator explains his ancestral heritage. Why do you think he sounds defensive?

WORD STUDY
In line 15, the narrator refers to the girl who comes into the shop as "Little Miss Gentrification." Often, as a result of gentrification, low-income people are forced to relocate. Why does the narrator give the girl this name?

Fluency

Successful readers are able to read fluently—clearly, easily, quickly, and without word identification problems. In most selections, you'll be given an opportunity to practice and improve your fluency.

Vocabulary

The vocabulary words that were pretaught are defined in the side column and set in boldface in the selection, allowing you to see them in context.

Meet the Writer

A short biography of the writer appears after each literature selection.

A Walk Through the Book   xv

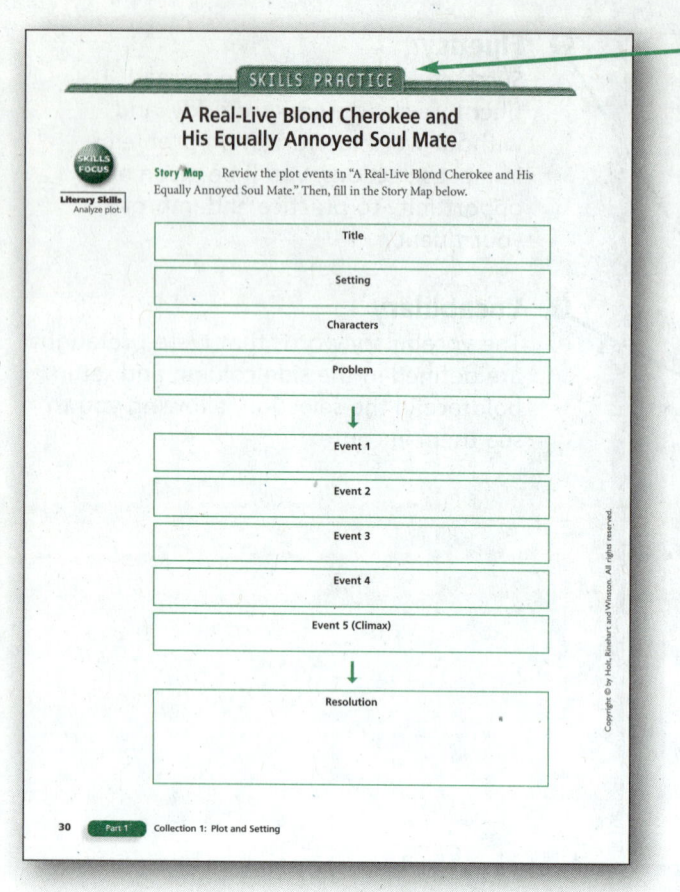

Skills Practice
Graphic organizers help reinforce your understanding of the literary focus in a highly visual and creative way.

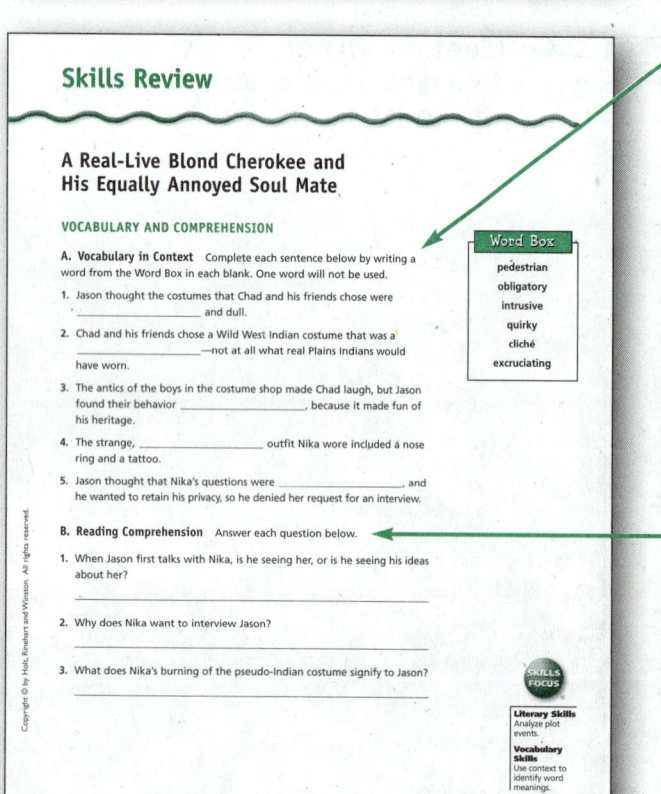

Skills Review: Vocabulary
Test your knowledge of the selection vocabulary and the vocabulary skill by completing this short activity.

Reading Comprehension
This feature allows you to see how well you've understood the selection you have just read.

xvi   A Walk Through the Book

Part One

Reading Literature

Collection 1   Plot and Setting

Collection 2   Character

Collection 3   Narrator and Voice

Collection 4   Comparing Themes

Collection 5   Irony and Ambiguity

Collection 6   Symbolism and Allegory

Collection 7   Poetry

Collection 8   Literary Criticism: Evaluating Style

Collection 9   Literary Criticism: Using Biographical and Historical Approaches

Collection 10 Drama

Collection 1

Plot and Setting

Academic Vocabulary for Collection 1

These are the terms you should know
as you read and analyze the selections in this collection.

Plot A series of related events, each connected to the next, like links in a chain.

Sequence The order in which a story's events take place. Most works take place in chronological order, or time order.

• • •

Flashback A scene that interrupts the narrative to introduce an event that took place in the past.

Flash-forward A scene that jumps ahead of the narrative to relate an event that happens in the future.

Foreshadowing Hints in the narrative that certain events are going to happen later.

• • •

Exposition The opening of a narrative, also called the **basic situation,** which presents the main characters and their conflicts.

Conflict A struggle between two opposing forces. An **external conflict** can take place between two characters, between a character and a group, or between a character and an animal or a force in nature. An **internal conflict** is a struggle that takes place within a character's mind or heart.

Complications The problems that come up during the story as the characters try to resolve, or deal with, the conflict.

Suspense The excitement and tension that build up in a story, making readers curious to find out how the story ends.

Climax The most exciting part of a story—the moment when the outcome of the major conflict is determined, usually at its point of greatest intensity. The climax usually comes near the end of a short story.

Resolution (also called denouement [dā′nōō·män′]) The very end of the narrative, when loose ends of the plot are tied up.

• • •

Setting The time and place in which the narrative happens.

Atmosphere Mood or feelings brought on by a narrative's setting.

Academic Vocabulary   3

Before You Read

POEM

Tony Went to the Bodega but He Didn't Buy Anything

by Martín Espada

The course of a successful life does not always follow a straight line from where we are to where we want to be. Sometimes we move in unexpected directions, as Tony does in this "rice and beans success story."

LITERARY FOCUS: PLOT AND SETTING

The **plot** in a narrative is the series of related events that occur as one or more characters confront **conflicts,** or problems, and try to resolve them.

Setting provides a frame of time and place within which the story's events unfold—whether that story is told in prose or, as in this case, in poetry. The setting in time can move back or forward through the use of **flashback** or **flash-forward.** In this way the passage of many years can be shown within a few lines.

As you read "Tony Went to the Bodega but He Didn't Buy Anything," note how the setting affects the main character, his choices, and thus, the plot.

READING SKILLS: READING A NARRATIVE POEM

A **narrative poem** is a poem that tells a story. It has a plot with a beginning, a middle, and an end. When you read "Tony Went to the Bodega but He Didn't Buy Anything," use the following strategies:

- Look for punctuation in the poem that tells you where sentences begin and end.
- Do not make a full stop at the end of a line if there is no punctuation there. If a line of poetry has no punctuation at its end, read right on to the next line to complete the sense of the sentence.
- Try to visualize what the poet is describing for you. Be alert for comparisons and figures of speech.
- Read the poem aloud.

SKILLS FOCUS

Literary Skills
Understand plot.
Understand setting.

Reading Skills
Read a narrative poem.

Tony Went to the Bodega but He Didn't Buy Anything

para Angel Guadalupe

Martín Espada

Tony's father left the family
and the Long Island City projects,
leaving a mongrel-skinny puertorriqueño° boy
nine years old
5 who had to find work.

Makengo the Cuban
let him work at the bodega.°
In grocery aisles
he learned the steps of the dry-mop mambo,
10 banging the cash register
like piano percussion
in the spotlight of Machito's orchestra,
polite with the abuelas° who bought on credit,
practicing the grin on customers
15 he'd seen Makengo grin
with his bad yellow teeth.

Tony left the projects too,
with a scholarship for law school.
But he cursed the cold primavera°
20 in Boston;

---

3. **puertorriqueño** (pwer′tə·rē·kā′nyō): Spanish for "Puerto Rican."
7. **bodega** (bō·dā′gə): small grocery shop in a Hispanic neighborhood.
13. **abuelas** (ä·bwä′läs): Spanish for "grandmothers."
19. **primavera** (prē′mä·ver′ä): Spanish for "spring."

"Tony Went to the Bodega but He Didn't Buy Anything" from *Trumpets from the Islands of Their Eviction* by Martín Espada. Copyright © 1987 by Bilingual Press/Editorial Bilingüe. Reproduced by permission of **Bilingual Press/Editorial Bilingüe**, Arizona State University, Tempe, AZ.

IDENTIFY CAUSE & EFFECT

Why does Tony have to find work?

IDENTIFY

Underline words that show what Tony did at his job at the bodega.

INFER

Do you think Tony likes his work? Why or why not?

PLOT

Underline the words that tell you how much time has passed.

CONFLICT

Underline the words in lines 19–24 that show Tony's **conflicts,** or problems, in Boston.

INTERPRET

Note how the author describes the "darkness" of the white faces (line 28). How can white faces be dark?

_____
_____
_____
_____
_____
_____
_____
_____
_____
_____
_____

FLUENCY

Read the boxed lines aloud, first for rhythm and next for mood. Use your tone of voice to convey the darkness of Tony's feelings until he discovers the projects.

Ambient Images Inc./Alamy

the cooking of his neighbors
left no smell in the hallway,
and no one spoke Spanish
(not even the radio).

25 So Tony walked without a map
through the city,
a landscape of hostile condominiums
and the darkness of white faces,
sidewalk-searcher lost
30 till he discovered the projects.

Tony went to the bodega
but he didn't buy anything:
he sat by the doorway satisfied
to watch la gente° (people
35 island-brown as him)

———————————————

34. **la gente** (la hän′tä): Spanish for "the people."

6   Part 1   Collection 1: Plot and Setting

crowd in and out,
hablando español,°
thought: this is beautiful,
and grinned
40   his bodega grin.

This is a rice and beans
success story:
today Tony lives on Tremont Street,
above the bodega.

37. **hablando español** (ä·blän′dō es·pä·nyōl′): Spanish for "speaking Spanish."

MEET THE WRITER

Martín Espada (1957–   ) was born in Brooklyn, New York, and moved to Boston to study law. Like Tony's trip through life, Espada's life journey has been varied and complex. It has taken him as far away as Nicaragua (where he worked as a radio journalist) and back to Boston (where he provides legal services for tenants and poor people). Along the way, Espada has worked as a hotel clerk, a bouncer, an attendant in a primate nursery, a groundskeeper in a minor-league ballpark, a welfare-rights activist, and an advocate for patients with mental disabilities. At the heart of his poetry are his experiences in the Latino communities of New York City and Boston. Espada now teaches English at the University of Massachusetts at Amherst.

SKILLS PRACTICE

Tony Went to the Bodega but He Didn't Buy Anything

Plot Chart In "Tony Went to the Bodega but He Didn't Buy Anything," there are two **settings.** Tony spends his childhood in the projects in Long Island City, New York, and then moves to Boston to go to law school.

Fill out the Plot Chart below to review the events in the narrative poem and the settings in which each took place.

SKILLS FOCUS

Literary Skills Analyze plot and setting.

	Setting #1: Long Island City projects (lines 1–16)	**Setting #2:** Boston (lines 17–29)
Plot events: Describe what happens in each setting.		
Setting and mood: What words are used to describe each setting, and what feelings are conveyed?		
Conflicts: Describe Tony's conflicts—internal, external, or both.		

Resolution: Is Tony's main conflict internal or external? How has he resolved his conflict by the end of the poem? Explain.

_____
_____
_____
_____

Tony Went to the Bodega but He Didn't Buy Anything   **9**

Skills Review

Tony Went to the Bodega but He Didn't Buy Anything

COMPREHENSION

Reading Comprehension Answer each question below.

1. Describe the first setting and how Tony feels there.

2. Describe the second setting and how Tony feels there.

3. How does Tony resolve his conflict?

4. What do you think the title means?

Before You Read

POEM

For My Sister Molly Who in the Fifties by Alice Walker

Do you know someone who has had a big effect on your life? In the following poem the narrator describes the influence her sister Molly had on her.

LITERARY FOCUS: CONFLICT

Conflict is a struggle or clash between opposing characters, forces, or emotions. In an **external conflict,** a character struggles against an outside force, such as another character, society as a whole, or something in nature. An **internal conflict** takes place within a character's own mind. It is a struggle between opposing needs, desires, or emotions.

- As you read "For My Sister Molly Who in the Fifties," notice the different kinds of conflicts experienced by the speaker of the poem and her sister Molly.

READING SKILLS: MAKING INFERENCES

In literature, we are not always told directly what is happening. We have to make **inferences,** or educated guesses. We base our guesses on information in the text and on our own prior experiences. As you read the poem "For My Sister Molly Who in the Fifties," pause at the end of each stanza and ask yourself the following questions:

- What is happening in the stanza?
- Where are events taking place?
- When are the events happening?
- Whom are the events happening to?
- Are any of the characters experiencing conflicts?

SKILLS FOCUS

Literary Skills
Understand plot and setting.

Reading Skills
Make inferences.

For My Sister Molly Who in the Fifties

Alice Walker

> Once made a fairy rooster from
> Mashed potatoes
> Whose eyes I forget
> But green onions were his tail
> 5 And his two legs were carrot sticks
> A tomato slice his crown.
> Who came home on vacation
> When the sun was hot
> and cooked
> 10 and cleaned
> And minded least of all
> The children's questions
> A million or more
> Pouring in on her
> 15 Who had been to school
> And knew (and told us too) that certain
> Words were no longer good
> And taught me not to say us for we
> No matter what "Sonny said" up the
> 20 road.
>
> FOR MY SISTER MOLLY WHO IN THE FIFTIES
> Knew Hamlet° well and read into the night
> And coached me in my songs of Africa
> A continent I never knew
> 25 But learned to love

---

22. **Hamlet:** hero of a play by William Shakespeare.

INFER

In lines 1–20, what is happening? When and where are the events taking place? Who is involved?

INTERPRET

In lines 16–17, the narrator explains that Molly "knew (and told us too) that certain / Words were no longer good." What does she mean?

IDENTIFY

In lines 22–23, circle two interests of Molly's.

"For My Sister Molly Who in the Fifties" from *Revolutionary Petunias and Other Poems* by Alice Walker. Copyright © 1972 by Alice Walker. Reproduced by permission of **Harcourt, Inc.**

Melon Season (1967) by Romare Bearden (1911–1988).
ESM – Ed Meneely/Art Resource, NY

INFER

In line 26, who might "they" be? In lines 26–29, how do "they" differ from the speaker?

_____
_____
_____
_____
_____
_____
_____
_____

INFER

Visualize Molly sitting by the low-burning fire reading and the speaker praying for snow. Why might the speaker be wishing for snow?

_____
_____
_____
_____
_____
_____
_____
_____

Because "they" she said could carry
A tune
And spoke in accents never heard
In Eatonton.
30 Who read from *Prose and Poetry*
And loved to read "Sam McGee from Tennessee"°
On nights the fire was burning low
And Christmas wrapped in angel hair
And I for one prayed for snow.

(continued)

---

31. **"Sam McGee from Tennessee"**: from the first line of a humorous poem by Robert W. Service, "The Cremation of Sam McGee."

For My Sister Molly Who in the Fifties   13

FLUENCY

Practice reading the boxed lines aloud. Remember not to stop at the end of every line but to look for groupings of ideas, pausing or stopping only when the punctuation requires you to. Try to convey the narrator's feelings as you read.

INFER

Based on what you learned in lines 1–50, describe how the speaker experiences Molly. What influence does Molly have on her?

_____
_____
_____
_____
_____
_____
_____
_____
_____
_____
_____

IDENTIFY

In line 66, underline the words that show Molly's mobility in the world.

35 WHO IN THE FIFTIES
    Knew all the written things that made
    Us laugh and stories by
    The hour   Waking up the story buds
    Like fruit. Who walked among the flowers
40 And brought them inside the house
    And smelled as good as they
    And looked as bright.
    Who made dresses, braided
    Hair. Moved chairs about
45 Hung things from walls
    Ordered baths
    Frowned on wasp bites
    And seemed to know the endings
    Of all the tales
50 I had forgot.

        WHO OFF INTO THE UNIVERSITY
        Went exploring   To London and
        To Rotterdam
        Prague and to Liberia
55   Bringing back the news to us
        Who knew none of it
        But followed
        crops and weather
        funerals and
60   Methodist Homecoming;
        easter speeches,
        groaning church.

        WHO FOUND ANOTHER WORLD
        Another life   With gentlefolk
65   Far less trusting
        And moved and moved and changed

14   Part 1   Collection 1: Plot and Setting

Her name
And sounded precise
When she spoke   And frowned away
70 Our sloppishness.

    WHO SAW US SILENT
    Cursed with fear   A love burning
    Inexpressible
    And sent me money not for me
75 But for "College."
    Who saw me grow through letters
    The words misspelled   But not
    The longing   Stretching
    Growth
80 The tied and twisting
    Tongue
    Feet no longer bare
    Skin no longer burnt against
    The cotton.

85 WHO BECAME SOMEONE OVERHEAD
    A light   A thousand watts
    Bright and also blinding
    And saw my brothers cloddish
    And me destined to be
90 Wayward
    My mother remote   My father
    A wearisome farmer
    With heartbreaking
    Nails.

95 FOR MY SISTER MOLLY WHO IN THE FIFTIES
    Found much
    Unbearable

                    (continued)

CONFLICT

What **internal conflicts** is Molly feeling in lines 96–104?

___

Who walked where few had
Understood   And sensed our
100 Groping after light
And saw some extinguished
And no doubt mourned.

FOR MY SISTER MOLLY WHO IN THE FIFTIES
Left us.

✶✶✶✶✶✶✶✶

MEET THE WRITER

Alice Walker (1944–   ) is best known for her novel *The Color Purple*, which was later made into a movie directed by Steven Spielberg and then adapted into a Broadway musical. The daughter of poor African American sharecroppers and the youngest of eight children, Walker grew up in a segregated society in Eatonton, Georgia. At the age of eight, Walker was accidentally shot in the eye by a brother with a BB gun. Scarred and partially blind from the accident, Walker withdrew from others and spent her time reading. Eventually she won a scholarship to Spelman College, a prestigious elite college for black women, and later to Sarah Lawrence College.

Today, Alice Walker is one of the best-known African American writers. Though she began her writing career in 1968 with a book of poems, *Once*, she has since written short stories, essays, and novels. Influenced greatly by her childhood in the rural South and by her hardworking, impoverished mother, Walker writes most often about the black woman and the importance of her legacy in the world today.

PLOT

The poem's last line may have more than one meaning. In what ways might Molly have "left" her family?

SKILLS PRACTICE

For My Sister Molly Who in the Fifties

Conflict Chart   This poem traces the relationship between an unnamed speaker and her sister Molly. Complete the Conflict Chart below by making inferences based on the text and on your prior knowledge.

SKILLS FOCUS

Literary Skills
Analyze conflict.

Reading Skills
Make inferences.

	Plot (Describe the interaction between Molly and her sister.)	**Conflict** (How do Molly and her sister feel about one another?)
Lines 1–50		
Lines 51–84		
Lines 85–104		

For My Sister Molly Who in the Fifties   17

Skills Review

For My Sister Molly Who in the Fifties

COMPREHENSION

Reading Comprehension Answer each question below.

1. What are the most important plot events in lines 1–50? How does the speaker feel about her sister?

   _____
   _____
   _____

2. What events occur in lines 51–84 to change things?

   _____
   _____
   _____

3. What happens at the end? Explain how the characters resolve their conflicts.

   _____
   _____
   _____

4. Compare Molly's resolution at the end of the poem with Tony's resolution in "Tony Went to the Bodega but He Didn't Buy Anything." Are their decisions similar or different? Explain.

   _____
   _____
   _____
   _____
   _____
   _____

Before You Read

A Real-Live Blond Cherokee and His Equally Annoyed Soul Mate

by Cynthia Leitich Smith

The narrator of "A Real-Live Blond Cherokee and His Equally Annoyed Soul Mate" is exactly what the title suggests—the son of a Cherokee mother who is annoyed by people who marvel at his blond hair.

LITERARY FOCUS: PLOT

A **plot** in a story is a series of related events. In most stories the events are told in **chronological order,** or the order in which they happened in real time. The opening of the story is called the **exposition,** or basic situation. The exposition usually introduces the main character(s) and his or her **conflicts,** or problems. As the story continues, the characters face complications, which cause a new or deeper set of problems. The high point of the plot is the **climax,** the story's most exciting moment, when something happens to decide the outcome of the conflict. Finally, the last element of the plot is the **resolution,** or **denouement,** when the problems are resolved and the story ends.

Watch for these different parts of the plot as you read the following story.

READING SKILLS: CAUSE AND EFFECT

A **cause** is what makes something happen. An **effect** is the result of what happens. In a well-written story the events that make up the plot are closely related. One event causes another event, which leads to another event. To find a cause, ask yourself, "Why did this event happen?" To identify an effect, ask yourself, "What happened as a result of this event?" Keep in mind that an effect, or result, can stem from several causes and that one cause can lead to several effects.

To help you track cause-and-effect relationships as you read, fill in a chart like the one below. In the left-hand column, list the cause; in the right-hand column, list the effect.

Cause	Effect

SKILLS FOCUS

Literary Skills
Understand plot.

Reading Skills
Understand cause and effect.

Vocabulary Skills
Use context clues.

SHORT STORY

VOCABULARY DEVELOPMENT

PREVIEW SELECTION VOCABULARY

Preview the following words from the story before you begin reading.

pedestrian (pi·des′trē·ən) *adj.:* ordinary.

> The costume collection ranges from **pedestrian** to truly bizarre outfits.

intrusive (in·trōō′siv) *adj.:* invading; uninvited.

> Jason finds Nika's interest in his Indian background **intrusive** because it is uninvited.

cliché (klē·shā′) *n.:* something trite or predictable; stereotype.

> Nika's tattoo looked like a **cliché,** because so many other people had the same one.

obligatory (ə·blig′ə·tôr′ē) *adj.:* required.

> Every cheap Indian costume includes the **obligatory** feather headdress.

quirky (kwurk′ē) *adj.:* peculiar; odd.

> Jason slowly realizes that Nika might be **quirky** but that she isn't a cliché.

excruciating (eks·krōō′shē·āt′iŋ) *adj.:* intensely painful.

> Jason found every minute of the extra work after closing time to be **excruciating.**

USING CONTEXT CLUES

A word's **context** is the sentence in which it is found and the surrounding sentences. You can use **clues** you find in the context to help you figure out the meanings of unfamiliar words.

For example, in "A Real-Live Blond Cherokee and His Equally Annoyed Soul Mate," the narrator, Jason, says, "Clown pants were on the pedestrian side of our collection." *Pedestrian* has several different meanings; which fits here? Because clown pants are not especially original as costumes go, this context calls for the meaning "ordinary" rather than the meaning "for those traveling on foot."

As you read, look for context clues to help you determine word meanings.

A Real-Live Blond Cherokee and His Equally Annoyed Soul Mate

Cynthia Leitich Smith

I'm a card-carrying, respectably thick-blood Oklahoma Cherokee. That's right, I said "Cherokee." And yeah, my hair is blond. Sandy blond.

Sure, I know every "take-me-to-your-sweat-lodge" wannabe claims he's a Cherokee. Yeah, Mama's mama is the full blood. No, I didn't call her a "princess," and don't make fun of my gramma. So what if I'm not dark like her or a redhead like Dad's mama? I took after my grandpas, the Swedes.

Really. Check out this picture in my wallet. It's from my cousin Robbie's wedding last spring. Here's my tribal ID. And if you're wondering how my family got to Austin, Texas—well, we drove a U-Haul truck south down I-35.

That's all right, nothing personal. But now, you understand.

Looks aside, I'm a real-live Indian, and I felt like one when Little Miss Gentrification[1] tapped my shoulder at work and said in this whooshy breath, "Mickey tells me that you're part Native American. My American history teacher, Mr. Cavazos, he says that we have to use primary sources because if you want to find out about a people's history, you have to hear their side. As it turns out, I'm getting a C minus in history, and I was wondering if I could interview you about—"

---

1. **gentrification** (jen'tri·fi·kā'shən) *n.:* conversion of a deteriorating area into a more affluent one.

VOCABULARY

pedestrian (pi·des′trē·ən) *adj.*: ordinary.

IDENTIFY CAUSE & EFFECT

Notice how the narrator interrupts the girl when she tries to talk to him. What **causes** him to interrupt her?

_____
_____
_____
_____
_____

VOCABULARY

intrusive (in·trōō′siv) *adj.*: invading; uninvited.

cliché (klē·shā′) *n.*: something trite or predictable; stereotype.

CLARIFY

Pause at and re-read lines 50–51. Who is being dismissed now? Explain.

_____
_____
_____
_____
_____

"No," I replied, hanging the frayed, oversized clown pants back up. I worked at this funky costume shop on South Congress called All The World's A Stage. Clown pants were on the **pedestrian** side of our collection.

It took the girl a second to recover, and I remembered seeing her earlier that day. She'd walked into the shop, flipped through the wands, swords, and umbrellas section, taken one look at me, and fled. As I checked the mesh skirt on a ballet tutu, she began again, "But Mickey said—"

"Mickey," I clarified, "is my boss. My heritage is not work related." I strode past her through a maze of stuffed clothes hangers to the stacks of magician and *The Cat in the Hat*–style hats.

She was harmless. Mildly offensive, definitely **intrusive,** but no different from a thousand other spoiled teenage girls when it came to things like Indian identity or, say, the fact that she was sporting dyed red hair, a gauzy green dress, two nose rings, and an infinity tattoo, which, in this neighborhood, made her a walking **cliché.**

The bell over the front door jangled, and the girl who'd been talking to me was gone. That's that, I figured. Easy come, easy . . . You know, she had these green eyes. They reminded me of someone else's eyes. While helping a frantic indie[2] filmmaker pick out three parasols and six pairs of white elbow gloves, I tried to remember whose.

A half hour or so later, a trio of very frat-looking guys cruised in.

"Can I help y'all?" I asked. Hey, it was my job.

One of them held up a hand, dismissing me. "In a minute, man."

I strolled from the makeup display past a row of soft rubber head masks to take my station behind a glass counter case

---

2. **indie:** slang for "independent." An indie filmmaker makes films without funding from a major studio.

Part 1 Collection 1: Plot and Setting

filled with plastic and rhinestone jewelry. Then I glanced around the store, watching the college guys pore through the racks of costumes.

Their behavior was textbook. Some guffaws at the classic horror capes, the Dracula and/or Frankenstein impression, a repeated joke or two from the latest slasher flick, and a jeering gibe at the most beta[3] of their pack, daring him to rent a showgirl feather boa. I checked the time on my runner's watch, already bored.

Just then, one of the college guys pulled out a Wild West Indian costume. It was ugly, cheap, and ridiculous looking—suede fringe and purple feathers on the **obligatory** pseudo-Plains headdress. He held the costume up to himself, and—as if all that wasn't enough—started making "war whoops."

The costume must be new for Halloween, I thought, gripping the edge of the glass counter until it cut into my palms. "Mickey!" I called, but nobody answered. He'd already taken off for lunch.

Maybe the minstrel show of an Indian costume was no big deal, not by itself. But it was one of a million little things (not to mention a few biggies), and they just kept on coming . . . like everybody who didn't believe in blond Cherokees . . . like a pretty but stupid girl who thought I was exotic. You know, I didn't even get her name.

Mine is Jason, like that *Friday the 13th* hockey mask on the shelf between the rubber skull and the Hillary Clinton face.

When the Indian costume landed on my glass counter, I was thinking about how much I needed that summer job. Even though the dot-commers were now all unemployed, they'd already driven up the cost of living near downtown. My dad wasn't high up at Dell. He was replaceable, and more recently, underemployed. Mama had her hands full at home with my baby brothers, the twins.

---

3. **beta:** Beta is the second letter of the Greek alphabet. Here, it is a term meaning "mild mannered or shy."

WORD STUDY

In line 57, the narrator refers to the behavior of the three guys as "textbook." From the context, what does this word mean?

_____

_____

_____

VOCABULARY

obligatory (ə·blig′ə·tôr′ē) *adj.:* required.

WORD STUDY

The term *minstrel show* (line 72) refers to variety shows especially popular between 1850 and 1870, in which white performers were made up in blackface and sang songs, told jokes, and paraded around in costume.

CONFLICT

In lines 80–86, the narrator gives us more information about his background. What conflict **causes** him to be thinking about how much he needs his job?

_____

_____

_____

_____

_____

A Real-Live Blond Cherokee and His Equally Annoyed Soul Mate   23

Rough Guides/Alamy

IDENTIFY CAUSE & EFFECT

Underline the words that describe the girl's mood now. What do you think **caused** her to cry?

_____
_____
_____
_____
_____

I was so busy mulling this over that I didn't hear the front doorbell and I didn't notice that Miss Gentrification had returned . . . at least not until she slammed her paper cup of cranberry tea on the glass counter in front of me. A tiny bit splashed out onto the *purple* fake Indian feathers, and I offered her my first smile of the day.

When I looked into those iced evergreen eyes, they were furious and a little teary. My fault, I realized, dropping my gaze to the amulet she wore around her neck. It was some kind of female power symbol, a little more mystic than you'd find at the neighborhood herb store.

24 Part 1 Collection 1: Plot and Setting

Her hand was still wrapped around the paper cup.

"I didn't come in here," she began, "to get your help with my report."

That was interesting.

"I'm not getting a C minus in history. A person could be in a coma in Mr. Cavazos's class and still pull a straight C."

She lied. I didn't like liars.

"The truth is that I came in here to ask you out, and I've never asked out a guy before, and I needed an excuse to talk to you. I'm not really good with guys."

I forgave her.

"But now, of course, since you're such a hugely unfriendly, mean, horrible, evil person, I just want to let you know that I have lost absolutely all interest." Before I could get a thought together, she'd spun in her wood sandals and headed toward the door, taking her tea with her.

"Wait!" I called, trying to think of something more to say.

"Nika!" shouted the war-whooping guy from the back of the store.

She stopped with her hand on the doorknob. But not for me. For him.

"Chad!" she replied.

Chad left his friends, made his way to the front of the store, and hugged . . . what was her name? Nika.

"Hey, *dude*," Chad called back to one of his pals, "pay for my costume, all right? I'll meet you back at the house." Then he wrapped a beefy arm around Nika and walked out of my costume shop with her.

Geez. I couldn't figure out how a **quirky** urban princess like that would even know . . . whatever he was. The Chad. And to boot, I had to spend the next five minutes ringing up his friends, who'd picked up such exciting, original costumes as the villain from the *Scream* series, George W, and an emergency room MD.

PLOT

In lines 99–111, the girl explains to the narrator why she is so upset. Explain in your own words what happened.

_____
_____
_____
_____
_____
_____
_____

INFER

In lines 124–125, Jason refers to Mickey's shop as "my costume shop." Why do you think he uses the word *my* here?

_____
_____
_____
_____
_____
_____
_____

VOCABULARY

quirky (kwûrk′ē) *adj.*: peculiar; odd.

A Real-Live Blond Cherokee and His Equally Annoyed Soul Mate   25

SUMMARIZE

Summarize Jason's thought process about Nika in lines 137–159.

_____
_____
_____
_____
_____
_____
_____
_____

FLUENCY

Read the boxed passage aloud, first for smoothness and then for emphasis. Note that Jason keeps mentioning the time and what he is doing. As you read, try to imagine how Jason feels.

VOCABULARY

excruciating
(eks·kroo′shē·āt′iŋ) *adj.*: intensely painful.

Why does he find taking time for the inventory to be "excruciating"?

_____
_____

As they finally jostled out of the front door, Mickey strolled in from the back. He was smiling and whistling. He'd gotten some *queso*[4] on his prized T-shirt that read "Note Vader" on one side and "Vote Nader"[5] on the other.

"Back from lunch," he said. "Did I miss anythin'?"

At one-fifteen, I rang up Jack and Jill and figured that fate was just like that.

> At two o'clock, I helped Liza straighten her wig and decided
> 140 that any girl who'd want Chad wasn't good enough for me.
>
> At three-nineteen, I watched Sonny and Cher leave hand in hand and worried that Chad was five or six years older than Nika.
>
> At three forty-one, the entire command crew of the *Enterprise*[6] (original series) needed new communicators, and I realized it was no big deal.
>
> At four-eleven, I looked into a crystal ball and it was clear that I should've been dating Indian girls anyway.
>
> At five-thirty, Catwoman salsa-danced in the aisles with Scooby Doo, and I remembered that Mickey was the one who
> 150 told Nika about me. I realized that he might know how I could get in contact with her.

At six o'clock, Mickey explained that Nika's family had started attending his Unitarian church last week, and that he'd invited them to stop by and check out the shop. Nice folks, he said. Lived by the microwave tower in Clarksville. Then he announced that we needed to do a little last-minute inventory before the Halloween rush. I spent **excruciating** minutes counting things like wax fangs, pirate hoop earrings, and the blow-up sheep belonging to Ms. Peep.

160 It still didn't get dark early yet, not in mid-October. I could see the smoke long before I found the house. It was a two-bedroom stone cottage in the hilly historic Clarksville neighborhood, and

---

4. *queso* (kā′sō) *n.*: Spanish for "cheese."
5. **"Vote Nader"**: a reference to Ralph Nader, who was the Green Party nominee for president of the United States in 1996 and 2000.
6. *Enterprise*: the spaceship commanded by the main characters on the popular television show *Star Trek.*

the front faced one of those long, steep alleys. To get there, I had to jog the hike-and-bike trail alongside downtown and cross the lake via the new pedestrian bridge. When I arrived, the temperature was still in the eighties, and sweat was pouring down my back and neck.

Ahead, the smoke billowed darker, denser.

Call me bold. Call me a trespasser. Call me an idiot. But I let myself into the gate and found Nika perched on a garden bench not far from a metal garbage can. I could see a low flame flickering out of the top. Leaves, I figured, burning leaves.

"Hi," I said, feeling daring. I considered mentioning that leaf burning was probably in violation of some city ordinance, but it wasn't really the kind of line I wanted to open with. I'd believed her when she confessed to being bad with guys. The truth was that I wasn't much of an expert with girls, either.

Nika had changed out of her quirky urban princess ensemble. She was wearing a plain white T-shirt and cutoff jeans. She didn't bother replying, but she didn't ask me to leave, either. For a while, we sat quietly side by side on the bench.

This is stupid, I thought. She's a mildly offensive, definitely intrusive, spoiled ... It didn't matter. I'd sought her out. I'd run to get there. But I still really hated Chad.

"He's my brother," she explained, even though I hadn't asked the question.

I was relieved and disappointed all at once.

"He's always good to me ... kind of overprotective ... sort of annoying. But good." Her tone was apologetic.

I glanced at her hair and realized it wasn't dyed red; it was natural. My gaze followed the blazing hue up to the flames from the garbage can a few feet away. The color wasn't quite the same; her hair was a deeper red, more alive. Staring more carefully at the small blaze, I realized that what was burning wasn't leaves.

IDENTIFY CAUSE & EFFECT

What has **caused** Jason to make the trip to Nika's house (lines 160–167)?

CONFLICT

In lines 176–177, what does Jason admit is his **internal conflict**?

A Real-Live Blond Cherokee and His Equally Annoyed Soul Mate 27

PLOT

What do you think is the story's **climax**—the moment when the outcome of the story is determined?

_____
_____
_____
_____
_____
_____

IDENTIFY CAUSE & EFFECT

Re-read lines 199–202. How do Nika's actions affect Jason? Circle the sentence that explains how he feels.

PLOT

In your own words, explain the **resolution** of the story (lines 210–212).

_____
_____
_____
_____
_____
_____
_____
_____

It was fake Indian fringe and fake Indian feathers. Some of them were purple. She'd torched the costume that her brother Chad had rented from my store.

Nika said, "I'll pay Mickey back."

I rubbed my eyes. "It's the smoke," I explained, surprised by how much the gesture affected me. Glad that somebody else got it for once, that it wasn't up to me to deal alone. I understood now why I'd had to find her. When I looked back down at Nika again, I saw hints of my grandmother. Not my Cherokee grandma, my Irish one. The one with those eyes people sing about on street corners and in late-night bars. The one who was annoyed by the Celtic fad and framed four-leaf clovers. The one who couldn't stand the folks who flocked to see _Lord of the Dance._[7] Wannabes, Gramma called them. Gramma with her iced evergreen eyes.

My hand moved as if I had no control over it, and my fingers gently threaded her crimson locks. I ran my palm down the curve of her freckled cheek, and I lifted her chin gently.

---

7. **_Lord of the Dance:_** musical production featuring traditional Irish elements.

28 Part 1 Collection 1: Plot and Setting

MEET THE WRITER

Like Jason, the narrator of "A Real-Live Blond Cherokee and His Equally Annoyed Soul Mate," **Cynthia Leitich Smith** (1967–   ) is an American Indian—she is a member of the Muscogee (Creek) Nation. When she was a child, Smith spent every weekend at the library. Her love of reading led her to writing, eventually to journalism, and then to law school, which she attended with the goal of becoming a legal journalist. Ultimately, her passion for writing led her to quit her legal job and write full time. Her first book, *Jingle Dancer*, is a children's book about Native American culture. Since becoming a published author, Smith has moved on to writing for young adults. She also has created and maintains a Web site on children's literature resources.

SKILLS PRACTICE

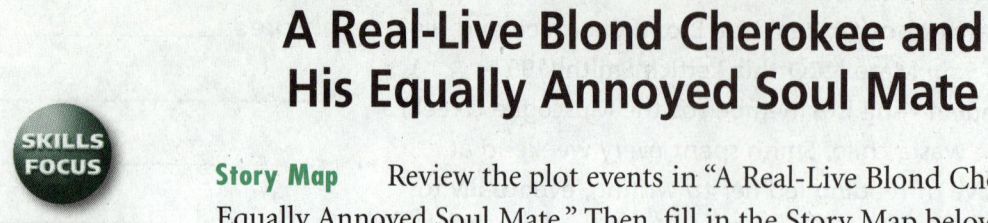

A Real-Live Blond Cherokee and His Equally Annoyed Soul Mate

SKILLS FOCUS
Literary Skills
Analyze plot.

Story Map Review the plot events in "A Real-Live Blond Cherokee and His Equally Annoyed Soul Mate." Then, fill in the Story Map below.

Title

Setting

Characters

Problem

↓

Event 1

Event 2

Event 3

Event 4

Event 5 (Climax)

↓

Resolution

30 Part 1 Collection 1: Plot and Setting

Skills Review

A Real-Live Blond Cherokee and His Equally Annoyed Soul Mate

VOCABULARY AND COMPREHENSION

Word Box
- pedestrian
- obligatory
- intrusive
- quirky
- cliché
- excruciating

A. Vocabulary in Context   Complete each sentence below by writing a word from the Word Box in each blank. One word will not be used.

1. Jason thought the costumes that Chad and his friends chose were _____ and dull.

2. Chad and his friends chose a Wild West Indian costume that was a _____—not at all what real Plains Indians would have worn.

3. The antics of the boys in the costume shop made Chad laugh, but Jason found their behavior _____, because it made fun of his heritage.

4. The strange, _____ outfit Nika wore included a nose ring and a tattoo.

5. Jason thought that Nika's questions were _____, and he wanted to retain his privacy, so he denied her request for an interview.

B. Reading Comprehension   Answer each question below.

1. When Jason first talks with Nika, is he seeing her, or is he seeing his ideas about her?
   _____

2. Why does Nika want to interview Jason?
   _____

3. What does Nika's burning of the pseudo-Indian costume signify to Jason?
   _____

SKILLS FOCUS

Literary Skills
Analyze plot events.

Vocabulary Skills
Use context to identify word meanings.

A Real-Live Blond Cherokee and His Equally Annoyed Soul Mate   31

Collection 2

Character

Thinkstock/Alamy

Academic Vocabulary for Collection 2

These are the terms you should know
as you read and analyze the selections in this collection.

Character traits The special qualities of a character, such as his or her behaviors, values, habits, likes, and dislikes.

Characterization The way writers reveal how and why characters think, feel, and act. In **direct characterization** the writer explains straight out, or directly, what the characters are like ("good" or "evil" or "lazy"). In **indirect characterization** the writer provides clues to what the characters are like. Clues are often found in the characters' words, private thoughts, and actions as well as in the ways they look and dress.

Motivation The reasons why a character acts or thinks in a certain way.

• • •

Protagonist The main character in a story, usually the one who sets the action in motion.

Antagonist The character or force that blocks the protagonist from achieving his or her goal.

Subordinate characters Less important characters.

• • •

Flat character A character who has only one or two key personality traits. A flat character is almost never the main character.

Round character A character who has many personality traits, just as a person in real life does.

Stock character A one-sided character whom we think of as a "type"—for example, the absent-minded professor.

• • •

Dynamic character A character who changes in an important way during the story. The change might involve recognition of some truth about life.

Static character A character who is the same at the end of the story as at the beginning; static characters are most often subordinate characters.

Before You Read

Museum Indians by Susan Power

What if you had to describe someone close to you—your mother, grandfather, cousin, or friend? What details about that person's life would you include? How would you explain how that person came to be who he or she is?

LITERARY FOCUS: CHARACTER—DESCRIBING A PERSON

In "Museum Indians," the narrator describes her mother, explaining the life-long journey she has made to bring the two of them where they are now. **Character traits** are the special qualities unique to a person, including that person's values, likes and dislikes, habits, and ways of speaking. In literature you can learn about a character's traits by paying attention to the details given by the narrator.

- In "Museum Indians," imagine that the narrator is turning the pages of a photo album and showing you various occasions and events in her mother's life. Along the way you will learn about her mother's past and her journey to the present.

READING SKILLS: MAKING INFERENCES ABOUT CHARACTERS

An **inference** is an educated guess based on evidence in the text and on what you already know. When you make inferences about characters, you should pay attention to what they say and do as well as how they are described by other people.

To track evidence and to make inferences about the characters in "Museum Indians," fill in a chart like this one:

Character	Text Evidence	What the Text Reveals About the Character

SKILLS FOCUS

Literary Skills
Understand character and characterization.

Reading Skills
Make inferences about a character.

Vocabulary Skills
Clarify word meanings using context clues.

ESSAY

VOCABULARY DEVELOPMENT

PREVIEW SELECTION VOCABULARY

The following words appear in "Museum Indians." Look them over before you begin reading.

integral (in′tə·grəl) *adj.:* necessary to the whole; essential.

*Certain details of her mother's history are **integral** to the daughter's narratives.*

petrified (pe′trə·fīd′) *v.* used as *adj.:* frozen in fear.

*On the long train ride from South Dakota to Chicago, Illinois, she was too **petrified** to leave her seat.*

anecdotes (an′ik·dōts′) *n.:* short, often humorous stories about personal events.

*The narrator prefers her mother's **anecdotes** to the stories found in history books, even if they cannot be proven.*

intrigues (in′trēgz) *n.:* plots; schemes.

*The Egyptian dead, despite their **intrigues**, still ended up on display in a Chicago museum.*

disconcerting (dis′·kən·surt′iŋ) *v.* used as *adj.:* startling; upsetting.

*The headless museum Indians are a **disconcerting** sight.*

CLARIFYING WORD MEANINGS: LOOK AT THE CONTEXT

When you come across an unfamiliar word, look at the **context**—the words or phrases surrounding the word—for clues to its meaning. Often, writers use a **definition**, a **restatement**, or an **example** near that word. Read the following sentence from "Museum Indians":

> "She was *petrified* of all the strange people and new surroundings; she stayed in her seat all the way from McLaughlin, South Dakota, to Chicago, Illinois, and didn't move once."

Notice how the author describes what her mother is *petrified* of: strange people, new surroundings. Also, because she is *petrified,* she doesn't move. From this context you might guess that the definition of *petrified* is "paralyzed with fear."

As you read "Museum Indians," look at the context of any unfamiliar words.

Museum Indians 35

Museum Indians

Susan Power

A snake coils in my mother's dresser drawer; it is thick and black, glossy as sequins. My mother cut her hair several years ago, before I was born, but she kept one heavy braid. It is the three-foot snake I lift from its nest and handle as if it were alive.

"Mom, why did you cut your hair?" I ask. I am a little girl lifting a sleek black river into the light that streams through the kitchen window. Mom turns to me.

"It gave me headaches. Now put that away and wash your hands for lunch."

"You won't cut *my* hair, will you?" I'm sure this is a whine.

"No, just a little trim now and then to even the ends."

I return the dark snake to its nest among my mother's slips, arranging it so that its thin tail hides beneath the wide mouth sheared by scissors. My mother keeps her promise and lets my hair grow long, but I am only half of her; my thin brown braids will reach the middle of my back, and in maturity will look like tiny garden snakes.

My mother tells me stories every day: while she cleans, while she cooks, on our way to the library, standing in the checkout line at the supermarket. I like to share her stories with other people, and chatter like a monkey when I am able to command adult attention.

"She left the reservation when she was sixteen years old," I tell my audience. Sixteen sounds very old to me, but I always state the number because it seems **integral** to my recitation. "She had never been on a train before, or used a telephone. She left Standing Rock to take a job in Chicago so she could help out the family during the war. She was **petrified** of all the strange people

"Museum Indians" from *Roofwalker* by Susan Power. Copyright © 2002 by Susan Power. Reproduced by permission of **Milkweed Editions**.

Entrance to the Field Museum of Natural History, Chicago, Illinois.
David Ball/CORBIS

and new surroundings; she stayed in her seat all the way from McLaughlin, South Dakota, to Chicago, Illinois, and didn't move once."

I usually laugh after saying this, because I cannot imagine my mother being afraid of anything. She is so tall, a true Dakota woman; she rises against the sun like a skyscraper, and when I draw her picture in my notebook, she takes up the entire page. She talks politics and attends sit-ins,[1] wrestles with the Chicago police and says what's on her mind.

I am her small shadow and witness. I am the timid daughter who can rage only on paper.

We don't have much money, but Mom takes me from one end of the city to the other on foot, on buses. I will grow up believing that Chicago belongs to me, because it was given to me

1. **sit-ins:** acts in which participants protest against a cause by sitting in a public place until they are forcibly removed or their complaints are answered.

CHARACTER

In this paragraph the author describes how she sees her mother. What can you infer about her mother's **character** from the author's description of her?

_____
_____
_____
_____
_____
_____
_____
_____
_____

Museum Indians 37

ANALYZE

Re-read lines 42–51. Why does the mother lecture the guides at the Historical Society?

_____
_____
_____
_____
_____
_____
_____
_____
_____
_____

VOCABULARY

anecdotes (an′ik·dōts′) *n.:* short, often humorous stories about personal events.

intrigues (in·trēgz′) *n.:* plots; schemes.

WORD STUDY

The word *buckskin* (line 74) means "leather made from deerskin." Many early Americans wore clothes and shoes made of buckskin, which was prized for its softness and was a yellowish gray color.

---

by my mother. Nearly every week we tour the Historical Society, and Mom makes a point of complaining about the statue that depicts an Indian man about to kill a white woman and her children: "This is the only monument to the history of Indians in this area that you have on exhibit. It's a shame because it is completely one-sided. Children who see this will think this is what Indians are all about."

50   My mother lectures the guides and their bosses, until eventually that statue disappears.

Some days we haunt the Art Institute, and my mother pauses before a Picasso.[2]

"He did this during his blue period," she tells me.

I squint at the blue man holding a blue guitar. "Was he very sad?" I ask.

"Yes, I think he was." My mother takes my hand and looks away from the painting. I can see a story developing behind her eyes, and I tug on her arm to release the words. She will tell me
60 why Picasso was blue, what his thoughts were as he painted this canvas. She relates **anecdotes** I will never find in books, never see footnoted in a biography of the master artist. I don't even bother to check these references because I like my mother's version best.

When Mom is down, we go to see the mummies at the Field Museum of Natural History. The Egyptian dead sleep in the basement, most of them still shrouded in their wrappings.

"These were people like us," my mother whispers. She pulls me into her waist. "They had dreams and **intrigues** and problems with their teeth. They thought their one particular life was of the
70 utmost significance. And now, just *look* at them." My mother never fails to brighten. "So what's the use of worrying too hard or too long? Might as well be cheerful."

Before we leave this place, we always visit my great-grandmother's buckskin dress. We mount the stairs and walk through the museum's main hall—past the dinosaur bones all

---

2. **Picasso:** Pablo Picasso (1881–1973), Spanish artist whose work is some of the most influential in modern art.

strung together, and the stuffed elephants lifting their trunks in a mute trumpet.

The clothed figures are **disconcerting** because they have no heads. I think of them as dead Indians. We reach the traditional outfits of the Sioux in the Plains Indian section, and there is the dress, as magnificent as I remembered. The yoke[3] is completely beaded—I know the garment must be heavy to wear. My great-grandmother used blue beads as a background for the geometrical design, and I point to the azure expanse.

"Was this her blue period?" I ask my mother. She hushes me unexpectedly, she will not play the game. I come to understand that this is a solemn call, and we stand before the glass case as we would before a grave.

"I don't know how this got out of the family," Mom murmurs. I feel helpless beside her, wishing I could reach through the glass to disrobe the headless mannequin. My mother belongs in a grand buckskin dress such as this, even though her hair is now too short to braid and has been trained to curl at the edges in a saucy flip.

We leave our fingerprints on the glass, two sets of hands at different heights pressing against the barrier. Mom is sad to leave.

"I hope she knows we visit her dress," my mother says.

There is a little buffalo across the hall, stuffed and staring. Mom doesn't always have the heart to greet him. Some days we slip out of the museum without finding his stall.

"You don't belong here," Mom tells him on those rare occasions when she feels she must pay her respects. "We honor you," she continues, "because you are a creature of great endurance and great generosity. You provided us with so many things that helped us to survive. It makes me angry to see you like this."

Few things can make my mother cry; the buffalo is one of them.

---

3. **yoke** *n.*: piece that supports the gathered parts of a garment.

COMPARE & CONTRAST

Pause at and re-read lines 113–120. In what ways is the author different from her mother here?

___

"I am just like you," she whispers. "I don't belong here either. We should be in the Dakotas, somewhere a little bit east of the Missouri River. This crazy city is not a fit home for buffalo or Dakotas."

I take my mother's hand to hold her in place. I am a city child, nervous around livestock and lonely on the plains. I am afraid of a sky without light pollution—I never knew there could be so many stars. I lead my mother from the museum so she will forget the sense of loss. From the marble steps we can see Lake Shore Drive spill ahead of us, and I sweep my arm to the side as if I were responsible for this view. I introduce my mother to the city she gave me. I call her home.

MEET THE WRITER

Susan Power (1961–   ) spent her early life hearing her mother tell her stories by day and her father read her stories by night. "Museum Indians," her autobiographical essay about her mother, is from her book *Roofwalker*. Power is a member of the Standing Rock Sioux, and most of her writing deals with contemporary Native American issues. Her first novel, *The Grass Dancer,* tells the story of a young Sioux and his heritage. Having graduated from Harvard Law School and then the Iowa Writers' Workshop, Power is happy to finally be out of school and able to concentrate on her writing.

SKILLS PRACTICE

Museum Indians

Inference and Character Chart The following chart will help you make inferences about both the author and her mother. The inferences are based in part on what the characters say about themselves and in part on what they do. Fill in the blank spaces with details from the selection. Then, write your inferences in the last box of each row.

SKILLS FOCUS

Literary Skills
Analyze character.

Reading Skills
Make inferences about character.

	What She Says	What She Does	My Inference
Author			
Mother			

Museum Indians   41

Skills Review

Museum Indians

VOCABULARY AND COMPREHENSION

Word Box
- integral
- petrified
- anecdotes
- intrigues
- disconcerting

A. Vocabulary in Context   Fill in each sentence below with a word from the Word Box.

1. Being part Cherokee is _____ to Susan Power's writing—she often writes about Native American themes.

2. Many of the _____ Power was told by her mother appear in different forms in her writing today.

3. Some of the stories her mother told her dealt with the _____, or schemes, of her ancestors.

4. Power might find it _____ if these stories of her heritage were lost or misinterpreted.

5. Power's mother was _____ on her first train journey to Chicago.

B. Reading Comprehension   Answer each question below.

1. What place does the mother most identify with?
   _____
   _____

2. What place does the daughter most identify with?
   _____
   _____

3. How does the mother's personal history affect her response to the museum display?
   _____
   _____

4. What is the significance of the story's title?
   _____
   _____

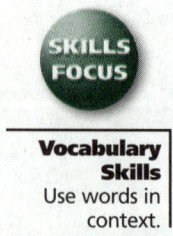

SKILLS FOCUS
Vocabulary Skills
Use words in context.

Collection 2: Character

Before You Read

GRAPHIC STORY

Super Unleaded by Derek Kirk Kim

Have you ever been stuck between two people who are not getting along? What if they were your parents or two of your best friends? How would you deal with the situation?

LITERARY FOCUS: CHARACTER AND MOTIVATION

Characters in stories, just like people in real life, form relationships with others. These relationships are important to the story, and often they can explain a character's **motivation**—the reasons he or she takes certain actions.

- As you read this graphic story, pay close attention to the interaction between the mother, father, and son.
- Look for the mother's motivations—the reasons she takes the actions she does. How does her relationship with her husband explain her actions? How does all of this affect their son?

READING SKILLS: READING GRAPHIC STORIES

A graphic story is sequential art—a combination of narrative text and panels of images that together tell a story. Instead of simply reading the text, as you would with a short story, you must also pay attention to the illustrations and make connections from one panel to the next. As you read "Super Unleaded," use the following tips:

- Read the panels as you would a printed page. Read from left to right and from the top of the page to the bottom.
- Read one panel at a time. First, read the text in the panel. Then, study the illustration.
- Look at the faces of the characters and how they change from panel to panel. Make inferences about how the characters look and how changes in their facial or body language may suggest a change in emotion.
- Ask yourself, "What do the pictures tell me that the text does not?"

SKILLS FOCUS

Literary Skills
Understand character and motivation.

Reading Skills
Read a graphic story.

Super Unleaded 43

SUPER UNLEADED

Derek Kirk Kim

IDENTIFY

Why is the narrator's room rumbling? What is the narrator doing in his room?

_____
_____
_____

INFER

In the third panel, circle the words that describe what the narrator is expecting that doesn't happen.

IDENTIFY CAUSE & EFFECT

Aware that something is wrong, the narrator decides to investigate. What does he do?

_____
_____
_____
_____

CHARACTER

What information does the narrator give you about his father?

_____
_____
_____
_____

> My room rumbled as the garage door opened below. I could hear the raindrops pebbling the hood of the Nissan as it pulled up the driveway.

> My mom got out of the passenger seat and raced into the garage, her heels clicking. Dad directed the car into the garage after her, and reclosed the door.

> I stretched away from my Trigonometry homework and rubbed my eyes. I waited for Mom to poke her head through my door and say hi, but she didn't.

> When I lumbered into the kitchen, Mom was near the sink, chopping up some Spam. Peas were frying over the stove.

> Dad was in the living room, sunk in his armchair and watching TV. He kept it on mute because his hearing wasn't any good and the subtitles were easier for him to follow. An Asian newscaster was silently mouthing some news of a flood somewhere.

"Hi, Mom."

> She unloaded the peas on a plate and replaced the pan with Spam. It hissed and popped.

"Super Unleaded" from *Same Difference and Other Stories* by Derek Kirk Kim. Copyright © 2004, 2005 by **Derek Kirk Kim**. Reproduced by permission of the author.

44 Part 1 Collection 2: Character

IDENTIFY

What does the mother do after she cooks dinner? Circle the words that explain what the narrator physically senses as she leaves.

Comic Panels

Panel 1:
"What's wrong? You look mad."
"What's there to be happy about?"

Panel 2:
"...I'm tired from work."

Panel 3:
After she finished fixing our dinner, she changed into casual clothes and went over to a friend's house. I felt the garage door open and close again as she left.

Panel 4:
Dad and I sat down at our round dinner table and chewed our omelets. We passed the salsa back and forth and commented on the rain.

Panel 5:
I only finished half of the omelet, so I saran wrapped the rest and placed it on the counter. We managed to finish off the bottle of salsa though. Once the table had been cleared, Dad began dealing himself a game of Solitaire.

Panel 6:
I started washing the dishes when the phone rang. Dad picked it up after the second ring like clockwork.
"Hello? ...Sure, okay, one second."

Panel 7:
"It's Mom. She says she wants to talk to you."

Panel 8:
"Hello, Mom?"

CHARACTER

Pause and reflect on Dad's **character**. What do you know about him so far?

PREDICT

Why do you think Mom wants to talk to her son?

Super Unleaded 45

CHARACTER

Why does the mother call her son? What does this tell you about her **character**?

_____
_____
_____
_____
_____

IDENTIFY

Why is the narrator's mom upset with his father?

_____
_____
_____
_____
_____
_____

INFER

What role is the narrator asked to play between his parents?

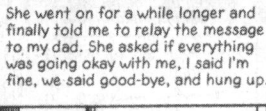

_____
_____
_____
_____
_____
_____
_____
_____

* **BART** (Bay Area Rapid Transit): San Francisco Bay Area's rail/subway system.

46   Part 1   Collection 2: Character

Comic Panels

Panel 1: After I told him what she had said, he shook his head without looking up from the cards.
"I'm disappointed she told you instead of me."

Panel 2: "Well, she said she told you three times before and she didn't want to face telling you again."
"No, she didn't. She never told me before. She said something once like, 'why don't you pick up gas before you pick me up?' or something... Like a question, but she never *told* me anything."

Panel 3: "She said she told you three times... She said since you don't do anything in the daytime, you should have plenty of time to get gas before you pick her up. And she said when she gets off work, she's tired and she wants to get home and relax and not wait for you to pump gas..."

Panel 4: "Huh! It takes me maybe five minutes to pump gas."
"I know, I was thinking the same thing."

Panel 5: "Here's what happened... She said she wanted to stop at the Korean market so I said, 'Okay, but first let me stop at the Shell to pump gas.' When I finished pumping and got back in the car, she said she doesn't wanna go anymore. When I asked her why, she just said she changed her mind."
HAPPY RETIREMENT

Panel 6: "...um... Well, anyway, now you know what she's mad about... And I agree with you... I don't know why she's getting so mad at such a trivial thing."
"It's hard to understand her sometimes..."

Panel 7: "It's probably not just this incident, Dad, but a series of things that led up to this."

IDENTIFY
In the third panel on this page, what do you see? Why do you think the author chooses to illustrate this?

INFER
What can you infer from the family photographs about the mother and father's relationship?

CHARACTER
What is the narrator's response to his father's explanation? What does the narrator's body language tell you about his **character**?

Super Unleaded

CHARACTER

How is the mother's behavior toward the father similar to her behavior toward her son? What might this tell you about her **character**?

_____
_____
_____
_____
_____
_____
_____
_____
_____
_____

ANALYZE

Notice that it has finally stopped raining but to the narrator the world looks as though it is underwater. What do you think this symbolizes?

_____
_____
_____
_____
_____
_____
_____
_____

MEET THE WRITER

Derek Kirk Kim (1974–) writes and illustrates short stories that are published in book form. He was born in Korea, where reading comics was a normal part of learning to read. He remembers imitating the style of those comics as soon as he learned how to draw. At the age of eight, he moved to the United States.

> I finished washing the dishes and took out the trash.
> My father packed the cards into a neat rectangle block and set it on the center of the glass table top.

> He hobbled across the living room relatively smoothly and fell into the armchair. His Multiple Sclerosis behaves much better on cool days. He turned on the TV again and clicked the sound back on.

> It was pumped up so loud I could barely stand it.

> I returned to my room and closed the door. A muffled commercial was thumping against the wall as I sat down in front of my Trigonometry homework again. I stared at an equation for a long time before picking up the pencil.

> I hoped to finish it soon, so I could jump into bed before the garage door roared open again.

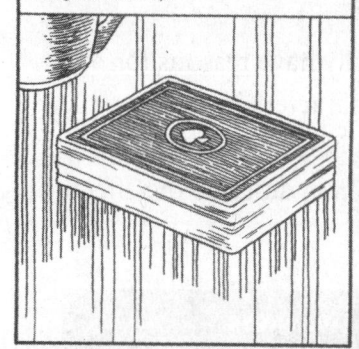

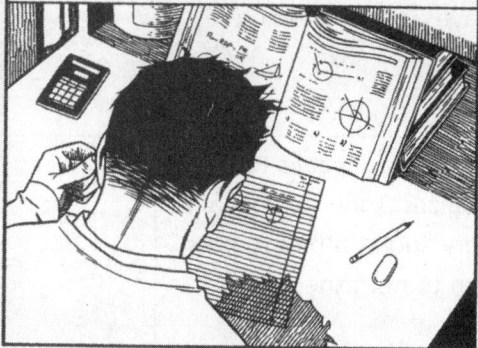

Growing up in Pacifica, California, where he still lives, he pursued his passion for writing and drawing realistic fiction. "Super Unleaded" is just one of the stories that appear in his award-winning collection *Same Difference and Other Stories*.

IDENTIFY

What important information do we learn about the father? Why does he turn the volume up on the television?

MOTIVATION

The narrator wants to be in bed before the garage door opens again. What is his **motivation**?

Super Unleaded 49

SKILLS PRACTICE

Super Unleaded

SKILLS FOCUS

Literary Skills Analyze characters' motivations.

Character Motivation Chart Characters in stories generally have reasons for the actions they take. Some of the actions taken by the characters in "Super Unleaded" are listed in the left-hand column of the chart below. In the right-hand column, fill in the **motivations** of the characters. Then, describe the effect of his parents' actions on the son.

Story Events	Motivations
1. Parents get home. The father puts the TV on mute. The mother makes dinner and leaves without eating.	
2. The mother phones, speaks to the son, and apologizes. Then she explains why she is angry and asks him to pass this message on to his father.	
3. The father says she has asked not three times but only once. The father and son agree that this is a trivial incident. The son thinks it's probably one in a series.	
4. The father plays solitaire, and the son finishes the dishes. The father goes back to the television. The son hopes to be in bed before his mother arrives home.	

How do you think the son feels about being in the middle of the fight between his parents? Explain, using the details from the text to support your answer.

_____

_____

_____

50   Part 1   Collection 2: Character

Skills Review

Super Unleaded

COMPREHENSION

Reading Comprehension Answer each question below.

1. What is the narrator's role in his family?
   _____
   _____
   _____
   _____

2. How does the narrator attempt to resolve the conflict between his parents?
   _____
   _____
   _____
   _____

3. How do both the mother and the father contribute to the conflict?
   _____
   _____
   _____
   _____

4. How does this conflict affect the narrator?
   _____
   _____
   _____
   _____

Collection

3

Narrator and Voice

Lisa Zador/Getty Images

Academic Vocabulary for Collection 3

These are the terms you should know
as you read and analyze the selections in this collection.

Narrator The storyteller, the voice telling you the story.

Point of view The vantage point, or perspective, from which a writer tells a story. There are three main points of view: omniscient (äm·nish′ənt), first person, and third person limited. *Omniscient* means "all knowing."

- In the **omniscient point of view,** the narrator knows everything that is going on in the story, including the characters' thoughts and feelings. This type of narrator rarely plays a direct role in the story.

- In the **first-person point of view,** one of the characters tells the story, using the personal pronoun *I*. We know only what this person knows and see only what this person sees. Some first-person narrators are **credible,** or reliable—we can believe what they tell us. Other first-person narrators are not credible—we can't believe everything they say because they may not be telling the truth, or they may not know what the truth is.

- In the **third-person-limited point of view,** the narrator tells the story from the vantage point of only one character. The narrator reveals the thoughts and feelings of this character, and events are limited to what this character experiences and observes.

• • •

Voice A term in literature that refers to a writer's special use of language in a story, including diction and tone.

- **Diction** is the kinds of words a writer chooses. Diction can be formal, informal, poetic, plain, full of slang, and so on. Diction has a powerful effect on the tone of a piece of writing.

- **Tone** is the attitude a writer takes toward an audience, a subject, or a character. Tone is conveyed through a writer's choice of words and details. For example, tone can be humorous, sad, or friendly.

Before You Read

Sweet Potato Pie by Eugenia Collier

The narrator of this story, Buddy, has reason to be thankful to his older siblings, but most of all to Charley, his oldest brother.

LITERARY FOCUS: FIRST-PERSON POINT OF VIEW AND VOICE

- "Sweet Potato Pie" is told from the **first-person point of view.** The narrator, Buddy, recounts adult experiences in New York City as well as childhood experiences in the South.
- **Voice** is the writer's distinctive use of language. It consists of diction (the choice of words) and tone (the attitude expressed).
- The writer of "Sweet Potato Pie," Eugenia Collier, uses different styles of **diction** to help establish characterization. As you read, notice how the way Buddy speaks differs from the way the rest of his family speaks.
- **Tone** is the attitude the writer has toward the subject, events, or characters. Tone can be sympathetic, critical, ironic, humorous, hopeful, angry, and so on. As you read, ask yourself, "What tone does the writer take toward the events in the story?"

READING SKILLS: IDENTIFYING CAUSE AND EFFECT

A cause-and-effect pattern shows how or why one thing leads to another. The **cause** is the reason an action takes place. The **effect** is the result or consequence of the action. To find a cause, ask yourself, "Why did this happen?" To find an effect, ask, "What happened because of this?"

You might want to record the cause-and-effect patterns you find in "Sweet Potato Pie" in a chart like this one:

Cause: Why did this happen?	Effect: What happened because of this?

SKILLS FOCUS

Literary Skills
Understand first-person narration. Understand voice.

Reading Skills
Understand cause and effect.

Vocabulary Skills
Understand figurative language.

Part 1 Collection 3: Narrator and Voice

VOCABULARY DEVELOPMENT

PREVIEW SELECTION VOCABULARY

The following words appear in "Sweet Potato Pie." Look them over before you begin the story.

entities (en′tə·tēz) *n.*: real beings or things.

> Buddy's parents often seemed like shadowy figures, but at church they were solid **entities.**

edifice (ed′i·fis) *n.*: building.

> Their church was a frail **edifice,** but it offered Buddy's parents security and hope.

ubiquitous (yoo·bik′wə·təs) *adj.*: appearing everywhere.

> Charley's **ubiquitous** wet rag appeared whenever Buddy stuttered.

apex (ā′peks′) *n.*: high point.

> Buddy's graduation may well have been the **apex** of his parents' life.

assailed (ə·sāld′) *v.*: attacked; forcefully affected.

> Buddy was **assailed** by the unfamiliar bright lights of the city.

RECOGNIZING FIGURATIVE LANGUAGE

Words and phrases that describe one thing in terms of a second, very different thing are called **figurative language**. Figurative language is not meant to be taken literally but instead uses comparison to create pictures as well as greater understanding in the mind of the reader.

- An **idiom** is an expression peculiar to a particular language, one that cannot be understood from the literal, or dictionary, definitions of its words. For example, *seven hungry mouths to feed* is an idiom that means "seven children."
- A **simile** uses connecting words such as *like, as, than,* or *resembles* in making a comparison between two unlike things. For example: *The children were as hungry as baby birds in a nest.*
- A **metaphor** makes a comparison by saying that something *is* something else. It does not use a connecting word. For example: *Mother hurried to make sandwiches for her hungry nestlings.*

As you read "Sweet Potato Pie," notice the author's use of figurative language.

Sweet Potato Pie

Eugenia Collier

POINT OF VIEW

Circle pronouns in lines 1–8 that reveal the story is told from the **first-person point of view.**

INFER

Underline the **simile** in the first sentence. What does this figure of speech reveal about the setting of the story?

_____

_____

_____

_____

VOICE

Underline the **simile** in lines 11–12. From the narrator's **diction,** or choice of words, what can you infer about his education? Explain.

_____

_____

_____

_____

WORD STUDY

In line 14, the narrator refers to his childhood home as a *shanty.* Circle the synonym for *shanty* in line 27.

From up here on the fourteenth floor, my brother Charley looks like an insect scurrying among other insects. A deep feeling of love surges through me. Despite the distance, he seems to feel it, for he turns and scans the upper windows, but failing to find me, continues on his way.

I watch him moving quickly—gingerly, it seems to me—down Fifth Avenue and around the corner to his shabby taxicab. In a moment he will be heading back uptown.

I turn from the window and flop down on the bed, shoes and all. Perhaps because of what happened this afternoon or maybe just because I see Charley so seldom, my thoughts hover over him like hummingbirds. The cheerful, impersonal tidiness of this room is a world away from Charley's walk-up flat in Harlem[1] and a hundred worlds from the bare, noisy shanty where he and the rest of us spent what there was of childhood. I close my eyes, and side by side I see the Charley of my boyhood and the Charley of this afternoon, as clearly as if I were looking at a split TV screen. Another surge of love, seasoned with gratitude, wells up in me.

As far as I know, Charley never had any childhood at all. The oldest children of sharecroppers never do. Mama and Pa were shadowy figures whose voices I heard vaguely in the morning when sleep was shallow and whom I glimpsed as they left for the field before I was fully awake or as they trudged wearily into the house at night when my lids were irresistibly heavy.

They came into sharp focus only on special occasions. One such occasion was the day when the crops were in and the sharecroppers were paid. In our cabin there was so much excitement

---

1. **Harlem:** neighborhood in New York City, whose residents are primarily African American and Hispanic.

"Sweet Potato Pie" by Eugenia Collier from *Black World*, August 1972. © 1972 by **Eugenia Collier.** Reproduced by permission of the author.

in the air that even I, the "baby," responded to it. For weeks we had been running out of things that we could neither grow nor get on credit. On the evening of that day we waited anxiously for our parents' return. Then we would cluster around the rough wooden table—I on Lil's lap or clinging to Charley's neck, little Alberta nervously tugging her plait,[2] Jamie crouched at Mama's elbow, like a panther about to spring, and all seven of us silent for once, waiting. Pa would place money on the table—gently, for it was made from the sweat of their bodies and from their children's tears. Mama would count it out in little piles, her dark face stern and, I think now, beautiful. Not with the hollow beauty of well-modeled features but with the strong radiance of one who has suffered and never yielded.

"This for store bill," she would mutter, making a little pile. "This for c'llection. This for piece o' gingham . . ."[3] and so on, stretching the money as tight over our collective needs as Jamie's outgrown pants were stretched over my bottom. "Well, that's the crop." She would look up at Pa at last. "It'll do." Pa's face would relax, and a general grin flitted from child to child. We would survive, at least for the present.

The other time when my parents were solid **entities** was at church. On Sundays we would don our threadbare Sunday-go-to-meeting clothes and tramp, along with neighbors similarly attired, to the Tabernacle Baptist Church, the frail **edifice** of bare boards held together by God knows what, which was all that my parents ever knew of security and future promise.

Being the youngest and therefore the most likely to err, I was plopped between my father and my mother on the long wooden bench. They sat huge and eternal like twin mountains at my sides. I remember my father's still, black profile silhouetted against the sunny window, looking back into dark recesses of time, into some dim antiquity, like an ancient ceremonial mask. My mother's face, usually sternly set, changed with the varying

---

2. **plait** (plāt) n.: braid.
3. **gingham** (giŋ'əm) n.: cotton fabric.

INTERPRET

Underline the **metaphor** in lines 35–37. What **tone**, or attitude toward the narrator's childhood, is revealed by this figure of speech?

INFER

Pause at line 47. From what you have read so far, what do you think the life of a sharecropper—someone who farms land that is owned by someone else for a share of the crop—was like?

VOCABULARY

entities (en'tə·tēz) n.: real beings or things.

edifice (ed'i·fis) n.: building.

Sweet Potato Pie 57

INTERPRET

In lines 71–77, underline details of what the narrator's sister Lil did. Circle details of how she sounded. What is your impression of this important sister?

_____
_____
_____
_____
_____

SUMMARIZE

Summarize what you learn of the narrator's brother Charley in lines 78–93.

_____
_____
_____
_____
_____
_____
_____
_____
_____
_____

nuances[4] of her emotion, its planes shifting, shaped by the soft highlights of the sanctuary, as she progressed from a subdued "amen" to a loud "Help me, Jesus" wrung from the depths of her gaunt frame.

My early memories of my parents are associated with special occasions. The contours of my everyday were shaped by Lil and Charley, the oldest children, who rode herd on the rest of us while Pa and Mama toiled in fields not their own. Not until years later did I realize that Lil and Charley were little more than children themselves.

Lil had the loudest, screechiest voice in the county. When she yelled, "Boy, you better git yourself in here!" you *got* yourself in there. It was Lil who caught and bathed us, Lil who fed us and sent us to school, Lil who punished us when we needed punishing and comforted us when we needed comforting. If her voice was loud, so was her laughter. When she laughed, everybody laughed. And when Lil sang, everybody listened.

Charley was taller than anybody in the world, including, I was certain, God. From his shoulders, where I spent considerable time in the earliest years, the world had a different perspective: I looked down at tops of heads rather than at the undersides of chins. As I grew older, Charley became more father than brother. Those days return in fragments of splintered memory: Charley's slender dark hands whittling a toy from a chunk of wood, his face thin and intense, brown as the loaves Lil baked when there was flour. Charley's quick fingers guiding a stick of charred kindling over a bit of scrap paper, making a wondrous picture take shape—Jamie's face or Alberta's rag doll or the spare figure of our bony brown dog. Charley's voice low and terrible in the dark, telling ghost stories so delightfully dreadful that later in the night the moan of the wind through the chinks in the wall sent us scurrying to the security of Charley's pallet,[5] Charley's sleeping form.

---

4. **nuances** (n̄oo′äns′iz) *n.:* shades of difference.
5. **pallet** (pal′it) *n.:* small bed or pad, placed on the floor.

MARGARET BOURKE-WHITE/Getty Images

Some memories are more than fragmentary. I can still feel the *whap* of the wet dish rag across my mouth. Somehow I developed a stutter, which Charley was determined to cure. Someone had told him that an effective cure was to slap the stutterer across the mouth with a sopping wet dish rag. Thereafter whenever I began, "Let's g-g-g—," *whap!* from nowhere would come the **ubiquitous** rag. Charley would always insist, "I don't want hurt you none, Buddy—" and *whap* again. I don't know when or why I stopped stuttering. But I stopped.

Already laid waste by poverty, we were easy prey for ignorance and superstition, which hunted us like hawks. We sought education feverishly—and, for most of us, futilely, for the sum total of our combined energies was required for mere brute survival. Inevitably each child had to leave school and bear his share of the eternal burden.

IDENTIFY CAUSE & EFFECT

Pause at line 102. What **caused** Charley to hit Buddy with a wet rag? What was the **effect** of this action?

_____
_____
_____
_____
_____

VOCABULARY

ubiquitous (yoo·bik′wə·təs) *adj.:* appearing everywhere.

Sweet Potato Pie 59

VOICE

The writer chooses to have Buddy's family speak in **dialect**—a way of speaking characteristic of a specific region or group of people. Circle examples of dialect in what Pa says in lines 115–121.

IDENTIFY CAUSE & EFFECT

Pause at line 127. Both Pa and Charley want Buddy to get the education they never had. Underline details that show what they think will be the **effect** of his education.

IDENTIFY CAUSE & EFFECT

Pause at line 135. Buddy's classmates make fun of him because of his poverty. What other **effect** does Buddy's poverty have on his life at school?

_____
_____
_____
_____
_____
_____

IDENTIFY CAUSE & EFFECT

In lines 136–139, circle what **caused** Buddy to be able to go to high school.

Eventually the family's hopes for learning fastened on me, the youngest. I remember—I *think* I remember, for I could not have been more than five—one frigid day Pa, huddled on a rickety stool before the coal stove, took me on his knee and studied me gravely. I was a skinny little thing, they tell me, with large, solemn eyes.

"Well, boy," Pa said at last, "if you got to depend on your looks for what you get out'n this world, you just as well lay down right now." His hand was rough from the plow, but gentle as it touched my cheek. "Lucky for you, you got a *mind*. And that's something ain't everybody got. You go to school, boy, get yourself some learning. Make something out'n yourself. Ain't nothing you can't do if you got learning."

Charley was determined that I would break the chain of poverty, that I would "be somebody." As we worked our small vegetable garden in the sun or pulled a bucket of brackish[6] water from the well, Charley would tell me, "You ain gon be no poor farmer, Buddy. You gon be a teacher or maybe a doctor or a lawyer. One thing, bad as you is you ain gon be no preacher."

I loved school with a desperate passion, which became more intense when I began to realize what a monumental struggle it was for my parents and brothers and sisters to keep me there. The cramped, dingy classroom became a battleground where I was victorious. I stayed on top of my class. With glee I out-read, out-figured, and out-spelled the country boys who mocked my poverty, calling me "the boy with eyes in back of his head"—the "eyes" being the perpetual holes in my hand-me-down pants.

As the years passed, the economic strain was eased enough to make it possible for me to go on to high school. There were fewer mouths to feed, for one thing: Alberta went North to find work at sixteen; Jamie died at twelve.

I finished high school at the head of my class. For Mama and Pa and each of my brothers and sisters, my success was a personal triumph. One by one they came to me the week before

---

6. **brackish** (brak′ish) *adj.:* salty or unpleasant in taste.

Collection 3: Narrator and Voice

commencement bringing crumpled dollar bills and coins long hoarded, muttering, "Here, Buddy, put this on your gradiation clothes." My graduation suit was the first suit that was all my own.

On graduation night our cabin (less crowded now) was a frantic collage of frayed nerves. I thought Charley would drive me mad.

"Buddy, you ain pressed out them pants right . . . Can't you git a better shine on them shoes? . . . Lord, you done messed up that tie!"

Overwhelmed by the combination of Charley's nerves and my own, I finally exploded. "Man, cut it out!" Abruptly he stopped tugging at my tie, and I was afraid I had hurt his feelings. "It's okay, Charley. Look, you're strangling me. The tie's okay."

Charley relaxed a little and gave a rather sheepish chuckle. "Sure, Buddy." He gave my shoulder a rough joggle. "But you gotta look good. You *somebody*."

My valedictory address[7] was the usual idealistic, sentimental nonsense. I have forgotten what I said that night, but the sight of Mama and Pa and the rest is like a lithograph[8] burned on my memory; Lil, her round face made beautiful by her proud smile; Pa, his head held high, eyes loving and fierce; Mama radiant. Years later when her shriveled hands were finally still, my mind kept coming back to her as she was now. I believe this moment was the **apex** of her entire life. All of them, even Alberta down from Baltimore—different now, but united with them in her pride. And Charley, on the end of the row, still somehow the protector of them all. Charley, looking as if he were in the presence of something sacred.

As I made my way through the carefully rehearsed speech it was as if part of me were standing outside watching the whole thing—their proud, work-weary faces, myself wearing the suit that was their combined strength and love and hope: Lil with

---

7. **valedictory** (val′ə·dik′tər·ē) **address**: speech given at a graduation ceremony by the highest-ranking student in the class.
8. **lithograph** (lith′ə·graf′) *n.*: picture printed by a process involving the retaining and repulsing of ink.

SUMMARIZE

Pause at line 189. What has happened to Buddy between his graduation day and "this afternoon"—the day he is telling his story?

IDENTIFY CAUSE & EFFECT

What **causes** Buddy to visit his brother without calling first (lines 190–194)?

IDENTIFY

Buddy's childhood took place in the South, but the **setting** for his story is now New York City. Circle the three New York City locations he mentions in lines 196–202.

---

her lovely, low-pitched voice, Charley with the hands of an artist, Pa and Mama with God knows what potential lost with their sweat in the fields. I realized in that moment that I wasn't necessarily the smartest—only the youngest.

And the luckiest. The war came along, and I exchanged three years of my life (including a fair amount of my blood and a great deal of pain) for the GI Bill[9] and a college education. Strange how time can slip by like water flowing through your fingers. One by one the changes came—the old house empty at last, the rest of us scattered; for me, marriage, graduate school, kids, a professorship, and by now a thickening waistline and thinning hair. My mind spins off the years, and I am back to this afternoon and today's Charley—still long and lean, still gentle-eyed, still my greatest fan, and still determined to keep me on the ball.

I didn't tell Charley I would be at a professional meeting in New York and would surely visit; he and Bea would have spent days in fixing up, and I would have had to be company. No, I would drop in on them, take them by surprise before they had a chance to stiffen up. I was anxious to see them—it had been so long. Yesterday and this morning were taken up with meetings in the posh Fifth Avenue hotel—a place we could not have dreamed in our boyhood. Late this afternoon I shook loose and headed for Harlem, hoping that Charley still came home for a few hours before his evening run. Leaving the glare and glitter of downtown, I entered the subway which lurks like the dark, inscrutable *id*[10] beneath the surface of the city. When I emerged, I was in Harlem.

Whenever I come to Harlem I feel somehow as if I were coming home—to some mythic ancestral home. The problems are real, the people are real—yet there is some mysterious epic

---

9. **GI Bill:** the 1944 bill that provided economic assistance to World War II veterans.
10. **inscrutable** (in·skro͞ot′ə·bəl) *adj.*: not easily understood; mysterious. *id n.*: in psychology, the part of the personality that controls instincts and the desire for pleasure.

quality about Harlem, as if all Black people began and ended there, as if each had left something of himself. As if in Harlem the very heart of Blackness pulsed its beautiful tortured rhythms. Joining the throngs of people that saunter Lenox Avenue late afternoons, I headed for Charley's apartment. Along the way I savored the panorama of Harlem—women with shopping bags trudging wearily home; little kids flitting saucily through the crowd; groups of adolescent boys striding boldly along—some boisterous, some ominously silent; tables of merchandise spread on the sidewalks with hawkers singing their siren songs[11] of irresistible bargains; a blaring microphone sending forth waves of words to draw passersby into a restless bunch around a slender young man whose eyes have seen Truth; defeated men standing around on street corners or sitting on steps, heads down, hands idle; posters announcing Garvey Day;[12] "Buy Black" stamped on pavements; store windows bright with things African; stores still boarded up, a livid scar from last year's rioting. There was a terrible tension in the air; I thought of how quickly dry timber becomes a roaring fire from a single spark.

    I mounted the steps of Charley's building—old and in need of paint, like all the rest—and pushed the button to his apartment. Charley's buzzer rang. I pushed open the door and mounted the urine-scented stairs.

    "It's Buddy!" roared Charley as I arrived on the third floor. "Bea! Bea! Come here, girl, it's Buddy!" And somehow I was simultaneously shaking Charley's hand, getting clapped on the back, and being buried in the fervor of Bea's gigantic hug. They swept me from the hall into their dim apartment.

    "Lord, Buddy, what you doing here? Whyn't you tell me you was coming to New York?" His face was so lit up with pleasure that in spite of the inroads of time, he still looked like the Charley of years gone by, excited over a new litter of kittens.

---

11. **siren songs:** allusion to the Sirens of Greek mythology, whose singing was irresistible to sailors.
12. **Garvey Day:** holiday that honors the African American leader Marcus Garvey (1887–1940).

INFER

Re-read the description in lines 203–224 of Harlem, a mostly African American neighborhood in New York City. What is your impression of Harlem at the time of this story? Why do you think there is "a terrible tension in the air"?

COMPARE & CONTRAST

Think about what you have learned about Buddy's and Charley's adult lives. Then, re-read the description in lines 225–228 of Charley's building. How are the lives of the two brothers different?

Notes

Street Scene (Boy with Kite) (1962) by Jacob Lawrence (1917–2000). Egg tempera on hardboard.
The Jacob and Gwendolyn Lawrence Foundation/Art Resource, NY

VOICE

Underline Buddy's comment in lines 246–247. How is his **diction** here, speaking to his family, different from his diction when addressing the reader? Why do you think it is different here?

"The place look a mess! Whyn't you let us know?" put in Bea, suddenly distressed.

240 "Looks fine to me, girl. And so do you!"

And she did. Bea is a fine-looking woman, plump and firm still, with rich brown skin and thick black hair.

"Mary, Lucy, look, Uncle Buddy's here!" Two neat little girls came shyly from the TV. Uncle Buddy was something of a celebrity in this house.

I hugged them heartily, much to their discomfort. "Charley, where you getting all these pretty women?"

We all sat in the warm kitchen, where Bea was preparing dinner. It felt good there. Beautiful odors mingled in the air.

250 Charley sprawled in a chair near mine, his long arms and legs akimbo.[13] No longer shy, the tinier girl sat on my lap, while her

---

13. **akimbo** (ə·kim′bō) *adj.:* in a bent position.

sister darted here and there like a merry little water bug. Bea bustled about, managing to keep up with both the conversation and the cooking.

I told them about the conference I was attending and, knowing it would give them pleasure, I mentioned that I had addressed the group that morning. Charley's eyes glistened.

"You hear that, Bea?" he whispered. "Buddy done spoke in front of all them professors!"

"Sure I hear," Bea answered briskly, stirring something that was making an aromatic steam. "I bet he weren't even scared. I bet them professors learnt something, too."

We all chuckled. "Well anyway," I said, "I hope they did."

We talked about a hundred different things after that—Bea's job in the school cafeteria, my Jess and the kids, our scattered family.

"Seem like we don't git together no more, not since Mama and Pa passed on," said Charley sadly. "I ain't even got a Christmas card from Alberta for three-four year now."

"Well, ain't no two a y'all in the same city. An' everybody scratchin to make ends meet," Bea replied. "Ain't nobody got time to git together."

"Yeah, that's the way it goes, I guess," I said.

"But it sure is good to see you, Buddy. Say, look, Lil told me bout the cash you sent the children last winter when Jake was out of work all that time. She sure preciated it."

"Lord, man, as close as you and Lil stuck to me when I was a kid, I owed her that and more. Say, Bea, did I ever tell you about the time—" and we swung into the usual reminiscences.[14]

They insisted that I stay for dinner. Persuading me was no hard job: fish fried golden, ham hocks and collard greens, corn bread—if I'd *tried* to leave, my feet wouldn't have taken me. It was good to sit there in Charley's kitchen, my coat and tie flung over a chair, surrounded by soul food and love.

---

14. reminiscences (rem′ə·nis′əns·iz) *n.*: remembrances.

IDENTIFY CAUSE & EFFECT

Pause at line 301. Explain in your own words the reason Charley doesn't want the student to know that Buddy has a brother who is a cab driver.

VOICE

Circle the **idiom** in lines 303–304. What does this figure of speech mean?

CONNECT

Pause at line 305. Do you agree with Buddy's reason for keeping silent? In a similar situation, would you have kept quiet or spoken up? Explain.

"Say, Buddy, a couple months back I picked up a kid from your school."

"No stuff."

"I axed him did he know you. He say he was in your class last year."

290 "Did you get his name?"

"No, I didn't ax him that. Man, he told me you were the best teacher he had. He said you were one smart cat!"

"He told you that cause you're my brother."

"Your *brother*—I didn't tell him I was your brother. I said you was a old friend of mine."

I put my fork down and leaned over. "What you tell him *that* for?"

Charley explained patiently as he had explained things when I was a child and had missed an obvious truth. "I didn't 300 want your students to know your brother wasn't nothing but a cab driver. You *somebody*."

"You're a nut," I said gently. "You should've told that kid the truth." I wanted to say, I'm proud of you, you've got more on the ball than most people I know, I wouldn't have been anything at all except for you. But he would have been embarrassed.

Bea brought in the dessert—homemade sweet potato pie! "Buddy, I must of knew you were coming! I just had a mind I wanted to make some sweet potato pie."

There's nothing in this world I like better than Bea's sweet 310 potato pie! "Lord, girl, how you expect me to eat all that?"

The slice she put before me was outrageously big—and moist and covered with a light, golden crust—I ate it all.

"Bea, I'm gonna have to eat and run," I said at last.

Charley guffawed. "Much as you et, I don't see how you gonna *walk*, let alone *run*." He went out to get his cab from the garage several blocks away.

Bea was washing the tiny girl's face. "Wait a minute, Buddy, I'm gon give you the rest of that pie to take with you."

---

66   Part 1   Collection 3: Narrator and Voice

"Great!" I'd eaten all I could hold, but my *spirit* was still hungry for sweet potato pie.

Bea got out some waxed paper and wrapped up the rest of the pie. "That'll do you for a snack tonight." She slipped it into a brown paper bag.

I gave her a long good-bye hug. "Bea, I love you for a lot of things. Your cooking is one of them!" We had a last comfortable laugh together. I kissed the little girls and went outside to wait for Charley, holding the bag of pie reverently.

In a minute Charley's ancient cab limped to the curb. I plopped into the seat next to him, and we headed downtown. Soon we were **assailed** by the garish[15] lights of New York on a sultry spring night. We chatted as Charley skillfully managed the heavy traffic. I looked at his long hands on the wheel and wondered what they could have done with artists' brushes.

We stopped a bit down the street from my hotel. I invited him in, but he said he had to get on with his evening run. But as I opened the door to get out, he commanded in the old familiar voice, "Buddy, you wait!"

For a moment I thought my fly was open or something. "What's wrong?"

"What's that you got there?"

I was bewildered. "That? You mean this bag? That's a piece of sweet potato pie Bea fixed for me."

"You ain't going through the lobby of no big hotel carrying no brown paper bag."

"Man, you *crazy!* Of course I'm going— Look, Bea fixed it for me— *That's my pie—*"

Charley's eyes were miserable. "Folks in that hotel don't go through the lobby carrying no brown paper bags. That's *country*. And you can't neither. You *somebody*, Buddy. You got to be *right*. Now, gimme that bag."

---

15. **garish** (gar′ish) *adj.*: too bright.

EVALUATE

Do you think Charley is right that Buddy has to keep up appearances, or is Buddy right that he has nothing to prove to anyone? Explain your position.

_____
_____
_____
_____
_____
_____
_____
_____

IDENTIFY

In lines 372–374, circle the **simile** expressing Buddy's emotions when he glances back.

INTERPRET

Charley wouldn't let Buddy carry the paper bag into the hotel, so why is Charley so proud to carry it himself?

_____
_____
_____
_____
_____

"I want that pie, Charley. I've got nothing to prove to anybody—"

I couldn't believe it. But there was no point in arguing. Foolish as it seemed to me, it was important to him.

"You got to look *right,* Buddy. Can't nobody look dignified carrying a brown paper bag."

So finally, thinking how tasty it would have been and how seldom I got a chance to eat anything that good, I handed over my bag of sweet potato pie. If it was that important to him—

360 I tried not to show my irritation. "Okay, man—take care now." I slammed the door harder than I had intended, walked rapidly to the hotel, and entered the brilliant, crowded lobby.

"That Charley!" I thought. Walking slower now, I crossed the carpeted lobby toward the elevator, still thinking of my lost snack. I had to admit that of all the herd of people who jostled each other in the lobby, not one was carrying a brown paper bag. Or anything but expensive attaché cases or slick packages from exclusive shops. I suppose we all operate according to the symbols that are meaningful to us, and to Charley a brown 370 paper bag symbolizes the humble life he thought I had left. I was *somebody.*

I don't know what made me glance back, but I did. And suddenly the tears and laughter, toil and love of a lifetime burst around me like fireworks in a night sky.

For there, following a few steps behind, came Charley, proudly carrying a brown paper bag full of sweet potato pie.

MEET THE WRITER

Eugenia Collier (1928–   ) was born and raised and has lived most of her life in the Baltimore, Maryland, area. She took her education very seriously, eventually earning a Ph.D. from the University of Maryland. Collier says that all her creative output is inspired and informed by her African American heritage. Her writings, teachings, and personal life celebrate the richness and diversity of black culture. Collier has been an educator most of her working life and has used her spare time to contribute stories, poems, and articles to various publications. She is now retired from teaching and is currently working on a collection of autobiographical sketches.

SKILLS PRACTICE

Sweet Potato Pie

Voice Chart When you examine a story to describe its **voice**, you look at the **diction** (word choice) and **tone** (author's attitude toward the characters or events). Diction might be formal, informal, or colloquial. Tone might be sad, humorous, angry, admiring, loving, or friendly. Diction and tone can both vary within a story according to the events or characters being described. The chart below lists quotations from "Sweet Potato Pie." In the right-hand side, describe the diction and tone of each quotation. Then, describe the overall voice of the author in this story.

Literary Skills Analyze an author's voice.

Details from the Text	Diction and Tone
"Lucky for you, you got a *mind*. And that's something ain't everybody got. You go to school, boy, get yourself some learning. Make something out'n yourself. Ain't nothing you can't do if you got learning." (lines 118–121)	
"As I made my way through the carefully rehearsed speech it was as if part of me were standing outside watching the whole thing—their proud, work-weary faces, myself wearing the suit that was their combined strength and love and hope. . . ." (lines 171–174)	
". . . there is some mysterious epic quality about Harlem, as if all Black people began and ended there, as if each had left something of himself. As if in Harlem the very heart of Blackness pulsed its beautiful, tortured rhythms." (lines 205–208)	
"Charley explained patiently as he had explained things when I was a child and had missed an obvious truth. 'I didn't want your students to know your brother wasn't nothing but a cab driver. You *somebody*." (lines 298–301)	
"And suddenly the tears and laughter, toil and love of a lifetime burst around me like fireworks in a night sky. "For there, following a few steps behind, came Charley, proudly carrying a brown paper bag full of sweet potato pie." (lines 372–376)	
The author's overall voice in the story:	

Skills Review

Sweet Potato Pie

VOCABULARY AND COMPREHENSION

A. Recognizing Figurative Language   Fill in the blanks in each sentence with the correct Word Box word. Then, circle the figure of speech in each sentence and, on the blank after the sentence, identify it as an **idiom**, **simile**, or **metaphor**.

Word Box

entities
edifice
ubiquitous
apex
assailed

1. The chairman of the board, who was at the _____ of his career, was the king of the jungle. _____

2. Mary was fed up with the _____ mosquitoes that always found her—in the city, in the country, wherever she went outdoors. _____

3. The hospital patients were _____ by the loud noise of the intercom, which sounded like the speakers at a railroad station. _____

4. The statues on Easter Island are stately _____, soldiers standing guard against invasion. _____

5. The tiny _____ sat between its neighbors like a penguin chick nestled between its tall parents. _____

B. Reading Comprehension   Answer each question below.

1. Why was Buddy the only one in his family able to get an education?
   _____
   _____

2. How does his education separate Buddy from the rest of his family?
   _____
   _____

3. What does Buddy continue to share with the rest of his family?
   _____
   _____

4. Why is Charley so proud that Buddy is *"somebody"*?
   _____
   _____

SKILLS FOCUS

Vocabulary Skills
Recognize figurative language.

Before You Read

Golden Glass by Alma Luz Villanueva

Sometimes it is good to be alone, to awake hearing only the birds. In this story a fourteen-year-old boy spends the summer in a fort he builds himself in the woods.

LITERARY FOCUS: POINT OF VIEW AND SETTING

This story is told from the **third-person-omniscient point of view.** The narrator, who does not appear in the story, focuses mainly on two characters, Ted and his mother, Vida, describing what they both see, think, and feel. The pronouns used are *he, she, they, his, her, their,* and so on.

- While reading "Golden Glass," pay attention to Ted's and Vida's individual thoughts and feelings as well as to their relationship with each other.

A sense of place is important to this story. The characters are very attuned to the **setting,** which is summertime in the country in northern California, where cypress and redwood trees grow.

- As you read, think about how the characters' reactions to the setting help reveal the story's message.

READING SKILLS: MAKING INFERENCES

Often writers do not directly state what they mean. To understand what is being said, the reader has to make **inferences,** or guesses based on the evidence. You make inferences about a story based on details in the text and on your own experience and prior knowledge.

You may want to keep track of the inferences you make as you read by filling in a chart like this one:

Story Detail	My Inference

SKILLS FOCUS

Literary Skills
Understand omniscient point of view. Understand setting.

Reading Skills
Understand inferences.

Vocabulary Skills
Understand suffixes.

72   Part 1   Collection 3: Narrator and Voice

VOCABULARY DEVELOPMENT

PREVIEW SELECTION VOCABULARY

Preview the following words from "Golden Glass" before you begin reading the story.

angular (aŋ′gyoo·lər) *adj.:* having sharp angles; bony and lean; awkward.

> At fourteen, Ted is becoming thin and **angular**—and clumsy.

communion (kə·myoon′yən) *n.:* sharing of thoughts; deep understanding.

> Ted and Vida share a silent **communion** over food, based on her provision and his enjoyment of it.

involuntarily (in·väl′ən·ter′ə·lē) *adv.:* instinctively; without control.

> Ted **involuntarily** thinks that he might like the moon, a thought that almost seems not his own.

concocted (kən·käkt′id) *v.:* made; devised; created.

> Once Ted has **concocted** a latch and door, he feels safer.

hysteria (hi·ster′ē·ə) *n.:* panic; overwhelming sense of alarm.

> Later, they all have a good laugh over their needless **hysteria**.

meticulous (mə·tik′yoo·ləs) *adj.:* extremely careful and precise.

> Ted crafted his stained-glass panel with **meticulous** care.

SUFFIXES: CLUES TO WORD MEANINGS

Sometimes you can figure out the meaning of an unfamiliar word if you analyze the meanings of its parts. A **suffix** is a word part added to the end of a word or root. The more suffixes you recognize, the more words you'll be able to figure out.

The chart below lists four suffixes that occur in the list of vocabulary words above. Study these suffixes to understand how their meanings influence the definitions of words. **Prefixes** (word parts added to the beginning of a word or root) play an equal role in influencing word meaning. What word above contains both a suffix and a prefix?

Suffix	Meaning	Other Examples
–ar	of; related to; resembling	sonar; polar
–ion; –tion	action; result; state	union; selection
–ly	in the manner of; like	vividly; especially
–ous	marked by; given to	religious; furious

Golden Glass 73

Golden Glass

Alma Luz Villanueva

It was his fourteenth summer. He was thinning out, becoming **angular** and clumsy, but the cautiousness, the old-man seriousness he'd had as a baby, kept him contained, ageless and safe. His humor, always dry and to the bone since a small child, let you know he was watching everything.

He seemed always to be at the center of his own universe, so it was no surprise to his mother to hear Ted say: "I'm building a fort and sleeping out in it all summer, and I won't come in for anything, not even food. Okay?"

This had been their silent **communion,** the steady presence of love that flowed regularly, daily—food. The presence of his mother preparing it, his great appetite and obvious enjoyment of it—his nose smelling everything, seeing his mother more vividly than with his eyes.

He watched her now for signs of offense, alarm, and only saw interest. "Where will you put the fort?" Vida asked.

She trusted him to build well and not ruin things, but of course she had to know where. She looked at his dark, contained face and her eyes turned in and saw him when he was small, with curly golden hair, when he wrapped his arms around her neck. Their quiet times—undemanding—he could be let down, and a small toy could delight him for hours. She thought of the year he began kissing her elbow in passing, the way he preferred. Vida would touch his hair, his forehead, his shoulders—the body breathing out at the touch, his stillness. Then the explosion out the door told her he needed her touch, still.

"I'll build it by the redwoods, in the cypress trees. Okay?"

"Golden Glass" by Alma Villanueva from *Hispanics in the U.S.: An Anthology of Creative Literature,* edited by Francisco Jimenez and Gary D. Keller. Reproduced by permission of **Bilingual Press/Editorial Bilingüe,** Arizona State University, Tempe, Arizona.

"Make sure you keep your nails together and don't dig into the trees. I'll be checking. If the trees get damaged, it'll have to come down."

"Jason already said he'd bring my food and stuff."

"Where do you plan to shower and go to the bathroom?" Vida wondered.

"With the hose when it's hot and I'll dig holes behind the barn," Ted said so quietly as to seem unspoken. He knew how to slither under her, smoothly, like silk.

"Sounds interesting, but it better stay clean—this place isn't that big. Also, on your dinner night, you can cook outdoors."

His eyes flashed, but he said, "Okay."

He began to gather wood from various stacks, drying it patiently from the long rains. He kept in his room one of the hammers and a supply of nails that he'd bought. It was early June and the seasonal creek was still running. It was pretty dark out there and he wondered if he'd meant what he'd said.

FLUENCY

Read the boxed passage aloud until you can do so smoothly. Then, try to express both the voices and the emotions of the mother and son.

SETTING

What do you learn about the **setting** of this story in lines 27–44?

___

Golden Glass 75

COMPARE & CONTRAST

Pause at line 51. Describe Ted's relationship with his father. How is it different from or similar to his relationship with his mother?

___

INFER

Re-read lines 52–60. Why does the fort, which is not far from the house, seem to Ted far away, especially at night?

___

ANALYZE

Pause at line 72. What might the moon **symbolize,** or represent, for Vida? What might it represent for Ted?

___

VOCABULARY

involuntarily
(in·väl′ən·ter′ə·lē) *adv.*:
instinctively; without control.

concocted (kən·käkt′id) *v.*:
made; devised; created.

Ted hadn't seen his father in nearly four years, and he didn't miss him like you should a regular father, he thought. His father's image blurred with the memory of a football hitting him too hard, pointed (a bullet), right in the stomach, and the punishment for the penny candies—a test his father had set up for him to fail. [50] His stomach hardened at the thought of his father, and he found he didn't miss him at all.

He began to look at the shapes of the trees, where the limbs were solid, where a space was provided (he knew his mother really would make him tear down the fort if he hurt the trees). The cypress was right next to the redwoods, making it seem very remote. Redwoods do that—they suck up sound and time and smell like another place. So he counted the footsteps, when no one was looking, from the fort to the house. He couldn't believe it was so close; it seemed so separate, alone—especially in the dark, [60] when the only safe way of travel seemed flight (invisible at best).

Ted had seen his mother walk out to the bridge at night with a glass of wine, looking into the water, listening to it. He knew she loved to see the moon's reflection in the water. She'd pointed it out to him once by a river where they camped, her face full of longing—too naked somehow, he thought. Then, she swam out into the water, at night, as though trying to touch the moon. He wouldn't look at her. He sat and glared at the fire and roasted another marshmallow the way he liked it: bubbly, soft and brown (maybe six if he could get away with it). Then she'd [70] be back, chilled and bright, and he was glad she went. Maybe I like the moon too, he thought, **involuntarily,** as though the thought weren't his own—but it was.

He built the ground floor directly on the earth, with a cover of old plywood, then scattered remnant rugs that he'd asked Vida to get for him. He **concocted** a latch and a door, with his hand ax over it, just in case. He brought his sleeping bag, some pillows, a transistor radio, some clothes, and moved in for the summer. The first week he slept with his buck knife[1] open in his

---

1. **buck knife:** knife made by the Buck Company; folding-style knives are its most popular type.

hand and his pellet gun loaded on the same side, his right. The second week Ted sheathed the knife and put it under his head, but kept the pellet gun loaded at all times. He missed no one in the house but the dog, so he brought him into the cramped little space, enduring dog breath and farts because he missed *someone.*

Ted thought of when his father left, when they lived in the city, with forty kids on one side of the block and forty on the other. He remembered that one little kid with the funny sores on his body who chose an apple over candy every time. He worried they would starve or something worse. That time he woke up screaming in his room (he forgot why), and his sister began crying at the same time, "Someone's in here," as though they were having the same terrible dream. Vida ran in with a chair in one hand and a kitchen knife in the other, which frightened them even more. But when their mother realized it was only their **hysteria,** she became angry and left. Later they all laughed about this till they cried, including Vida, and things felt safer.

He began to build the top floor now but he had to prune some limbs out of the way. Well, that was okay as long as he was careful. So he stacked them to one side for kindling and began to brace things in place. It felt weird going up into the tree, not as safe as his small, contained place on the ground. He began to build it, thinking of light. He could bring his comic books, new ones, sit up straight, and eat snacks in the daytime. He would put in a side window facing the house to watch them, if he wanted, and a tunnel from the bottom floor to the top. Also, a ladder he'd found and repaired—he could pull it up and place it on hooks, out of reach. A hatch at the top of the ceiling for leaving or entering, tied down inside with a rope. He began to sleep up here, without the dog, with the tunnel closed off.

Vida noticed Ted had become cheerful and would stand next to her, to her left side, talking sometimes. But she realized she mustn't face him or he'd become silent and wander away. So she stood listening, in the same even breath and heartbeat she kept when she spotted the wild pheasants with their long, lush

---

SETTING

In lines 84–95, Ted remembers his life in a city. How is his life in this **setting** different from his life in the country? How is it similar?

VOCABULARY

hysteria (hi·ster′ē·ə) *n.:* panic; any outbreak of uncontrolled excitement or feeling.

INFER

How do you think Ted is feeling as he expands his fort? Support your response with details from lines 96–108.

Golden Glass 77

INFER

In lines 109–116, Vida uses an **analogy** that compares Ted to wild pheasants. What do you learn about Ted from this analogy?

_____
_____
_____
_____
_____
_____
_____
_____
_____
_____
_____

VOCABULARY

meticulous (mə·tik′yōō·ləs) *adj.:* extremely careful and precise.

IDENTIFY

Underline in lines 130–131 the task that Ted sets himself and accomplishes this summer.

Colorful glass pieces.
Royalty-Free Corbis

tails trailing the grape arbor, picking delicately and greedily at the unpicked grapes in the early autumn light. So sharp, so perfect, so rare to see a wild thing at peace.

She knew he ate well—his brother brought out a half gallon of milk that never came back, waiting to be asked to join him, but never daring to ask. His sister made him an extra piece of ham for his four eggs; most always he ate cold cereal and fruit or got a hot chocolate on the way to summer school. They treated Ted somewhat like a stranger, because he was.

Ted was taking a makeup course and one in stained glass. There, he talked and acted relaxed, like a boy; no one expected any more or less. The colors of the stained glass were deep and beautiful, and special—you couldn't waste this glass. The sides were sharp, the cuts were slow and **meticulous** with a steady pressure. The design's plan had to be absolutely followed or the beautiful glass would go to waste, and he'd curse himself.

It was late August and Ted hadn't gone inside the house once. He liked waking up, hearing nothing but birds—not his mother's voice or his sister's or his brother's. He could tell the various bird calls and liked the soft brown quail call the best. He imagined their taste and wondered if their flesh was as soft

78 Part 1 Collection 3: Narrator and Voice

as their song. Quail would've been okay to kill, as long as he ate it, his mother said. Instead, he killed jays because they irritated him so much with their shrill cries. Besides, a neighbor paid Ted per bird because he didn't want them in his garden. But that was last summer and he didn't do that anymore, and the quail were proud and plump and swift, and Ted was glad.

The stained glass was finished and he decided to place it in his fort facing the back fields. In fact, it looked like the back fields—trees and the sun in a dark sky. During the day the glass sun shimmered a beautiful yellow, the blue a much better color than the sky outside: deeper, like night.

He was so used to sleeping outside now he didn't wake up during the night, just like in the house. One night, toward the end when he'd have to move back with everyone (school was starting, frost was coming and the rains), Ted woke up to see the stained glass full of light. The little sun was a golden moon and the inside glass sky and the outside sky matched.

In a few days he'd be inside, and he wouldn't mind at all.

MEET THE WRITER

Alma Luz Villanueva (1944–   ) was born in Lompoc, California, and grew up in the Mission District of San Francisco. She later moved to the mountains in California. Villanueva is of both Chicano and Yaqui Indian ancestry, and she draws inspiration from both cultures. Villanueva's first book of poetry, *Bloodroot,* was published in 1977. She has since published numerous poetry collections as well as short stories and novels.

ANALYZE

Re-read lines 141–151. What does the image in lines 150–151 **symbolize**, or represent?

INFER

Ted has been happy living in his fort during the summer. Why, then, will he not "mind at all" moving back indoors?

SKILLS PRACTICE

Golden Glass

SKILLS FOCUS

Literary Skills Analyze point of view and setting.

Point of View and Setting Chart An **omniscient narrator** is able to describe the actions, thoughts, and feelings of all the characters. In the chart below, fill in examples of Ted's and Vida's actions, thoughts, and feelings. Finally, describe what you think the **setting** means to each character.

	Ted	Vida
Actions		
Thoughts		
Feelings		
Setting		

80 Part 1 Collection 3: Narrator and Voice

Skills Review

Golden Glass

VOCABULARY AND COMPREHENSION

A. Recognizing Suffixes Fill in the blanks with the correct Word Box word. Then, circle all the examples of the suffixes –ar, –ly, –ion, and –ous that you find in the sentences. Finally, below the sentences, state what the suffixes mean.

Word Box
angular
communion
involuntarily
concocted
hysteria
meticulous

1. Marta _____ a delicious new drink by combining six juices.

2. When the bird flew into the room, the class reaction was _____.

3. Keisha and her grandfather felt a deep _____ when they worked together silently in the garden.

4. Joe hardly ever cleaned his messy room, but his homework was always _____.

5. The puppet made the children laugh with its jerky, _____ motion.

6. Students go to detention _____; attendance is required.

Meanings: 7. –ar: _____ 8. –ly: _____
9. –ion: _____ 10. –ous: _____

B. Reading Comprehension Answer each question below.

1. What is Ted's plan for his fourteenth summer? _____
_____
_____

2. How does Ted's mother, Vida, feel about his plan? _____
_____
_____

3. How does Ted's summer plan work out? What effect does it have on him?
_____
_____

SKILLS FOCUS

Vocabulary Skills
Recognize suffixes.

Golden Glass **81**

Collection 4

Comparing Themes

Royalty-Free/Corbis

Academic Vocabulary for Collection 4

These are the terms you should know
as you read and analyze the selections in this collection.

Generalization A statement that conveys a general truth, drawn from a number of specific instances. A statement about a story's theme is a kind of generalization.

Genres The different forms of literature, such as stories, novels, plays, essays, and poems.

Theme A truth about life and human nature that gives meaning to a story. Different readers may discover different themes in a story, depending on their own attitudes and backgrounds. The meaning of a story comes from both the writer and the reader.

Universal themes Themes that appear in the literature of many cultures and historical periods.

• • •

Conflict A struggle between two forces. Usually conflict results when a character wants something badly but encounters obstacles in trying to get it. An **external conflict** takes place between two characters, between a character and a group, or between a character and an animal or a force in nature. An **internal conflict** is a struggle that takes place within a character's mind or heart.

Main character The character who drives the action in a story. The way the main character changes during the story can provide clues to the story's theme.

Motivation The reason a character behaves in a certain way.

Before You Read

Learning to Read and Write
by Frederick Douglass

Robert Louis Stevenson wrote, "To be what we are, and to become what we are capable of becoming, is the only end of life." As you read the next selection, think about how this quotation applies to Frederick Douglass's account.

LITERARY FOCUS: THEME AND CONFLICT

A **theme** is the truth a story reveals about life or human nature. Theme is different from subject. A subject can often be stated in a single word, such as *luck*. A theme is a revelation about the subject, such as *What we call luck is often more persistence and less good fortune.* One way to discover a theme is to pay close attention to **conflicts** faced by the main character. Theme can often be found in the outcome of these struggles.

- As you read about Frederick Douglass's struggle to learn to read and write, ask yourself what **conflicts** arise for him and observe how he confronts them.
- What **theme** do you think is revealed by the way Douglass faces his conflicts?

READING SKILLS: PARAPHRASE AND SUMMARIZE

Frederick Douglass was one of the great orators and writers of his time. However, modern writers generally use simpler language than was typical in Douglass's day, so you may find his vocabulary, sentence length, and syntax (word order) difficult or confusing.

- To make sure you understand Douglass's text, **paraphrase** it—restate it in your own words. Paraphrasing is different from summarizing, although both skills require that you restate ideas in your own words. When you **summarize**, you include only the most important ideas. When you paraphrase, you include all the information.

SKILLS FOCUS

Literary Skills
Understand theme and conflict.

Reading Skills
Paraphrase and summarize text.

Vocabulary Skills
Understand connotation and denotation.

Sentence from the Text	Sample Paraphrase
"My mistress, who had kindly commenced to instruct me, had, in compliance with the advice and direction of her husband, not only ceased to instruct, but had set her face against my being instructed by any one else."	My mistress kindly began to teach me, until her husband told her not to; then she not only stopped teaching me but also refused to let anyone else do so.

84   Part 1   Collection 4: Comparing Themes

VOCABULARY DEVELOPMENT

PREVIEW SELECTION VOCABULARY

The following words appear in "Learning to Read and Write." Look them over before you begin the selection.

divest (də·vest′) *v.*: rid; remove.

> Douglass saw slavery quickly **divest** the mistress of her humanity.

precepts (prē′septs′) *n.*: principles; teachings.

> Under the influence of her husband's **precepts,** she stopped teaching Douglass.

apprehension (ap′rē·hen′shən) *n.*: dread; fear.

> The mistress felt great **apprehension** whenever she suspected Douglass of reading.

denunciation (dē·nun′sē·ā′shən) *n.*: condemnation.

> Douglass finds in Sheridan's writing a **denunciation** of slavery.

vindication (vin′də·kā′shən) *n.*: defense; justification.

> In the same writing he finds a **vindication** of human rights.

CONNOTATION AND DENOTATION

The **connotations** of a word are the ideas or emotions associated with the word. The connotations of a word are different from its **denotation,** which is its literal meaning. Writers' word choice depends on their audience, their subject, and the effect they want to produce. Words with the same denotation may have very different connotations. Consider this sentence from "Learning to Read and Write":

> She at first lacked the **depravity** indispensable to shutting me up in mental darkness.

The denotations of *corruption, wickedness,* and *immorality* are similar to those of *depravity,* but they all carry less emotional intensity.

As you read "Learning to Read and Write," notice the powerful impression produced by the connotations of Douglass's words.

Learning to Read and Write

from *The Narrative of the Life of Frederick Douglass*

Frederick Douglass

I lived in Master Hugh's family about seven years. During this time, I succeeded in learning to read and write. In accomplishing this, I was compelled to resort to various stratagems.[1] I had no regular teacher. My mistress, who had kindly commenced to instruct me, had, in compliance with the advice and direction of her husband, not only ceased to instruct, but had set her face against my being instructed by any one else. It is due, however, to my mistress to say of her, that she did not adopt this course of treatment immediately. She at first lacked the depravity indispensable to shutting me up in mental darkness. It was at least necessary for her to have some training in the exercise of irresponsible power, to make her equal to the task of treating me as though I were a brute.

My mistress was, as I have said, a kind and tender-hearted woman; and in the simplicity of her soul she commenced, when I first went to live with her, to treat me as she supposed one human being ought to treat another. In entering upon the duties of a slaveholder, she did not seem to perceive that I sustained to her the relation of a mere chattel,[2] and that for her to treat me as a human being was not only wrong, but dangerously so. Slavery proved as injurious to her as it did to me. When I went there, she was a pious, warm, and tender-hearted woman. There was no sorrow or suffering for which she had not a tear. She had bread for the hungry, clothes for the naked, and comfort for every mourner that came within her reach. Slavery soon proved its

---

CONFLICT

Pause at line 13. What is Douglass's **conflict** with the mistress? How does he respond to the conflict?

PREDICT

How do you think slavery will prove as injurious (line 21), or harmful, to Douglass's mistress as it is to him?

---

1. **stratagems** (strat′ə·jəmz) *n.*: tricks or plans used to gain a result.
2. **chattel** (chat′'l) *n.*: property; slave.

Frederick Douglass.
Bettmann/CORBIS

ability to **divest** her of these heavenly qualities. Under its influence, the tender heart became stone, and the lamblike disposition gave way to one of tiger-like fierceness. The first step in her downward course was in her ceasing to instruct me. She now commenced to practice her husband's **precepts**. She finally became even more violent in her opposition than her husband himself. She was not satisfied with simply doing as well as he had commanded; she seemed anxious to do better. Nothing seemed to make her more angry than to see me with a newspaper. She seemed to think that here lay the danger. I have had her rush at me with a face made all up of fury, and snatch from me a newspaper, in a manner that fully revealed her **apprehension**. She was an apt woman; and a little experience soon demonstrated, to her satisfaction, that education and slavery were incompatible with each other.

30

SUMMARIZE

Pause at line 39. Summarize Douglass's description of his mistress. What is she like when Douglass first comes into contact with her? What is she like after she learns "the duties of a slaveholder"?

VOCABULARY

divest (də·vest′) v.: rid; remove.

precepts (prē′septs′) n.: principles; teachings.

apprehension (ap′rē·hen′shən) n.: dread; fear.

Learning to Read and Write 87

WORD STUDY

The word *ell* (line 46) comes from an Old English word for "arm." It came to mean "a measure of length" because cloth was measured out for sale by arm lengths. Still later, *ell* came to mean forty-five inches. The Old English saying was "if you give him an inch, he'll take an ell"; the modern version is "if you give him an inch, he'll take a mile."

SUMMARIZE

Re-read lines 47–60. How is Douglass able to learn to read?

_____
_____
_____
_____

WORD STUDY

The word *urchins* (line 58) comes from the Middle English word for "hedgehog." The word came to mean "poor, undisciplined boys" because boys who behaved in an unruly manner often seemed prickly to those they annoyed.

ANALYZE

It is commonly said that children have to be taught prejudice. Underline details that support this idea in lines 71–74.

---

40 From this time I was most narrowly watched. If I was in a separate room any considerable length of time, I was sure to be suspected of having a book, and was at once called to give an account of myself. All this, however, was too late. The first step had been taken, Mistress, in teaching me the alphabet, had given me the *inch*, and no precaution could prevent me from taking the *ell*.

The plan which I adopted, and the one by which I was most successful, was that of making friends of all the little white boys whom I met in the street. As many of these as I could, I 50 converted into teachers. With their kindly aid, obtained at different times and in different places, I finally succeeded in learning to read. When I was sent of errands, I always took my book with me, and by going one part of my errand quickly, I found time to get a lesson before my return. I used also to carry bread with me, enough of which was always in the house and to which I was always welcome; for I was much better off in this regard than many of the poor white children in our neighborhood. This bread I used to bestow upon the hungry little urchins, who, in return, would give me that more valuable bread of 60 knowledge. I am strongly tempted to give the names of two or three of those little boys, as a testimonial of the gratitude and affection I bear them; but prudence forbids;—not that it would injure me, but it might embarrass them; for it is almost an unpardonable offense to teach slaves to read in this Christian country. It is enough to say of the dear little fellows, that they lived on Philpot Street, very near Durgin and Bailey's ship-yard. I used to talk this matter of slavery over with them. I would sometimes say to them, I wished I could be as free as they would be when they got to be men. "You will be free as soon as you are 70 twenty-one, *but I am a slave for life!* Have not I as good a right to be free as you have?" These words used to trouble them; they would express for me the liveliest sympathy, and console me with the hope that something would occur by which I might be free.

I was now about twelve years old, and the thought of being a *slave* for *life* began to bear heavily upon my heart. Just about this time, I got hold of a book entitled "The Columbian Orator." Every opportunity I got, I used to read this book. Among much of other interesting matter, I found in it a dialogue between a master and his slave. The slave was represented as having run away from his master three times. The dialogue represented the conversation which took place between them, when the slave was retaken the third time. In this dialogue, the whole argument in behalf of slavery was brought forward by the master, all of which was disposed of by the slave. The slave was made to say some very smart as well as impressive things in reply to his master—things which had the desired though unexpected effect; for the conversation resulted in the voluntary emancipation of the slave on the part of the master.

In the same book, I met with one of Sheridan's mighty speeches on and in behalf of Catholic emancipation.[3] These were choice documents to me. I read them over and over again with unabated interest. They gave tongue to interesting thoughts of my own soul, which had frequently flashed through my mind, and died away for want of utterance. The moral which I gained from the dialogue was the power of truth over the conscience of even a slaveholder. What I got from Sheridan was a bold **denunciation** of slavery, and a powerful **vindication** of human rights. The reading of these documents enabled me to utter my thoughts, and to meet the arguments brought forward to sustain slavery; but while they relieved me of one difficulty, they brought on another even more painful than the one of which I was relieved. The more I read, the more I was led to abhor and detest my enslavers. I could regard them in no other light than a band of successful robbers, who had left their homes, and gone to Africa, and stolen us from our homes, and in a strange land reduced us to slavery. I loathed them as being the meanest as

---

3. **Sheridan's . . . emancipation:** Richard B. Sheridan (1751–1816) was an Irish-born playwright and essayist who argued for freedom for Catholics in Ireland.

IDENTIFY

Circle Douglass's age at this point in his narrative (line 75).

PARAPHRASE

Restate in your own words the ideas expressed in the sentence in lines 85–89.

IDENTIFY

Underline the moral Douglass finds in the dialogue between a slave and a slaveholder (lines 95–97).

VOCABULARY

denunciation (dē·nun′sē·ā′shən) *n.:* condemnation.

vindication (vin′də·kā′shən) *n.:* defense; justification.

Learning to Read and Write   89

CONFLICT

Pause at line 120. What **conflict** does Douglass face now? Is it an **internal** or an **external conflict**? Explain.

ANALYZE

Writers often use parallel construction—phrases or sentences that are similar in grammatical form. Underline examples in lines 126–128. How do you think this kind of construction adds to the power of a text?

---

well as the most wicked of men. As I read and contemplated the subject, behold! that very discontentment which Master Hugh had predicted would follow my learning to read had already come, to torment and sting my soul to unutterable anguish. As I writhed under it, I would at times feel that learning to read had been a curse rather than a blessing. It had given me a view of my wretched condition, without the remedy. It opened my eyes to the horrible pit, but to no ladder upon which to get out. In moments of agony, I envied my fellow slaves for their stupidity. I have often wished myself a beast. I preferred the condition of the meanest reptile to my own. Any thing, no matter what, to get rid of thinking! It was this everlasting thinking of my condition that tormented me. There was no getting rid of it. It was pressed upon me by every object within sight or hearing, animate or inanimate. The silver trump of freedom had roused my soul to eternal wakefulness. Freedom now appeared, to disappear no more forever. It was heard in every sound, and seen in every thing. It was ever present to torment me with a sense of my wretched condition. I saw nothing without seeing it, I heard nothing without hearing it, and felt nothing without feeling it. It looked from every star, it smiled in every calm, breathed in every wind, and moved in every storm.

I often found myself regretting my own existence, and wishing myself dead; and but for the hope of being free, I have no doubt but that I should have killed myself, or done something for which I should have been killed. While in this state of mind, I was eager to hear any one speak of slavery. I was a ready listener. Every little while, I could hear something about the abolitionists. It was some time before I found what the word meant. It was always used in such connections as to make it an interesting word to me. If a slave ran away and succeeded in getting clear, or if a slave killed his master, set fire to a barn, or did anything very wrong in the mind of a slaveholder, it was spoken of as the fruit of *abolition*. Hearing the word in this connection very often, I set about learning what it meant. The dictionary afforded me little or no help. I found it was "the act of abolishing"; but then I did not know what was to be abolished. Here I was perplexed. I did not dare to ask any one about its meaning, for I was satisfied that it was something they wanted me to know very little about. After a patient waiting, I got one of our city papers, containing an account of the number of petitions from the north, praying for the abolition of slavery in the District of Columbia, and of the slave trade between the States. From this time I understood the words *abolition* and *abolitionist,* and always drew near when that word was spoken, expecting to hear something of importance to myself and fellow slaves. The light broke in upon me by degrees. I went one day down on the wharf of Mr. Waters; and seeing two Irishmen unloading a scow[4] of stone, I went, unasked, and helped them. When we had finished, one of them came to me and asked me if I were a slave. I told him I was. He asked, "Are ye a slave for life?" I told him that I was. The good Irishman seemed to be deeply affected by the statement. He said to the other that it was a pity so fine a little fellow as myself should be a slave for life. He said it was a shame to hold me. They both advised me to run away to the north; that I should find friends there, and that I should be free. I pretended not to be interested in what they said, and treated them as if I did not understand them; for I feared they might be treacherous. White men have been known to encourage slaves to escape, and then, to get the reward, catch them and return them to their masters. I was afraid that these seemingly good men might use me so; but I nevertheless remembered their advice, and from that time I resolved to run away. I looked forward to a time at which it would be safe for me to escape. I was too young to think of doing so immediately; besides, I wished to learn how to write, as I might have occasion to write my own pass. I consoled myself with the hope that I should one day find a good chance. Meanwhile, I would learn to write.

---

4. **scow** (skou) *n.:* large, flat-bottomed boat used to carry bulk materials.

MPI/Getty Images

WORD STUDY

The word *larboard* (line 181) is an old name for the left side of a ship from the point of view of someone facing forward. *Starboard* is the name for the right side. Shouted over the noise of wind and waves, *larboard* and *starboard* sounded too much alike, so in 1844, *larboard* was replaced by *port*. The word *aft* (line 185) means "near or toward the back of a ship."

The idea as to how I might learn to write was suggested to me by being in Durgin and Bailey's ship-yard, and frequently seeing the ship carpenters, after hewing, and getting a piece of timber ready for use, write on the timber the name of that part of the ship for which it was intended. When a piece of timber was intended for the larboard side, it would be marked thus—"L." When a piece was for the starboard side, it would be marked thus—"S." A piece for the larboard side forward, would be marked thus—"L.F." When a piece was for starboard side forward, it would be marked thus—"S.F." For larboard aft, it would be marked thus—"L.A." For starboard aft, it would be marked thus—"S.A." I soon learned the names of these letters, and for what they were intended when placed upon a piece of timber in the ship-yard. I immediately commenced copying them, and in a short time was able to make the four letters named. After that, when I met with any boy who I knew could write, I would tell him I could write as well as he. The next word would be, "I don't believe you. Let me see you try it." I would then make the letters which I had been so fortunate as to learn, and ask him to beat that. In this way I got a good many lessons in writing, which it is quite possible I should never have gotten in any other way. During this time, my copy-book was the board fence, brick wall, and pavement; my pen and ink was a lump of chalk. With these, I learned mainly how to write. I then commenced and continued copying the Italics in Webster's Spelling Book, until I could make them all without looking on the book. By this time, my little Master Thomas had gone to school, and learned how to write, and had written over a number of copy-books. These had been brought home, and shown to some of our near neighbors, and then laid aside. My mistress used to go to class meeting at the Wilk Street meeting house every Monday afternoon, and leave me to take care of the house. When left thus, I used to spend the time in writing in the spaces left in Master Thomas's copy-book, copying what he had written. I continued to do this until I could write a hand very similar to that of Master Thomas. Thus, after a long, tedious effort for years, I finally succeeded in learning how to write.

MEET THE WRITER

Frederick Douglass (1818–1895) was born in Maryland to an enslaved woman and a white man. He was raised by his grandmother and saw his mother only a few times before her death when he was seven. When he was eight, he was sent to Baltimore to live with a ship carpenter named Hugh Auld. When he was twenty, he borrowed papers from a free black sailor and escaped to New York. There he married Ann Murray, a free black woman who joined him from Baltimore. They moved to New Bedford, Massachusetts, where Douglass became a popular abolitionist speaker. When he toured Great Britain with William Lloyd Garrison, another famous abolitionist speaker, English friends raised the money to buy Douglass's freedom from Hugh Auld for $711.66.

THEME
What theme might Douglass's struggle to learn to read and write reveal?

Before You Read

from The Autobiography of Malcolm X by Malcolm X

For most people, imprisonment is the very opposite of freedom. Read this excerpt from his autobiography to learn how Malcolm X used his time in prison to set his mind free.

LITERARY FOCUS: UNIVERSAL THEMES

A **theme** is a message or insight about life revealed in a work of literature. Some themes can be found again and again in works from different periods and different parts of the world. Such themes are called a **universal themes**. Here are some examples of universal themes:

- Arrogance and pride can bring destruction.
- Love endures and triumphs over adversity.
- Perseverance often leads to success.

As you read the selection from *The Autobiography of Malcolm X,* think about its themes. Then, think of other works you have read that have similar themes.

READING SKILLS: COMPARING AND CONTRASTING

"Learning to Read and Write" by Frederick Douglass and the following selection by Malcolm X are similar in some ways. Both are taken from autobiographies—people's accounts of their own lives. Both deal with the subject of learning to read and write.

These statements are points of comparison. When you **compare** two works of literature, you look for ways they are alike. When you **contrast** two works of literature, you look for ways they are different.

As you read the selection from *The Autobiography of Malcolm X,* compare and contrast it with "Learning to Read and Write" by asking yourself these questions:

- What are the two writers' circumstances?
- What methods do the writers devise for learning to read and write?
- What do the writers learn from pursuing their goal?
- What are characteristics of the writers' styles?

SKILLS FOCUS

Literary Skills
Understand universal themes.

Reading Skills
Compare and contrast.

Vocabulary Skills
Understand synonyms and antonyms.

AUTOBIOGRAPHY

VOCABULARY DEVELOPMENT

PREVIEW SELECTION VOCABULARY

Become acquainted with the following words before you read the selection from *The Autobiography of Malcolm X*.

articulate (är·tik′yoo·lit) *adj.*: well-spoken; expressing oneself clearly.

On the streets, Malcolm was the most **articulate** man around; he could outtalk anyone.

emulate (em′yoo·lāt) *v.*: imitate (someone or something admired).

Malcolm tried to **emulate** the most knowledgeable man in the prison.

succeeding (sək·sēd′iŋ) *v.* used as *adj.*: following.

With each **succeeding** page in the dictionary, Malcolm learned more and more.

inevitable (in·ev′i·tə·bəl) *adj.*: certain to happen; unavoidable.

It was **inevitable** that as Malcolm expanded his vocabulary, he could understand more of what he read.

SYNONYMS AND ANTONYMS

You can help build your vocabulary by learning synonyms and antonyms of new words or of words you already know. **Synonyms** are words with similar meanings. **Antonyms** are words with opposite meanings. The chart below lists synonyms and antonyms of some common words.

	Synonyms	Antonyms
glad	delighted; pleased; cheerful; joyful	discontented; irritated; irate; sorry
young	youthful; fresh; immature	elderly; ancient; antique; venerable
hot	sweltering; burning	cold; chilly; frigid; icy; freezing

Not all words have synonyms and antonyms, but try to remember the ones you discover when you read or when you look up the meaning of an unfamiliar word.

from The Autobiography of Malcolm X

from THE AUTOBIOGRAPHY OF MALCOLM X

Malcolm X

It was because of my letters that I happened to stumble upon starting to acquire some kind of homemade education.

I became increasingly frustrated at not being able to express what I wanted to convey in letters that I wrote, especially those to Mr. Elijah Muhammad.[1] In the street, I had been the most **articulate** hustler out there—I had commanded attention when I said something. But now, trying to write simple English, I not only wasn't articulate, I wasn't even functional. How would I sound writing in slang, the way I would say it, something such as, "Look, daddy, let me pull your coat about a cat, Elijah Muhammad—"

Many who today hear me somewhere in person, or on television, or those who read something I've said, will think I went to school far beyond the eighth grade. This impression is due entirely to my prison studies.

It had really begun back in the Charlestown Prison, when Bimbi first made me feel envy of his stock of knowledge. Bimbi had always taken charge of any conversation he was in, and I had tried to **emulate** him. But every book I picked up had few sentences which didn't contain anywhere from one to nearly all of the words that might as well have been in Chinese. When I just skipped those words, of course, I really ended up with little idea of what the book said. So I had come to the Norfolk Prison Colony still going through only book-reading motions. Pretty soon, I would have quit even these motions, unless I had received the motivation that I did.

---

1. **Elijah Muhammad** (1897–1975): leader of the Nation of Islam, a black nationalist religious organization Malcolm X joined.

From pages 174–176 from *The Autobiography of Malcolm X* by Malcolm X, with the assistance of Alex Haley. Copyright © 1964 by Alex Haley and Malcolm X; copyright © 1965 by Alex Haley and Betty Shabazz. Reproduced by permission of **Random House, Inc.**

I saw that the best thing I could do was get hold of a dictionary—to study, to learn some words. I was lucky enough to reason also that I should try to improve my penmanship. It was sad. I couldn't even write in a straight line. It was both ideas together that moved me to request a dictionary along with some tablets and pencils from the Norfolk Prison Colony school.

I spent two days just riffling[2] uncertainly through the dictionary's pages. I'd never realized so many words existed! I didn't know *which* words I needed to learn. Finally, just to start some kind of action, I began copying.

In my slow, painstaking, ragged handwriting, I copied into my tablet everything printed on that first page, down to the punctuation marks.

---

2. **riffling** (rif′liŋ) *v.* used as *adv.:* leafing quickly through the pages of a book.

COMPARE & CONTRAST

Malcolm X and Frederick Douglass make plans for the same goal: to educate themselves and develop their language skills. How do their plans differ?

_____
_____
_____
_____
_____
_____

Malcolm X in front of the Connecticut Capitol Building, 1963.
Bettmann/CORBIS

from The Autobiography of Malcolm X

COMPARE & CONTRAST

What do Malcolm X's and Frederick Douglass's plans for education tell you about their **characters**?

_____
_____
_____
_____
_____
_____
_____
_____
_____
_____
_____
_____
_____
_____
_____

VOCABULARY

succeeding (sək·sēd′iŋ) v. used as *adj.*: following.

inevitable (in·ev′i·tə·bəl) *adj.*: certain to happen; unavoidable.

Aardvark.
Andrew Bannister/Getty Images

40 I believe it took me a day. Then, aloud, I read back, to myself, everything I'd written on the tablet. Over and over, aloud, to myself, I read my own handwriting.

I woke up the next morning, thinking about those words—immensely proud to realize that not only had I written so much at one time, but I'd written words that I never knew were in the world. Moreover, with a little effort, I also could remember what many of these words meant. I reviewed the words whose meanings I didn't remember. Funny thing, from the dictionary's first page right now, that "aardvark" springs to my mind. The diction-
50 ary had a picture of it, a long-tailed, long-eared, burrowing African mammal, which lives off termites caught by sticking out its tongue as an anteater does for ants.

I was so fascinated that I went on—I copied the dictionary's next page. And the same experience came when I studied that. With every **succeeding** page, I also learned of people and places and events from history. Actually the dictionary is like a miniature encyclopedia. Finally the dictionary's A section had filled a whole tablet—and I went on into the B's. That was the way I started copying what eventually became the entire dictionary.
60 It went a lot faster after so much practice helped me to pick up handwriting speed. Between what I wrote in my tablet, and writing letters, during the rest of my time in prison I would guess I wrote a million words.

I suppose it was **inevitable** that as my word-base broadened, I could for the first time pick up a book and read and now begin

98   Part 1   Collection 4: Comparing Themes

to understand what the book was saying. Anyone who has read a great deal can imagine the new world that opened. Let me tell you something: from then until I left that prison, in every free moment I had, if I was not reading in the library, I was reading on my bunk. You couldn't have gotten me out of books with a wedge. Between Mr. Muhammad's teachings, my correspondence, my visitors—usually Ella and Reginald—and my reading of books, months passed without my even thinking about being imprisoned. In fact, up to then, I never had been so truly free in my life.

MEET THE WRITER

Malcolm X (1925–1965) was born Malcolm Little in Omaha, Nebraska. He was a good student and at the top of his class in junior high school, but when he was told that his goal of becoming a lawyer was unrealistic for an African American, he dropped out of school. In 1946, he was convicted of burglary and was sentenced to seven years in prison. There he joined the Nation of Islam and determined to further his education. When he was paroled in 1952, he came out of prison with excellent communication skills and a new surname, X, chosen as a symbol of his lost African name. Malcolm X served as minister of the Nation of Islam's New York temple but broke with the organization in 1964 and formed his own. Malcolm X was assassinated as he began speaking at the Audubon Ballroom in New York City on February 21, 1965.

> **INTERPRET**
>
> Pause at line 75. Why do you think Malcolm X feels free even though he is in prison?

> **THEME**
>
> What theme, or message about life, is revealed by both Malcolm X's and Frederick Douglass's accounts? What might make this a **universal theme**?

from The Autobiography of Malcolm X

SKILLS PRACTICE

Learning to Read and Write/ from *The Autobiography of Malcolm X*

SKILLS FOCUS

Literary Skills Analyze theme.

Reading Skills Compare and contrast.

Comparison-and-Contrast Chart **Universal themes** are messages about life that occur again and again in literature. Fill in the chart below to compare "Learning to Read and Write" by Frederick Douglass and the excerpt from *The Autobiography of Malcolm X*. Then, review your completed chart to identify the theme the two selections share.

	"Learning to Read and Write" by Frederick Douglass	from *The Autobiography of Malcolm X*
Conflicts (external and internal)		
What happens		
What the writer learns or discovers		
Theme(s)		

Shared or universal theme:

Collection 4: Comparing Themes

Skills Review

Learning to Read and Write/*from* The Autobiography of Malcolm X

VOCABULARY AND COMPREHENSION

A. Recognizing Synonyms and Antonyms Fill in each of the blanks below with the Word Box word that matches the synonym-antonym pair. Note that not all words have synonyms and antonyms.

1. dread / anticipation _____

2. certain / avoidable _____

3. rid / add _____

4. following / preceding _____

5. condemnation / praise _____

6. defense / attack _____

7. well-spoken / incomprehensible _____

> **Word Box**
> divest
> precepts
> apprehension
> denunciation
> vindication
> articulate
> emulate
> succeeding
> inevitable

B. Reading Comprehension Answer each question below.

1. What motivated Frederick Douglass to learn to read and write?
   _____
   _____
   _____

2. What motivated Malcolm X to increase his vocabulary?
   _____
   _____
   _____

3. What character traits do Frederick Douglass and Malcolm X share?
   _____
   _____
   _____

SKILLS FOCUS

Vocabulary Skills
Recognize synonyms and antonyms.

Before You Read

Superman and Me by Sherman Alexie

LITERARY FOCUS: THEME AND CHARACTER

One way to identify the **theme** of a work of literature—its underlying message about life—is to pay close attention to its **main character.** In the personal essay you are about to read, the author writes about his thoughts and experiences, so you may consider him the main character. His experiences and the lessons he learns may help you pinpoint the essay's major themes.

- As you read "Superman and Me," observe how the author handles his conflicts, both external and internal.
- Look for details that show the forces that shape his attitude toward life. These details may help you identify the theme of the essay.
- As you read, think about the title, "Superman and Me." The title of a work may hint at its theme.

READING SKILLS: MAKING GENERALIZATIONS

When you make a **generalization,** you look at evidence and make a broad statement about what it tells you. Someone who says "All stories contain conflicts" is making a generalization on the basis of her or his experience reading many stories. A generalization about the message of a work of literature can often be stated as its theme. To make a generalization stating a selection's theme, you have to

- think about the main events and conflicts
- identify what the characters have learned
- relate these lessons to your own experiences

SKILLS FOCUS

Literary Skills
Understand theme and character.

Reading Skills
Make generalizations.

Vocabulary Skills
Understand connotation and denotation.

102 Part 1 Collection 4: Comparing Themes

ESSAY

VOCABULARY DEVELOPMENT

PREVIEW SELECTION VOCABULARY

The following words appear in "Superman and Me." Look them over before you begin the story.

avid (av′id) *adj.*: eager; enthusiastic.

> Sherman Alexie and his father were **avid** readers, devouring any books they could find.

prodigy (präd′ə·jē) *n.*: child with unusual talent; child genius.

> Alexie was a **prodigy** who learned to read at a very young age.

subverted (səb·vurt′id) *v.*: overturned.

> Many Indian children **subverted** their teachers' low expectations outside the classroom.

monosyllabic (män′ō·si·lab′ik) *adj.*: using only one-syllable words.

> The children are **monosyllabic** in class but tell complicated stories in private.

submissively (səb·mis′iv·lē) *adv.*: obediently; without resisting.

> The children **submissively** follow adults' instructions but will fight a bully ten years older.

CONNOTATIONS AND DENOTATIONS

The **connotations** of a word are the ideas and emotions associated with it. The connotations of a word are different from its **denotation**, its literal meaning.

In "Superman and Me" Sherman Alexie several times calls himself *arrogant*. Synonyms of *arrogant* include *proud* and *haughty*. The three words have similar meanings, but their connotations, or emotional overtones, are quite different.

- *Proud* often has the positive connotation of "having a proper self-esteem."
- *Haughty* usually has the negative connotation of "scorning those of lower status."
- *Arrogant* usually has the negative connotation of "aggressively asserting superiority." As you read the essay, think about why Alexie chooses this word to describe himself.

As you read the essay, keep track of words or phrases that have strong connotations. List them in a chart like this one. In the column on the right, use the symbol + if you think the word or phrase has a positive connotation. Use the symbol ✓ if the connotation seems neutral. Use the symbol − if the connotation seems negative. Don't forget to include *arrogant* in your chart.

Word or Phrase	+, ✓, or −

Superman and Me   103

Superman and Me

from The Most Wonderful Books:
Writers on Discovering the Pleasures of Reading

Sherman Alexie

> **INFER**
>
> Judging from the information in lines 8–12, what do you think life was like on the Spokane Indian Reservation when Alexie was a boy?

I learned to read with a *Superman* comic book. Simple enough, I suppose. I cannot recall which particular *Superman* comic book I read, nor can I remember which villain he fought in that issue. I cannot remember the plot, nor the means by which I obtained the comic book. What I can remember is this: I was three years old, a Spokane Indian boy living with his family on the Spokane Indian Reservation in eastern Washington state. We were poor by most standards, but one of my parents usually managed to find some minimum-wage job or another, which made us middle class by reservation standards. I had a brother and three sisters. We lived on a combination of irregular paychecks, hope, fear, and government-surplus food.

My father, who is one of the few Indians who went to Catholic school on purpose, was an **avid** reader of westerns, spy thrillers, murder mysteries, gangster epics, basketball-player biographies, and anything else he could find. He bought his books by the pound at Dutch's Pawn Shop,[1] Goodwill, Salvation Army, and Value Village. When he had extra money, he bought new novels at supermarkets, convenience stores, and hospital gift shops. Our house was filled with books. They were stacked in crazy piles in the bathroom, bedrooms, and living room. In a fit of unemployment-inspired creative energy, my father built a set of bookshelves and soon filled them with a random assortment

> **VOCABULARY**
>
> **avid** (av´id) *adj.*: eager; enthusiastic.
>
> Which of the three synonyms above has the most intense connotation? Circle the word.

1. **Dutch's Pawn Shop:** Pawnshops hold personal goods as security for a loan of money. If the loan is not repaid, the goods are sold as secondhand merchandise.

"Superman and Me" by Sherman Alexie from *The Most Wonderful Books: Writers on Discovering the Pleasures of Reading,* edited by Michael Dorris and Emile Buchwald. Copyright © 1997 by Sherman Alexie. Reproduced by permission of **Milkweed Editions.**

Sherman Alexie.
Ulf Andersen/Getty Images

of books about the Kennedy assassination, Watergate,[2] the Vietnam War, and the entire twenty-three book series of the Apache westerns. My father loved books, and since I loved my father with an aching devotion, I decided to love books as well.

I can remember picking up my father's books before I could read. The words themselves were mostly foreign, but I still remember the exact moment when I first understood, with a sudden clarity, the purpose of a paragraph. I didn't have the vocabulary to say "paragraph," but I realized that a paragraph was a fence that held words. The words inside a paragraph worked together for a common purpose. They had some specific reason for being inside the same fence. This knowledge delighted me. I began to think of everything in terms of paragraphs. Our

2. **Watergate:** hotel in Washington, D.C., that was the site of a 1972 political-information burglary that later resulted in President Richard Nixon's resignation.

GENERALIZE

Using the information in lines 13–27, make a **generalization** about books and Alexie's father.

WORD STUDY

Circle the word that has more positive or intense connotations: *devotion* (line 27) or its synonym *affection*.

ANALYZE

Circle the **metaphor** Alexie uses in lines 32–33 to describe a paragraph. Then, underline the example of **personification** in lines 33–34. What do these figures of speech add to your understanding of paragraphs?

Superman and Me 105

ANALYZE

In lines 36–45, Alexie uses the word *paragraph* as a **metaphor** for many things in life. Circle the things he says are paragraphs. How are all these things like paragraphs?

_____
_____
_____
_____

SUMMARIZE

How does Alexie teach himself to read (lines 46–58)?

_____
_____
_____
_____
_____

CHARACTER

Judging from the information in lines 59–68, how would you describe Alexie?

_____
_____
_____
_____

VOCABULARY

prodigy (präd′ə·jē) *n.:* child with unusual talent; child genius.

---

reservation was a small paragraph within the United States. My family's house was a paragraph, distinct from the other paragraphs of the LeBrets to the north, the Fords to our south, and the Tribal School to the west. Inside our house, each family member existed as a separate paragraph, but still had genetics and common experiences to link us. Now, using this logic, I can see my changed family as an essay of seven paragraphs: mother, father, older brother, the deceased sister, my younger twin sisters, and our adopted little brother.

At the same time I was seeing the world in paragraphs, I also picked up that *Superman* comic book. Each panel, complete with picture, dialogue, and narrative, was a three-dimensional paragraph. In one panel, Superman breaks through a door. His suit is red, blue, and yellow. The brown door shatters into many pieces. I look at the narrative above the picture. I cannot read the words, but I assume it tells me that Superman is breaking down the door. Aloud, I pretend to read the words and say "Superman is breaking down the door." Words, dialogue, also float out of Superman's mouth. Because he is breaking down the door, I assume he says, "I am breaking down the door." Once again, I pretend to read the words and say aloud, "I am breaking down the door." In this way, I learned to read.

This might be an interesting story all by itself. A little Indian boy teaches himself to read at an early age and advances quickly. He reads *Grapes of Wrath*[3] in kindergarten when other children are struggling through Dick and Jane.[4] If he'd been anything but an Indian boy living on the reservation, he might have been called a **prodigy**. But he is an Indian boy living on the reservation, and is simply an oddity. He grows into a man who often speaks of his childhood in the third-person, as if it will somehow dull the pain and make him sound more modest about his talents.

---

3. *Grapes of Wrath:* long novel by John Steinbeck (1902–1968).
4. **Dick and Jane:** characters in a series of beginning readers that were widely used in schools in the United States from the 1930s to the 1960s.

A smart Indian is a dangerous person, widely feared and ridiculed by Indians and non-Indians alike. I fought with my classmates on a daily basis. They wanted me to stay quiet when the non-Indian teacher asked for answers, for volunteers, for help. We were Indian children who were expected to be stupid. Most lived up to those expectations inside the classroom, but **subverted** them on the outside. They struggled with basic reading in school, but could remember how to sing a few dozen powwow[5] songs. They were **monosyllabic** in front of their non-Indian teachers, but could tell complicated stories and jokes at the dinner table. They **submissively** ducked their heads when confronted by a non-Indian adult, but would slug it out with the Indian bully who was ten years older. As Indian children, we were expected to fail in the non-Indian world. Those who failed were ceremonially accepted by other Indians and appropriately pitied by non-Indians.

I refused to fail. I was smart. I was arrogant. I was lucky. I read books late into the night, until I could barely keep my eyes open. I read books at recess, then during lunch, and in the few minutes left after I had finished my classroom assignments. I

5. **powwow** n.: North American Indian ceremony or meeting.

Students using computers at the Wellpinit Elementary/High School on the Spokane Indian Reservation.
Ed Kashi/CORBIS

VOCABULARY

subverted (səb·vurt′id) v.: overturned.

monosyllabic (män′ō·si·lab′ik) adj.: using only one-syllable words.

submissively (səb·mis′iv·lē) adv.: obediently; without resisting.

CHARACTER

Circle the four things Alexie says about himself in line 85. What details in this essay support his description of himself?

Superman and Me 107

INFER

Pause at line 100. How do you think all this reading could save Alexie's life?

_____
_____
_____
_____
_____
_____

FLUENCY

Read the boxed passage aloud until you are comfortable with the words. Then, use your voice to convey the feelings Alexie is expressing.

THEME

What **themes,** or messages about life, are revealed in lines 101–121? (You will probably be able to find more than one.)

_____
_____
_____
_____
_____
_____

90 read books in the car when my family traveled to powwows or basketball games. In shopping malls, I ran to the bookstores and read bits and pieces of as many books as I could. I read the books my father brought home from the pawnshops and second-hand stores. I read the books I borrowed from the library. I read the backs of cereal boxes. I read the newspaper. I read the bulletins posted on the walls of the school, the clinic, the tribal offices, the post office. I read junk mail. I read auto-repair manuals. I read magazines. I read anything that had words and paragraphs. I read with equal parts joy and desperation. I loved those books, but I also knew that love had only one purpose. I was trying to
100 save my life.

> Despite all the books I read, I am still surprised I became a writer. I was going to be a pediatrician.[6] These days, I write novels, short stories, and poems. I visit schools and teach creative writing to Indian kids. In all my years in the reservation school system, I was never taught how to write poetry, short stories, or novels. I was certainly never taught that Indians wrote poetry, short stories, and novels. Writing was something beyond Indians. I cannot recall a single time that a guest teacher visited the reservation. There must have been visiting teachers. Who were they?
> 110 Where are they now? Do they exist? I visit the schools as often as possible. The Indian kids crowd the classroom. Many are writing their own poems, short stories, and novels. They have read my books. They have read many other books. They look at me with bright eyes and arrogant wonder. They are trying to save their lives. Then there are the sullen and already defeated Indian kids who sit in the back rows and ignore me with theatrical precision. The pages of their notebooks are empty. They carry neither pencil nor pen. They stare out the window. They refuse and resist. "Books," I say to them. "Books," I say. I throw my weight
> 120 against their locked doors. The door holds. I am smart. I am arrogant. I am lucky. I am trying to save our lives.

6. **pediatrician** (pē′dē·ə·trish′ən): doctor who specializes in the care of children.

MEET THE WRITER

Sherman Alexie (1966–   ), a Spokane/Coeur d'Alene Indian, had a serious brain operation when he was only six months old. It was feared he would not survive or that if he did, he would be severely mentally retarded. Alexie surprised everyone. Despite suffering side effects such as seizures throughout his childhood, he learned to read by age three and had read many novels by age five. When he was a teenager, he chose to attend high school outside the reservation, where he could get a better education. He planned to become a doctor but found that he kept fainting in his anatomy class. In a poetry workshop at Washington State University, he discovered a love of writing. His first book of poetry, *The Business of Fancydancing,* was published in 1992, when he was twenty-six years old. He has since published more than seventeen books of poetry, fiction, and nonfiction as well as the screenplay for a movie, *Smoke Signals,* based on one of his stories. Alexie has also done stand-up comedy, won poetry competitions, and received many awards.

Notes

SKILLS PRACTICE

Superman and Me

Literary Skills
Analyze character and theme.

Character and Theme Chart One way to discover the **theme,** or truth about life revealed in a work of literature, is to think about the **main character.** In "Superman and Me," the main character is the author. Ask yourself, "What conflicts does he face? How does he respond to them? What does he learn from them?" Then, state the themes revealed by this information. Finally, pick a theme and compare or contrast it to the universal theme you found in "Learning to Read" and the excerpt from *The Autobiography of Malcolm X.*

Main Character: Sherman Alexie	Themes
His conflicts:	
His actions:	
Lessons he learns:	

Comparison of themes:

_____

_____

_____

110 Part 1 Collection 4: Comparing Themes

Skills Review

Superman and Me

VOCABULARY AND COMPREHENSION

A. Evaluating Word Connotations Fill in each blank with a word from the Word Box. Then, decide whether the connotations of the word are positive, neutral, or negative, and check the appropriate box. Note that decisions about connotations may vary.

> **Word Box**
> avid
> prodigy
> subverted
> monosyllabic
> submissively

1. Jose was an _____ baseball player who spent every minute he could practicing.
   ☐ positive   ☐ neutral   ☐ negative

2. Mozart was a musical _____ who began composing at the age of five.
   ☐ positive   ☐ neutral   ☐ negative

3. The well-trained dog comes _____ whenever his master calls.
   ☐ positive   ☐ neutral   ☐ negative

4. Jocelyn had every intention of finishing her homework, but her resolve was _____ by the sound of the party next door.
   ☐ positive   ☐ neutral   ☐ negative

5. The teacher was frustrated by the student's _____ answers to her questions.
   ☐ positive   ☐ neutral   ☐ negative

B. Reading Comprehension Answer each question below.

1. How does Sherman Alexie first learn to read? _____

2. Why isn't Alexie celebrated as a prodigy for learning to read so young?

3. How does Alexie overcome the expectation that he will fail? _____

4. Why does Alexie continue to visit and teach creative writing in Indian schools?

SKILLS FOCUS

Vocabulary Skills Evaluate connotations.

Superman and Me   111

Collection 5

Irony and Ambiguity

Relativity (1953) by M. C. Escher (1898–1972). Lithograph.
Art Resource, NY

Academic Vocabulary for Collection 5

These are the terms you should know as you read and analyze this collection.

Irony The difference between what we expect or what seems suitable and what actually happens. There are three main types of irony:

- **Verbal irony** occurs when someone *says* one thing but *means* the opposite. "Great hair," you say as you eye your friend's crooked haircut.
- In **situational irony** an event occurs that is the opposite of what we expect. Example: A convicted felon is hired as a security guard.
- **Dramatic irony** takes place when we know what is going to happen to a character but the character does not know. Example: *We* know, but Ron does *not* know, that when he flicks on his computer, a horrible virus will begin destroying his hard drive.

• • •

Ambiguity A quality that allows readers to interpret a story or other work in more than one way. Ambiguity is not something that can be cleared up by careful interpretation. Sometimes, writers deliberately make stories ambiguous to reinforce the idea that the things that happen in life itself can be interpreted in more than one way. There is no single correct interpretation to an ambiguous story.

Before You Read

Van Gogh's Ear by Moacyr Scliar

The bill collectors are threatening, and Father doesn't have the money. Perhaps Van Gogh's ear will save the day.

LITERARY FOCUS: SITUATIONAL IRONY

Irony is the difference between what we expect to happen and what actually happens.

Situational irony occurs when a story takes a surprising turn or concludes with an ending that most readers don't expect. This surprise is not tacked onto the story, but rather is an integral part of it, in no way contradicting the details of the plot.

- In "Van Gogh's Ear" the narrator's family is desperate to pay off the father's creditors. How might someone in debt get him- or herself out of it?
- As you read, think about what you expect to happen next.

READING SKILLS: CAUSE AND EFFECT

A plot is a series of causes and effects. A **cause** is the reason an action occurs. An **effect** is the result of an action. One event causes something else to happen: It has an effect. That event causes another event to happen, and so on. "Van Gogh's Ear" opens with the sentence "We were, as usual, on the brink of ruin." Ask yourself what the cause of this situation might be. As you read, look out for details that explain what events cause the next events to happen.

SKILLS FOCUS

Literary Skills
Understand situational irony.

Reading Skills
Understand cause and effect.

Vocabulary Skills
Understand affixes.

114 Part 1 Collection 5: Irony and Ambiguity

VOCABULARY DEVELOPMENT

PREVIEW SELECTION VOCABULARY

Review the following words from the story before you begin reading:

repulsed (ri·pulsd′) v.: drove back; resisted.

> For a while Father successfully **repulsed** his creditors' attempts to collect their money.

ruthless (rooth′lis) adj.: cruel; unfeeling.

> The man whom Father owed money to was **ruthless** and unforgiving about our late payments.

emerged (ē·murjd′) v.: came out; appeared.

> We **emerged** from the store onto the street, looking around for our enemy.

bequeathed (bē·kwēthd′) v.: handed down; given by means of a will at someone's death.

> Our family had only a modest income because Father was not **bequeathed** anything at the time of his own parents' deaths.

inevitable (in·ev′i·tə·bəl) adj.: unavoidable; certain.

> A confrontation between Father and his creditor was **inevitable,** and I thought we were better off facing him than hiding.

AFFIXES

An **affix** is a word part that is added to a base word or root and changes its meaning. Affixes that come *before* a base word are called **prefixes**. Affixes that come *after* a base word are called **suffixes**. Learning about affixes will help you understand and use a wider variety of words.

Below are some examples of commonly used prefixes and suffixes.

Prefix (Meaning)	Example
re– (again)	return
e– (out, away)	evict
be– (make)	befriend
im–, in– (not)	impossible
un– (opposite of; not)	unnecessary

Suffix (Meaning)	Example
–less (without)	thoughtless
–able (is; can be)	comfortable
–ness (state or quality of being)	kindness
–ful (full of)	wonderful
–ment (action or process)	government

Van Gogh's Ear

Van Gogh's Ear

Moacyr Scliar

We were, as usual, on the brink of ruin. My father, the owner of a small grocery store, owed a substantial amount of money to one of his suppliers. And there was no way he could pay off the debt.

But if Father was short of money, he certainly wasn't lacking in imagination... He was an intelligent, cultured man with a cheerful disposition. He hadn't finished school; fate had confined him to a modest grocery store where, amid bratwursts and other sausages, he bravely **repulsed** the attacks of existence. His customers liked him because, amongst other things, he granted them credit and never exacted payment. With his suppliers, however, it was a different story. Those strong-willed gentlemen wanted their money. The man whom Father owed money at that point was known as being a particularly **ruthless** creditor.

Any other person would have been driven to despair. Any other person would have considered running away, or even committing suicide. Not Father, though. Ever the optimist, he was convinced that he would find a way out. This man must have a weakness, he would say, and that's how we're going to get him. By making enquiries here and there, Father dug up something promising. This creditor, who to all appearances was a boorish and insensitive man, had a secret passion for Van Gogh. His house was full of reproductions of works by the great painter. And he had seen the movie about the tragic life of the artist, with Kirk Douglas in the star role, at least half a dozen times.

Father borrowed a biography of Van Gogh from the library and spent the weekend immersed in the book. Then, late on Sunday afternoon, the door of his bedroom opened and he **emerged**, triumphant:

"Van Gogh's Ear" by Moacyr Scliar, translated by Eloah F. Giacomelli from *The Vintage Book of Latin American Stories*, edited by Carlos Fuentes and Julio Ortega. Copyright © 1989 by Moacyr Scliar; translation copyright © 1989 by Eloah F. Giacomelli. Reproduced by permission of **Vintage Books**, a division of Random House, Inc.

"I've found it!"

Taking me aside—at the age of twelve I was his confidant and accomplice—he then whispered, his eyes glittering: "Van Gogh's ear. The ear will save us."

"What are the two of you whispering about?" asked Mother, who didn't have much tolerance for what she called the shenanigans of her husband.

"Nothing, nothing," replied Father, and then to me, lowering his voice, "I'll explain later."

Which he did. As the story went, Van Gogh had cut his ear off in a fit of madness and sent it to his beloved. This fact led Father to devise a scheme: He would go to his creditor and tell him that his great-grandfather, the lover of the woman Van Gogh had fallen in love with, had **bequeathed** him the mummified ear of the painter. Father would let his creditor have this relic in exchange for the cancellation of his debt and for additional credit.

Self Portrait (1889) by Vincent Van Gogh (1853–1890). Oil on canvas.
Private Collection, Zurich, Switzerland/Bridgeman Art Library

INFER
Why does Father believe his creditor will find his offer of Van Gogh's ear irresistible?

VOCABULARY
bequeathed (bē·kwēthd′) v.: handed down; given by means of a will at someone's death.

IDENTIFY
Explain Father's scheme to cancel his debt and get additional credit.

IRONY

Pause and re-read lines 46–52. What is **ironic** in Father's reaction to the son's question about the ear?

_____
_____
_____
_____
_____

SITUATIONAL IRONY

Circle what Father says about the creditor's behavior when he refuses the ear. Do you think Father is more upset about the refusal of the proposal or the creditor's behavior? Explain.

_____
_____
_____
_____
_____
_____

VOCABULARY

inevitable (in·ev′i·tə·bəl) *adj.*: unavoidable; certain.

"What do you think?"

Mother was right: he lived in another world, in a fantasy world. However, the main problem wasn't the absurdity of his idea; after all, we were in such dire straits that anything was worth a try. It was something else.

"But what about the ear?"

"The ear?" He looked at me astounded, as if the matter had never crossed his mind.

"Yes," I said, "Van Gogh's ear, where in the world are you going to get it?"

"Ah," he said, "no problem, we can get one from the morgue. A friend of mine is a janitor there, he'll do anything for me."

On the following day he left early in the morning. He came home at noon, radiant, carrying a parcel, which he then proceeded to unwrap carefully. It was a flask of formaldehyde[1] with something dark, of an indefinite shape, in it. Van Gogh's ear, he announced, triumphant. And who would say that it wasn't? Anyhow, just in case, he stuck a label on the flask: Van Gogh—ear.

In the afternoon the two of us headed for the creditor's house. Father went in, and I waited outside. Five minutes later he came out, disconcerted, and really furious. The man had not only rejected the proposal but he had also snatched the flask from Father and thrown it out of the window.

"Disrespectful!"

I had to agree with him, although I thought that such an outcome was to a certain extent **inevitable**. We started to walk along the tranquil street, with Father muttering all the time: disrespectful, disrespectful. Suddenly he stopped dead in his tracks, and stared fixedly at me:

> "Was it the right one, or the left one?"
>
> "What?" I said, without getting it.
>
> "The ear that Van Gogh cut off. Was it the right one or the left one?"

---

1. **formaldehyde:** strong-smelling substance used to preserve things such as body parts.

"How should I know?" I said, already irritated by the whole thing. "You're the one who read the book. You're the one who should know."

"But I don't," he said, disconsolate. "I admit I don't know."

We stood in silence for a while. I was then assailed by a nagging doubt, a doubt I didn't dare to articulate because I knew that the answer could be the end of my childhood. However:

"And the one in the flask?" I asked. "Was it the right one or the left?"

He stared at me, dumbfounded.

"You know what? I haven't the faintest," he murmured in a weak, hoarse voice.

We then continued to walk, heading for home. If you examine an ear carefully—any ear, whether Van Gogh's or not—you'll see that it is designed much like a labyrinth.[2] In this labyrinth I got lost. And I would never find my way out again.

---

2. **labyrinth** (lab′ə·rinth′) *n.:* maze.

MEET THE WRITER

Moacyr Scliar (1937–   ) was born and raised in Porto Alegre, Brazil, where he still lives and works as a public health physician. Scliar began writing fiction after hearing his parents' stories about life in Bessarabia, a region of Eastern Europe that is now part of Moldavia and Ukraine. His mother, a teacher in a Yiddish school in Brazil, first introduced him to literature. Commenting on his own work, Scliar has described it as influenced by both the Jewish literary tradition and Latin American magic realism. His novel *The Centaur in the Garden* was his first to be translated into English and was named by the National Yiddish Book Center one of the "100 Greatest Works of Modern Jewish Literature."

FLUENCY

Read the boxed passage aloud with a partner. Pay attention to the words describing each character's mood, and try to convey that mood in your reading.

Notes

SKILLS PRACTICE

Van Gogh's Ear

Literary Skills
Analyze irony.

Irony Chart The contrast between expectations and reality is referred to as **irony**. To help you appreciate the irony in "Van Gogh's Ear," fill in the blanks in this chart.

Story Passage	How Passage Creates Irony
Lines 8–10: "His customers liked him because, amongst other things, he granted them credit and never exacted payment."	
Lines 20–24: "This creditor . . . had a secret passion for Van Gogh. . . . And he had seen the movie about the tragic life of the artist, with Kirk Douglas in the star role, at least half a dozen times."	
Lines 76–77: " 'The ear that Van Gogh cut off. Was it the right one or the left one?' "	

Skills Review

Van Gogh's Ear

VOCABULARY AND COMPREHENSION

A. Using Affixes Match each affix with its definition by writing the correct letter on the line.

1. _____ re–   a. make
2. _____ un–   b. full of
3. _____ –less   c. again
4. _____ –ful   d. not
5. _____ be–   e. lacking

Word Box

repulsed
ruthless
emerged
bequeathed
inevitable

B. Vocabulary in Context Use a word from the Word Box to fill in each blank below.

1. The _____ creditor refused to cut a deal with the desperate man.

2. My grandparents _____ Father hardly anything when they died.

3. Because Father never received payment from his own customers, his financial ruin was _____.

4. He shut himself in the library for days before he finally _____.

5. Father _____ his creditors' efforts to collect the money he owed.

C. Reading Comprehension Answer each question below.

1. Explain Father's plan to make a deal with the creditor.
   _____

2. How does Father get the ear? _____
   _____

3. What happens when Father presents the ear to the creditor?
   _____
   _____

SKILLS FOCUS

Vocabulary Skills
Use affixes to help determine word meaning. Use words in context.

Before You Read

The Third Bank of the River
by João Guimarães Rosa

Father was out on the river in a boat. The river was so wide you couldn't see across it. But every once in a while the family would see Father in his boat rowing on its great expanse. What was he doing there?

LITERARY FOCUS: AMBIGUITY

When a story offers more than one meaning or interpretation, it is ambiguous, or shows **ambiguity.** Works that contain ambiguity are thought provoking because there is no single, correct interpretation. Instead, you are left to think and rethink story events, characters' actions, and the meanings you extract from them.

- As you read "The Third Bank of the River," you may be left with more questions than answers. How, in your view, should the story be interpreted?

READING SKILLS: MAKING INFERENCES

In literary works containing ambiguity, you, the reader, are not told everything; in fact, you may not be told much of *anything.* Instead, it is up to you to make inferences, or careful guesses, about what is happening and why. Making inferences about an ambiguous work won't lead you to one correct answer because one doesn't exist. By making inferences, however, you actively participate in the literary work's ongoing debate or puzzle.

To make an inference about a character or event:

- Identify all the details you can find that describe the character or the event.
- Think about how that character or event is like or unlike people or situations you've encountered in your own life or perhaps even in other stories.
- Make a careful guess about the kind of person you are meeting in the story and about the significance of the events in the story.
- Revise your inferences as the story goes on. Often in stories, as in life, we are surprised by people or by situations.

SKILLS FOCUS

Literary Skills
Understand ambiguity.

Reading Skills
Understand inference.

Vocabulary Skills
Understand roots and affixes.

SHORT STORY

VOCABULARY DEVELOPMENT

PREVIEW SELECTION VOCABULARY

The following words appear in "The Third Bank of the River." Get to know them before you read the story.

exhilarated (eg·zil′ə·rāt′ed) *v.* used as *adj.*: excited; stimulated.

My father's strange behavior made me feel bold and **exhilarated.**

appalled (ə·pôld′) *v.* used as *adj.*: horrified; dismayed.

Father's relatives and neighbors were **appalled** *when they learned of his decision.*

composure (kəm·pō′zhər) *n.*: calmness; self-possession.

Although she was ashamed of what Father did, Mother reacted with **composure.**

derelict (der′ə·likt′) *n.*: person without a home or means to live.

He shows no purpose, drifting aimlessly like a homeless **derelict.**

imperceptibly (im′pər·sep′tə·blē) *adv.*: without being noticed.

Father's boat drifted **imperceptibly** *across the wide river.*

impedimenta (im·ped′ə·men′tə) *n.*: obstacles; things that hinder progress.

The **impedimenta** *of my life kept me from moving forward.*

UNDERSTANDING ROOTS AND AFFIXES

An **affix** is a part that is added to a base word, or **root**. There are two kinds of affixes: **Prefixes** come before the root, and **suffixes** come after it. Learning the root meaning of one word can often help you understand related words. For example, look at the structure of the word *ambiguous*:

Prefix	Root Word	Suffix
ambi– (both, on both sides)	*agere* (act, do)	*–ous* (characterized by)

Knowledge of the root and affixes can help you figure out the meaning of *ambiguous*: "acting on both sides" hints at the real meaning: "able to be interpreted in different ways."

English contains many more words in the family derived from the root word *agere*, and they all have something to do with a form of "acting or doing." Here are just a few:

- as *act*: **act**ing, **act**ress, **act**ivate, **act**ual, en**act**, re**act**
- as *gate*: fumi**gate**, navi**gate**, liti**gate**
- as *gen*: co**gen**t, **agen**da, **agen**t
- as *gi, gu*: co**gi**tate, a**gi**le, ambi**gu**ous, coa**gu**late

The Third Bank of the River   123

The Third Bank of the River

João Guimarães Rosa

My father was a dutiful, orderly, straightforward man. And according to several reliable people of whom I inquired, he had had these qualities since adolescence or even childhood. By my own recollection, he was neither jollier nor more melancholy than the other men we knew. Maybe a little quieter. It was Mother, not Father, who ruled the house. She scolded us daily—my sister, my brother, and me. But it happened one day that Father ordered a boat.

He was very serious about it. It was to be made specially for him, of mimosa wood. It was to be sturdy enough to last twenty or thirty years and just large enough for one person. Mother carried on plenty about it. Was her husband going to become a fisherman all of a sudden? Or a hunter? Father said nothing. Our house was less than a mile from the river, which around there was deep, quiet, and so wide you couldn't see across it.

I can never forget the day the rowboat was delivered. Father showed no joy or other emotion. He just put on his hat as he always did and said good-by to us. He took along no food or bundle of any sort. We expected Mother to rant and rave, but she didn't. She looked very pale and bit her lip, but all she said was: "If you go away, stay away. Don't ever come back!"

Father made no reply. He looked gently at me and motioned me to walk along with him. I feared Mother's wrath, yet I eagerly obeyed. We headed toward the river together. I felt bold and **exhilarated,** so much so that I said: "Father, will you take me with you in your boat?"

He just looked at me, gave me his blessing, and by a gesture, told me to go back. I made as if to do so but, when his back was turned, I ducked behind some bushes to watch him. Father got

"The Third Bank of the River" by João Guimarães Rosa from *Modern Brazilian Short Stories*, edited and translated by William L. Grossman. Copyright © 1967 by the Regents of the University of California. Reproduced by permission of the **University of California Press.**

WORD STUDY

Inquired (line 2) derives from the Latin root *quaerere*, "to seek." It has this root in common with *question, request, exquisite,* and *acquire.*

COMPARE & CONTRAST

The narrator's father and mother are quite different. What do you learn about them in lines 1–13?

INTERPRET

What do you think of Mother's statement in line 21? Is it an order, a threat, or an attempt to have the last word? Explain.

VOCABULARY

exhilarated (eg·zil′ə·rāt′ed) *v.* used as *adj.:* excited; stimulated.

into the boat and rowed away. Its shadow slid across the water like a crocodile, long and quiet.

Father did not come back. Nor did he go anywhere, really. He just rowed and floated across and around, out there in the river. Everyone was **appalled.** What had never happened, what could not possibly happen, was happening. Our relatives, neighbors, and friends came over to discuss the phenomenon.

Mother was ashamed. She said little and conducted herself with great **composure.** As a consequence, almost everyone thought (though no one said it) that Father had gone insane. A few, however, suggested that Father might be fulfilling a promise

VOCABULARY

appalled (ə·pôld′) v. used as adj.: horrified; dismayed.

composure (kəm·pō′zhər) n.: calmness; self-possession.

WORD STUDY

Phenomenon (line 36) derives from the Latin *phaenomenon,* "things that appear." Note how little its meaning has changed since the Caesars ruled the Roman Empire two thousand years ago.

The Third Bank of the River 125

VOCABULARY

derelict (der′ə·likt′) *n.:* person without a home or means to live.

imperceptibly (im′pər·sep′tə·blē) *adv.:* without being noticed.

AMBIGUITY

Father doesn't tell anyone what he is doing or why. He floats in his boat without really going anywhere. What do you think he is doing, and why?

_____
_____
_____
_____

CONNECT

Underline the new information about Mother in lines 65–67. Are you as surprised as the narrator? Why or why not?

_____
_____
_____
_____

WORD STUDY

Vestments (line 71), meaning "ritual robes," derives from the Latin root word *vestis*, meaning "garment."

---

he had made to God or to a saint, or that he might have some horrible disease, maybe leprosy, and that he left for the sake of the family, at the same time wishing to remain fairly near them.

Travelers along the river and people living near the bank on one side or the other reported that Father never put foot on land, by day or night. He just moved about on the river, solitary, aimless, like a **derelict**. Mother and our relatives agreed that the food which he had doubtless hidden in the boat would soon give out and that then he would either leave the river and travel off somewhere (which would be at least a little more respectable) or he would repent and come home.

How far from the truth they were! Father had a secret source of provisions: me. Every day I stole food and brought it to him. The first night after he left, we all lit fires on the shore and prayed and called to him. I was deeply distressed and felt a need to do something more. The following day I went down to the river with a loaf of corn bread, a bunch of bananas, and some bricks of raw brown sugar. I waited impatiently a long, long hour. Then I saw the boat, far off, alone, gliding almost **imperceptibly** on the smoothness of the river. Father was sitting in the bottom of the boat. He saw me but he did not row toward me or make any gesture. I showed him the food and then I placed it in a hollow rock on the riverbank; it was safe there from animals, rain, and dew. I did this day after day, on and on and on. Later I learned, to my surprise, that Mother knew what I was doing and left food around where I could easily steal it. She had a lot of feelings she didn't show.

Mother sent for her brother to come and help on the farm and in business matters. She had the schoolteacher come and tutor us children at home because of the time we had lost. One day, at her request, the priest put on his vestments, went down to the shore, and tried to exorcise[1] the devils that had got into my father. He shouted that Father had a duty to cease his unholy

---

1. **exorcise** (eks′ôr·sīz′) *v.:* drive away an evil spirit.

126 Part 1 Collection 5: Irony and Ambiguity

obstinacy. Another day she arranged to have two soldiers come and try to frighten him. All to no avail. My father went by in the distance, sometimes so far away he could barely be seen. He never replied to anyone and no one ever got close to him. When some newspapermen came in a launch to take his picture, Father headed his boat to the other side of the river and into the marshes, which he knew like the palm of his hand but in which other people quickly got lost. There in his private maze, which extended for miles, with heavy foliage overhead and rushes on all sides, he was safe.

We had to get accustomed to the idea of Father's being out on the river. We had to but we couldn't, we never could. I think I was the only one who understood to some degree what our father wanted and what he did not want. The thing I could not understand at all was how he stood the hardship. Day and night, in sun and rain, in heat and in the terrible midyear cold spells, with his old hat on his head and very little other clothing, week after week, month after month, year after year, unheedful of the waste and emptiness in which his life was slipping by. He never set foot on earth or grass, on isle or mainland shore. No doubt he sometimes tied up the boat at a secret place, perhaps at the tip of some island, to get a little sleep. He never lit a fire or even struck a match and he had no flashlight. He took only a small part of the food that I left in the hollow rock—not enough, it seemed to me, for survival. What could his state of health have been? How about the continual drain on his energy, pulling and pushing the oars to control the boat? And how did he survive the annual floods, when the river rose and swept along with it all sorts of dangerous objects—branches of trees, dead bodies of animals—that might suddenly crash against his little boat?

He never talked to a living soul. And we never talked about him. We just thought. No, we could never put our father out of mind. If for a short time we seemed to, it was just a lull from which we would be sharply awakened by the realization of his frightening situation.

AMBIGUITY

Pause at line 83. No one—not the family, priest, soldiers, newspapermen—is able to get close to Father. What do you think this means?

_____
_____
_____

ANALYZE

To sustain human life, certain basic needs for food, clothing, and shelter have to be met. In father's existence out on the river (lines 84–108), are those needs being met? Explain.

_____
_____
_____
_____

ANALYZE

The characters in this story are identified by their roles—father, mother, sister, brother—and not by any given names. Why do you think the author made this choice?

_____
_____
_____
_____

The Third Bank of the River 127

INFER

What do lines 109–118 reveal about the way the family feels about the father?

_____
_____
_____
_____
_____
_____

FLUENCY

Read the boxed passage aloud until you can read it smoothly. Then, use your voice to express the feelings behind the words.

AMBIGUITY

The narrator says that only Father knows whether he cares for his family. In lines 123–133, underline details suggesting that he cares, and circle details suggesting that he doesn't care.

VOCABULARY

impedimenta
(im·ped′ə·men′tə) n.: obstacles; things that hinder progress.

The word *impedimenta* entered English unchanged from its Latin plural form, but you can also use the English plural form, *impediments*.

---

110 My sister got married, but Mother didn't want a wedding party. It would have been a sad affair, for we thought of him every time we ate some especially tasty food. Just as we thought of him in our cozy beds on a cold, stormy night—out there, alone and unprotected, trying to bail out the boat with only his hands and a gourd. Now and then someone would say that I was getting to look more and more like my father. But I knew that by then his hair and beard must have been shaggy and his nails long. I pictured him thin and sickly, black with hair and sunburn, and almost naked despite the articles of clothing I occasionally left for him.

120 He didn't seem to care about us at all. But I felt affection and respect for him, and, whenever they praised me because I had done something good, I said: "My father taught me to act that way."

It wasn't exactly accurate but it was a truthful sort of lie. As I said, Father didn't seem to care about us. But then why did he stay around there? Why didn't he go up the river or down the river, beyond the possibility of seeing us or being seen by us? He alone knew the answer.

My sister had a baby boy. She insisted on showing Father his grandson. One beautiful day we all went down to the river-
130 bank, my sister in her white wedding dress, and she lifted the baby high. Her husband held a parasol above them. We shouted to Father and waited. He did not appear. My sister cried; we all cried in each other's arms.

My sister and her husband moved far away. My brother went to live in a city. Times changed with their usual imperceptible rapidity. Mother finally moved too; she was old and went to live with her daughter. I remained behind, a leftover. I could never think of marrying. I just stayed there with the **impedimenta** of my life. Father, wandering alone and forlorn on the river, needed
140 me. I knew he needed me, although he never even told me why he was doing it. When I put the question to people bluntly and insistently, all they told me was that they heard that Father had explained it to the man who made the boat. But now this man was dead and nobody knew or remembered anything. There was

just some foolish talk, when the rains were especially severe and persistent, that my father was wise like Noah and had the boat built in anticipation of a new flood; I dimly remember people saying this. In any case, I would not condemn my father for what he was doing. My hair was beginning to turn gray.

I have only sad things to say. What bad had I done, what was my great guilt? My father always away and his absence always with me. And the river, always the river, perpetually renewing itself. The river, always. I was beginning to suffer from old age, in which life is just a sort of lingering. I had attacks of illness and of anxiety. I had a nagging rheumatism.² And he? Why, why was he doing it? He must have been suffering terribly. He was so old. One day, in his failing strength, he might let the boat capsize; or he might let the current carry it downstream, on and on, until it plunged over the waterfall to the boiling turmoil below. It pressed upon my heart. He was out there and I was forever robbed of my peace. I am guilty of I know not what, and my pain is an open wound inside me. Perhaps I would know—if things were different. I began to guess what was wrong.

Out with it! Had I gone crazy? No, in our house that word was never spoken, never through all the years. No one called anybody crazy, for nobody is crazy. Or maybe everybody. All I did was go there and wave a handkerchief so he would be more likely to see me. I was in complete command of myself. I waited. Finally he appeared in the distance, there, then over there, a vague shape sitting in the back of the boat. I called to him several times. And I said what I was so eager to say, to state formally and under oath. I said it as loud as I could:

"Father, you have been out there long enough. You are old. . . . Come back, you don't have to do it anymore. . . . Come back and I'll go instead. Right now, if you want. Any time. I'll get into the boat. I'll take your place."

And when I had said this my heart beat more firmly.

---

2. **rheumatism** (rōō′mə·tiz′əm) *n.*: pain in the joints or muscles.

> **AMBIGUITY**
>
> Underline the reason the narrator gives in line 183 for running in fear. Do you think his father is of this world? Explain.
>
> _____
> _____
> _____
> _____
> _____

> **AMBIGUITY**
>
> Do you think the narrator is a failure? Is he sane or crazy? Explain.
>
> _____
> _____
> _____
> _____
> _____

> **ANALYZE**
>
> What do you think the river stands for in this story? What does the "third bank" of the title stand for?
>
> _____
> _____
> _____
> _____
> _____

Giuseppe Ceschi/Jupiter Images

He heard me. He stood up. He maneuvered with his oars and headed the boat toward me. He had accepted my offer. And suddenly I trembled, down deep. For he had raised his arm and waved—the first time in so many, so many years. And I couldn't. . . . In terror, my hair on end, I ran, I fled madly. For he seemed to come from another world. And I'm begging forgiveness, begging, begging.

I experienced the dreadful sense of cold that comes from deadly fear, and I became ill. Nobody ever saw or heard about him again. Am I a man, after such a failure? I am what never should have been. I am what must be silent. I know it is too late. I must stay in the deserts and unmarked plains of my life, and I fear I shall shorten it. But when death comes I want them to take me and put me in a little boat in this perpetual water between the long shores; and I, down the river, lost in the river, inside the river . . . the river. . . .

MEET THE WRITER

João Guimarães Rosa (1908–1967) acquired the world's languages the way some people collect cars. As a Brazilian, his native language was Portuguese, and he taught himself French before he was seven years old. As an adult, he spoke Portuguese, German, French, English, Spanish, Italian, Esperanto, and some Russian. He read Swedish, Dutch, Latin, and Greek with the aid of a dictionary. He studied the grammar of Hungarian, Arabic, Sanskrit, Lithuanian, Polish, Tupi, Hebrew, Japanese, Czech, Finnish, and Danish. He studied languages and wrote novels and stories for his own pleasure. For work, he was a medical doctor and a diplomat to Europe and Latin America. Guimarães Rosa is considered one of Brazil's greatest novelists.

SKILLS PRACTICE

The Third Bank of the River

SKILLS FOCUS

Literary Skills Analyze ambiguity.

Reading Skills Make inferences.

Ambiguity Chart   An **ambiguous** story is one that is open to two or more interpretations. The chart below lists some ambiguous details from the story. In the right-hand column, list two possible interpretations of each detail. Remember, with ambiguity, there is no one correct answer.

Ambiguous Detail	Possible Interpretations
A. The father floats in a boat on the river, continually moving but not really going anywhere.	1. 2.
B. The father lives for many years without clothing or shelter and with very little food.	1. 2.
C. The father seems not to care about his family but never goes far from where they live.	1. 2.
D. The narrator offers to take the father's place but then flees, fearing that his father is not of this world.	1. 2.
E. The narrator wishes to be put in a boat on the river when he dies.	1. 2.

Collection 5: Irony and Ambiguity

Skills Review

The Third Bank of the River

VOCABULARY AND COMPREHENSION

A. Recognizing Word Roots and Affixes Write the word from the Word Box next to its root and affix. Then, write the meaning of the Word Box word. (An intensifier just adds emphasis to the meaning of the word.)

1. *im–*, "not"; *pedis*, "foot" _____
   Meaning: _____

2. *a–*, "to"; *pallere*, "to be pale" _____
   Meaning: _____

3. *de–* (intensifier); *re–*, "from"; *linquere*, "to leave"
   _____
   Meaning: _____

4. *ex–* (intensifier); *hilaris*, "glad" _____
   Meaning: _____

5. *im–*, "not"; *per–*, "through"; *capere*, "to take" _____
   Meaning: _____

6. *com–*, "with"; *poser*, "to place" _____
   Meaning: _____

Word Box
exhilarated
appalled
composure
derelict
imperceptibly
impedimenta

B. Reading Comprehension Answer each question below.

1. How does the speaker describe the father before he gets into the boat?
   _____
   _____

2. What does the father do in the boat? _____
   _____

3. What happens to the rest of the family? _____
   _____

4. How does the narrator feel about his life? _____
   _____

SKILLS FOCUS

Vocabulary Skills
Use roots and affixes.

The Third Bank of the River   133

Collection 6

Symbolism and Allegory

Academic Vocabulary for Collection 6

These are the terms you should know
as you read and analyze the selections in this collection.

Symbol An object, setting, animal, or person that functions both as itself and as something other than itself, usually something abstract.

Figurative Language Language that describes one thing in terms of another and is not meant to be understood on a literal level. Common figures of speech include similes, metaphors, and personification.

Theme An idea or insight about life or human nature revealed in a work of literature.

• • •

Allegory A work of literature in which characters and places stand for abstract or moral ideas. Sometimes the characters and places stand for abstract qualities such as virtues and vices and have names that describe what they symbolize, such as a character called Mr. Mean or a place called the Sea of Troubles.

Fable An allegory in which animal characters, who usually symbolize vices and virtues, act out a story that teaches a practical lesson about life.

Parable An allegory in the form of a brief story, set in the everyday world, told to teach a lesson about ethics or morality.

Before You Read

My Wonder Horse by Sabine R. Ulibarrí

Do dreams come true? This is a story about a dream that comes true. It doesn't last, but for a timeless moment, there it is—a dream realized.

LITERARY FOCUS: SYMBOLIC MEANING

A **symbol** is something—a person, place, object, or event—that stands both for itself and for something beyond itself. For example, literally speaking, a horse is a horse is a horse; however, it can also symbolize strength, beauty, or freedom.

- As you read "My Wonder Horse," decide when the horse is just a horse and when it is a symbol of something else.
- When you have finished reading, think about what the symbol means.

READING SKILLS: VISUALIZING THE STORY

Writers use language to help readers **visualize**, or imagine, a story's setting and characters. When you visualize, you use the writer's words to create a mental picture of what's going on—almost as if you were watching a movie. Visualizing makes it easier to enter into a story and to understand what you are reading.

To visualize a story:

- Pay special attention to figurative language and imagery. Stop and imagine what the author hopes to convey through the use of these particular types of expression.
- Pause at the end of a paragraph or another logical stopping point to imagine the scene.
- Look for sensory details—those that appeal to one or all of your senses. Re-read the paragraph to catch any sensory details you might have missed.

SKILLS FOCUS

Literary Skills
Understand symbolism.

Reading Skills
Visualize the story.

Vocabulary Skills
Understand words in context.

VOCABULARY DEVELOPMENT

PREVIEW SELECTION VOCABULARY

The following words appear in "My Wonder Horse." Get to know them before you begin the story.

fabricated (fab′ri·kāt′ed) *v.* used as *adj.*: invented or made up.

*Some horse stories are true; others are **fabricated**.*

lethargy (leth′ər·jē) *n.*: great lack of energy; sluggishness.

*After hard riding, **lethargy** overcomes his horse.*

languor (laŋ′gər) *n.*: stillness; sluggishness.

*Lazing around the campfire, the men enjoy the **languor** of the still afternoon.*

inexplicable (in·eks′pli·kə·bəl) *adj.*: not able to be explained or understood.

*The sun seems to stand still in the sky in some **inexplicable** way.*

invincible (in·vin′sə·bəl) *adj.*: not able to be overcome; unconquerable.

*Many men try to capture him, but the horse remains **invincible**.*

turmoil (tur′moil′) *n.*: tumult; commotion; uproar; confusion.

*Dreaming of the horse leaves the young man upset and in **turmoil**.*

indomitable (in·däm′i·tə·bəl) *adj.*: not able to be defeated; unconquerable.

*The young man admired the horse's **indomitable** spirit.*

WORDS IN CONTEXT

You can sometimes use **context clues** to help you figure out the meanings of unfamiliar words. When you come across an unfamiliar word, look at its **context**—the words and sentences surrounding it. You may find a definition, a restatement, or an example of the unknown word to help you unlock its meaning.

> He thought of the horse as a **talisman,** one that would bring him luck with the girls if only he could capture it and bring it into town.

The word *talisman* in the sentence above is defined by an example. You can tell from reading the rest of the sentence that a talisman is an object that brings luck or power.

My Wonder Horse

My Wonder Horse

Sabine R. Ulibarrí

He was white. White as memories lost. He was free. Free as happiness is. He was fantasy, liberty, and excitement. He filled and dominated the mountain valleys and surrounding plains. He was a white horse that flooded my youth with dreams and poetry.

Around the campfires of the country and in the sunny patios of the town, the ranch hands talked about him with enthusiasm and admiration. But gradually their eyes would become hazy and blurred with dreaming. The lively talk would die down. All thoughts fixed on the vision evoked by the horse. Myth of the animal kingdom. Poem of the world of men.

White and mysterious, he paraded his harem through the summer forests with lordly rejoicing. Winter sent him to the plains and sheltered hillsides for the protection of his females. He spent the summer like an Oriental potentate[1] in his woodland gardens. The winter he passed like an illustrious warrior celebrating a well-earned victory.

He was a legend. The stories told of the Wonder Horse were endless. Some true, others **fabricated.** So many traps, so many snares, so many searching parties, and all in vain. The horse always escaped, always mocked his pursuers, always rose above the control of man. Many a valiant cowboy swore to put his halter and his brand on the animal. But always he had to confess later that the mystic[2] horse was more of a man than he.

SYMBOL

Circle the two **metaphors** in line 10 that describe the horse. What do these figures of speech tell you about the **symbolic meaning** of the Wonder Horse?

VISUALIZE

Underline the **similes** in lines 14–15. How do you picture the horse in summer and in winter?

VOCABULARY

fabricated (fab′ri·kāt′ed) v. used as adj.: invented or made up.

---

1. **Oriental potentate** (ôr′ē·ent″l pōt″n·tāt): Asian ruler.
2. **mystic** (mis′tik) adj.: mysterious; having magic powers.

"My Wonder Horse" from *Tierra Amarilla: Stories of New Mexico* by Sabine R. Ulibarrí. Copyright © 1971 by **Sabine R. Ulibarrí.** Reproduced by permission of the author.

I was fifteen years old. Although I had never seen the Wonder Horse, he filled my imagination and fired my ambition. I used to listen open-mouthed as my father and the ranch hands talked about the phantom horse who turned into mist and air and nothingness when he was trapped. I joined in the universal obsession—like the hope of winning the lottery—of putting my lasso on him some day, of capturing him and showing him off on Sunday afternoons when the girls of the town strolled through the streets.

It was high summer. The forests were fresh, green, and gay. The cattle moved slowly, fat and sleek in the August sun and shadow. Listless and drowsy in the **lethargy** of late afternoon, I was dozing on my horse. It was time to round up the herd and go back to the good bread of the cowboy camp. Already my comrades would be sitting around the campfire, playing the guitar, telling stories of past or present, or surrendering to the **languor** of the late afternoon. The sun was setting behind me in a riot of streaks and colors. Deep, harmonious silence.

I sit drowsily still, forgetting the cattle in the glade. Suddenly the forest falls silent, a deafening quiet. The afternoon comes to a standstill. The breeze stops blowing, but it vibrates. The sun flares hotly. The planet, life, and time itself have stopped in an **inexplicable** way. For a moment, I don't understand what is happening.

Then my eyes focus. There he is! The Wonder Horse! At the end of the glade, on high ground surrounded by summer green. He is a statue. He is an engraving. Line and form and white stain on a green background. Pride, prestige, and art incarnate[3] in animal flesh. A picture of burning beauty and virile freedom. An ideal, pure and **invincible**, rising from the eternal dreams of humanity. Even today my being thrills when I remember him.

A sharp neigh. A far-reaching challenge that soars on high, ripping the virginal fabric of the rosy clouds. Ears at the point. Eyes flashing. Tail waving active defiance. Hoofs glossy and destructive. Arrogant ruler of the countryside.

---

3. **incarnate** (in·kär′nit) *adj.:* having bodily form; being a living example of.

> **INTERPRET**
>
> In line 28, the narrator describes the horse as a "universal obsession." Underline the example in line 29 that he uses to clarify his meaning. How are capturing the horse and winning the lottery alike?
>
> **VOCABULARY**
>
> **lethargy** (leth′ər·jē) *n.:* great lack of energy; sluggishness.
>
> **languor** (laŋ′gər) *n.:* stillness; sluggishness.
>
> Notice how *lethargy* and *languor* can have the same meaning.
>
> **inexplicable** (in·eks′pli·kə·bəl) *adj.:* not able to be explained or understood.
>
> **invincible** (in·vin′sə·bəl) *adj.:* not able to be overcome; unconquerable.
>
> **VISUALIZE**
>
> Re-read lines 47–57. How do you picture the horse from these details?

Notes

PREDICT

Pause at line 63. How do you think seeing the horse will change the narrator's life?

VOCABULARY

turmoil (tʉr′moil′) *n.:* tumult; commotion; uproar; confusion.

SYMBOL

Circle the three things in line 73 that the Wonder Horse symbolizes for the narrator.

© Hugh Beebower/CORBIS

The moment is never-ending, a momentary eternity. It no longer exists, but it will always live.... There must have been mares. I did not see them. The cattle went on their indifferent way. My horse followed them, and I came slowly back from the land of dreams to the world of toil. But life could no longer be what it was before.

That night under the stars I didn't sleep. I dreamed. How much I dreamed awake and how much I dreamed asleep, I do not know. I only know that a white horse occupied my dreams and filled them with vibrant sound, and light, and **turmoil**.

Summer passed and winter came. Green grass gave place to white snow. The herds descended from the mountains to the valleys and the hollows. And in the town they kept saying that the Wonder Horse was roaming through this or that secluded area. I inquired everywhere for his whereabouts. Every day he became for me more of an ideal, more of an idol, more of a mystery.

140 Part 1 Collection 6: Symbolism and Allegory

It was Sunday. The sun had barely risen above the snowy mountains. My breath was a white cloud. My horse was trembling with cold and fear like me. I left without going to mass. Without any breakfast. Without the usual bread and sardines in my saddlebags. I had slept badly but had kept the vigil well. I was going in search of the white light that galloped through my dreams.

On leaving the town for the open country, the roads disappear. There are no tracks, human or animal. Only a silence, deep, white, and sparkling. My horse breaks trail with his chest and leaves an unending wake, an open rift, in the white sea. My trained, concentrated gaze covers the landscape from horizon to horizon, searching for the noble silhouette of the talismanic horse.

It must have been midday. I don't know. Time had lost its meaning. I found him! On a slope stained with sunlight. We saw one another at the same time. Together, we turned to stone. Motionless, absorbed, and panting, I gazed at his beauty, his pride, his nobility. As still as sculptured marble, he allowed himself to be admired.

A sudden, violent scream breaks the silence. A glove hurled into my face.[4] A challenge and a mandate.[5] Then something surprising happens. The horse that in summer takes his stand between any threat and his herd, swinging back and forth from left to right, now plunges into the snow. Stronger than they, he is breaking trail for his mares. They follow him. His flight is slow in order to conserve his strength.

I follow. Slowly. Quivering. Thinking about his intelligence. Admiring his courage. Understanding his courtesy. The afternoon advances. My horse is taking it easy.

One by one the mares become weary. One by one, they drop out of the trail. Alone! He and I. My inner ferment bubbles to my lips. I speak to him. He listens and is quiet.

---

4. **A glove . . . face:** In the past a thrown glove was a challenge to a duel.
5. **mandate** (man'dāt') *n.:* command; order.

My Wonder Horse **141**

INFER

Why do you think the narrator feels like an executioner (line 114)?

_____
_____
_____
_____
_____

VISUALIZE

Re-read the poetic description of the horse in lines 121–125. How do you picture this scene? What made the "wide, white pool"?

_____
_____
_____
_____
_____
_____

INFER

Why is the narrator able to catch the Wonder Horse when no one else has been able to?

_____
_____
_____
_____
_____

He still opens the way, and I follow in the path he leaves me. Behind us a long, deep trench crosses the white plain. My horse, which has eaten grain and good hay, is still strong. Undernourished as the Wonder Horse is, his strength is waning. But he keeps on because that is the way he is. He does not know how to surrender.

I now see black stains over his body. Sweat and the wet snow have revealed the black skin beneath the white hair. Snorting breath, turned to steam, tears the air. White spume[6] above white snow. Sweat, spume, and steam. Uneasiness.

I felt like an executioner. But there was no turning back. The distance between us was growing relentlessly shorter. God and Nature watched indifferently.

I feel sure of myself at last. I untie the rope. I open the lasso and pull the reins tight. Every nerve, every muscle is tense. My heart is in my mouth. Spurs pressed against trembling flanks. The horse leaps. I whirl the rope and throw the obedient lasso.

A frenzy of fury and rage. Whirlpools of light and fans of transparent snow. A rope that whistles and burns the saddletree.[7] Smoking, fighting gloves. Eyes burning in their sockets. Mouth parched. Fevered forehead. The whole earth shakes and shudders. The long, white trench ends in a wide, white pool.

Deep, gasping quiet. The Wonder Horse is mine! Both still trembling, we look at one another squarely for a long time. Intelligent and realistic, he stops struggling and even takes a hesitant step toward me. I speak to him. As I talk, I approach him. At first, he flinches and recoils. Then he waits for me. The two horses greet one another in their own way. Finally, I succeed in stroking his mane. I tell him many things, and he seems to understand.

Ahead of me, along the trail already made, I drove him toward the town. Triumphant. Exultant. Childish laughter gathered in my throat. With my newfound manliness, I controlled it. I wanted to sing, but I fought down the desire. I wanted to shout, but I kept quiet. It was the ultimate in happiness. It was the pride of the male adolescent. I felt myself a conqueror.

---

6. **spume** (spyo͞om) _n._: froth; foam.
7. **saddletree:** frame of a saddle.

Occasionally the Wonder Horse made a try for his liberty, snatching me abruptly from my thoughts. For a few moments, the struggle was renewed. Then we went on.

It was necessary to go through the town. There was no other way. The sun was setting. Icy streets and people on the porches. The Wonder Horse full of terror and panic for the first time. He ran, and my well-shod horse stopped him. He slipped and fell on his side. I suffered for him. The indignity. The humiliation. Majesty degraded. I begged him not to struggle, to let himself be led. How it hurt me that other people should see him like that!

Finally we reached home.

"What shall I do with you, Mago?[8] If I put you into the stable or the corral, you are sure to hurt yourself. Besides, it

---

8. **Mago:** Spanish for "wizard."

> **SYMBOL**
>
> Think about what this horse symbolizes for the narrator. Then, explain why he is suffering for the horse in lines 142–149.

My Wonder Horse

PREDICT

Pause at line 157. Do you think a friendship will develop between the narrator and the horse? Why or why not?

_____

_____

_____

_____

FLUENCY

Read the boxed passage aloud, first for smoothness and then for meaning. Try to express the narrator's growing anxiety with your voice.

CONNECT

The Greek philosopher Aristotle (384–322 B.C.) said that all human actions have one or more of these seven causes: chance, nature, compulsion, habit, reason, passion, and desire. In your opinion, which of these causes apply to the Wonder Horse's actions? Explain.

_____

_____

_____

_____

_____

---

would be an insult. You aren't a slave. You aren't a servant. You aren't even an animal."

I decided to turn him loose in the fenced pasture. There, little by little, Mago would become accustomed to my friendship and my company. No animal had ever escaped from that pasture.

My father saw me coming and waited for me without a word. A smile played over his face, and a spark danced in his eyes. He watched me take the rope from Mago, and the two of us thoughtfully observed him move away. My father clasped my hand a little more firmly than usual and said, "That was a man's job." That was all. Nothing more was needed. We understood one another very well. I was playing the role of a real man, but the childish laughter and shouting that bubbled up inside me almost destroyed the impression I wanted to create.

> That night I slept little, and when I slept, I did not know that I was asleep. For dreaming is the same when one really dreams, asleep or awake. I was up at dawn. I had to go to see my Wonder Horse. As soon as it was light, I went out into the cold to look for him.
>
> The pasture was large. It contained a grove of trees and a small gully. The Wonder Horse was not visible anywhere, but I was not worried. I walked slowly, my head full of the events of yesterday and my plans for the future. Suddenly I realized that I had walked a long way. I quicken my steps. I look apprehensively around me. I begin to be afraid. Without knowing it, I begin to run. Faster and faster.

He is not there. The Wonder Horse has escaped. I search every corner where he could be hidden. I follow his tracks. I see that during the night he walked incessantly, sniffing, searching for a way out. He did not find one. He made one for himself.

I followed the track that led straight to the fence. And I saw that the trail did not stop but continued on the other side. It was a barbed-wire fence. There was white hair on the wire. There was blood on the barbs. There were red stains on the snow and little red drops in the hoofprints on the other side of the fence.

I stopped there. I did not go any farther. The rays of the morning sun on my face. Eyes clouded and yet filled with light. Childish tears on the cheeks of a man. A cry stifled in my throat. Slow, silent sobs.

Standing there, I forgot myself and the world and time. I cannot explain it, but my sorrow was mixed with pleasure. I was weeping with happiness. No matter how much it hurt me, I was rejoicing over the flight and the freedom of the Wonder Horse, the dimensions of his **indomitable** spirit. Now he would always be fantasy, freedom, and, excitement. The Wonder Horse was transcendent.[9] He had enriched my life forever.

My father found me there. He came close without a word and laid his arm across my shoulders. We stood looking at the white trench with its flecks of red that led into the rising sun.

---

9. **transcendent** *adj.:* exceeding regular limits or understanding.

MEET THE WRITER

Sabine R. Ulibarrí (1919–2003), a short story writer, poet, essayist, critic, and university professor, was born in Tierra Amarilla, a small village in New Mexico. As a young man, he received the Distinguished Flying Cross for having flown thirty-five combat missions over Europe during World War II. When he returned home, he continued his education under the G.I. Bill at the University of New Mexico and at the University of California, Los Angeles. He later became a well-known writer and won many awards. Although born in the United States, Ulibarrí always wrote in Spanish, and his works were then translated into English.

VOCABULARY

indomitable (in·däm′i·tə·bəl) *adj.:* not able to be defeated; unconquerable.

What other Vocabulary word has the same meaning?

_____

SYMBOL

Circle the three things in line 197 that the Wonder Horse will always symbolize for the narrator.

SYMBOL

What does the rising sun in the last line symbolize?

_____

My Wonder Horse 145

SKILLS PRACTICE

My Wonder Horse

Literary Skills
Analyze symbolism.

Reading Skills
Visualize a story.

Symbolism Chart "The Wonder Horse" uses vivid imagery in its descriptions of the horse. The images help you visualize the action and understand symbolic meanings. In the first column of the chart below, you will find some passages from the story. In the second column, note what the images in the passages suggest to you. In the third column, infer what the images might symbolize. Item 1 has been completed for you.

Passage from the Story	What the Images Suggest	Symbolic Meaning
1. "I used to listen open-mouthed as my father and the ranch hands talked about the phantom horse who turned into mist and air and nothingness when he was trapped."	The horse has become a legend to the men, who are unable to catch him.	The horse symbolizes myth, legend, fantasy.
2. "He is a statue. He is an engraving. Line and form and white stain on a green background. Pride, prestige, and art incarnate in animal flesh. A picture of burning beauty and virile freedom. An ideal, pure and invincible, rising from the eternal dreams of humanity."		
3. "No matter how much it hurt me, I was rejoicing over the flight and the freedom of the Wonder Horse, the dimensions of his indomitable spirit. Now he would always be fantasy, freedom, and excitement. The Wonder Horse was transcendent. He had enriched my life forever."		

Collection 6: Symbolism and Allegory

Skills Review

My Wonder Horse

VOCABULARY AND COMPREHENSION

A. Using Context Clues In each sentence below, underline the context clues that help you understand the meaning of the boldfaced word. Then, write a definition of the word.

1. After cleaning out the basement, Mario was overcome with **lethargy**, so he stretched out on a lounge chair and took a nap. **Definition:** _____

2. On a hot summer day it feels good to lie still and enjoy the **languor** of the afternoon. **Definition:** _____

3. Juanita's mother scolded at her when she **fabricated** tales, but when she made up stories in class, her teacher gave her an A+. **Definition:** _____

4. Peter's singing ability was **inexplicable** to the rest of his family; none of them could carry a tune, so they couldn't understand where he got his talent. **Definition:** _____

5. When Georgia got back on her horse after a nasty fall, everyone admired her **indomitable** spirit. **Definition:** _____

6. After the basketball team won their first ten games, they thought they were **invincible**. **Definition:** _____

7. When Carlos's pet rat escaped from his backpack, the class erupted in **turmoil**; everyone was running around trying to catch the speedy rodent. **Definition:** _____

Word Box
- fabricated
- lethargy
- languor
- inexplicable
- invincible
- turmoil
- indomitable

B. Reading Comprehension Answer each question below.

1. What ambition does the fifteen-year-old narrator have at the beginning of the story? _____

2. How does the narrator feel at the end of the story? _____

SKILLS FOCUS

Vocabulary Skills Use context clues.

My Wonder Horse 147

Before You Read

The Alligator War by Horacio Quiroga

The story you are about to read is an amusing tale about alligators at war—or is it?

LITERARY FOCUS: ALLEGORY

An **allegory** is a story in which characters and places stand for abstract or moral ideas. Allegories are intended to be read on two levels. On one level is the literal story, telling us who does what to whom. On another level is the story's allegorical, or symbolic, meaning—the issues that the story is really about.

- First read the story for its basic meaning—and enjoy it! Then, think about the allegorical meaning of the story. The title offers a broad hint of what the allegory is about.

READING SKILLS: IDENTIFYING RELATIONSHIPS

We don't exist in a vacuum. We interact with other people—at home, in school, at work, even on public transportation. Our relationships affect our lives profoundly. Most stories are about relationships. Analyzing these relationships—trying to understand the characters' behaviors and motivations—can help us understand our own relationships in life.

- As you read, look for characters who have influence over other characters.
- Take note of alliances—friendships between characters for mutual benefits.
- Look for characters who dislike each other and the reasons for their dislike.
- Look for characters who take on leadership roles.

SKILLS FOCUS

Literary Skills
Understand symbolism and allegory.

Reading Skills
Identify relationships between characters.

Vocabulary Skills
Understand word roots.

VOCABULARY DEVELOPMENT

PREVIEW SELECTION VOCABULARY
You probably won't find many unfamiliar words in "The Alligator War," but here are a few you may not know.

obstruction (əb·struk′shən) *n.:* something blocking the way; obstacle.

*The new **obstruction** across the river surprises the men in the boat.*

derision (di·rizh′ən) *n.:* ridicule; scorn.

*The alligators laughed at the sailors with **derision**.*

detonation (det′′n·ā′shən) *n.:* explosion.

*A loud **detonation** came suddenly from the warship.*

IDENTIFYING GREEK AND LATIN ROOTS
What do *evidence, video,* and *provide* have in common? All three words share the Latin root *vid,* meaning "see." Learning to recognize Greek and Latin roots will help you unlock the meanings of many English words. Several of the roots in the charts below can be found in words in "The Alligator War."

Greek Root	Meaning	Example
–astro–, –aster–	"star"	astronaut
–auto–	"self"	automobile
–geo–	"earth"	geology
–graph–	"write"	telegraph
–psych–	"mind"	psychology

Latin Root	Meaning	Example
–rid–	"laugh"	ridiculous
–struct–	"build"	construction
–ton–	"thunder"	thunderous
–ven–	"come"	convention
–volv–	"turn"	revolve

Use your knowledge of roots and affixes to guess the meanings of unfamiliar words, and then check to see how close your guesses come to each word's dictionary definition.

The Alligator War 149

The Alligator War

Horacio Quiroga

VISUALIZE

Pause at line 11. Describe the setting in which the alligators live.

_____
_____
_____
_____
_____
_____

IDENTIFY RELATIONSHIPS

Judging from what you have read on this page, what kind of relationships do the alligators have with one another?

_____
_____
_____
_____
_____
_____
_____

It was a very big river in a region of South America that had never been visited by white men; and in it lived many, many alligators—perhaps a hundred, perhaps a thousand. For dinner they ate fish, which they caught in the stream, and for supper they ate deer and other animals that came down to the waterside to drink. On hot afternoons in summer they stretched out and sunned themselves on the bank. But they liked nights when the moon was shining best of all. Then they swam out into the river and sported and played, lashing the water to foam with their tails, while the spray ran off their beautiful skins in all the colors of the rainbow.

These alligators had lived quite happy lives for a long, long time. But at last one afternoon, when they were all sleeping on the sand, snoring and snoring, one alligator woke up and cocked his ears—the way alligators cock their ears. He listened and listened, and, to be sure, faintly, and from a great distance, came a sound: *Chug! Chug! Chug!*

"Hey!" the alligator called to the alligator sleeping next to him, "Hey! Wake up! Danger!"

"Danger of what?" asked the other, opening his eyes sleepily and getting up.

"I don't know!" replied the first alligator. "That's a noise I never heard before. Listen!"

The other alligator listened: *Chug! Chug! Chug!*

In great alarm the two alligators went calling up and down the riverbank: "Danger! Danger!" And all their sisters and brothers and mothers and fathers and uncles and aunts woke up and began running this way and that with their tails curled up in the air. But the excitement did not serve to calm their fears. *Chug! Chug! Chug!* The noise was growing louder every moment; and at last, away off down the stream, they could see something moving along the surface of the river, leaving a trail of gray smoke behind it and beating the water on either side to foam: *Chush! Chush! Chush!*

The alligators looked at each other in the greatest astonishment: "What on earth is that?"

But there was one old alligator, the wisest and most experienced of them all. He was so old that only two sound teeth were left in his jaws—one in the upper jaw and one in the lower jaw. Once, also, when he was a boy, fond of adventure, he had made a trip down the river all the way to the sea.

PREDICT

Pause at line 36. What do you think is coming up the river?

WORD STUDY

The word *sound* has multiple meanings. What does *sound* mean in line 38?

Alligator.
© Charles Philip Cangialosi/CORBIS

The Alligator War 151

IDENTIFY RELATIONSHIPS

Pause at line 52. What is the relationship between the wise old alligator and the little alligators?

_____
_____
_____
_____
_____
_____

WORD STUDY

Steamer (line 63) is another word for a steamboat—a boat driven by steam power. In this boat, the steam drives paddle wheels—the "revolving things it had on either side" (lines 61–62), which move the boat through the water.

PREDICT

Underline what the old alligator predicts will happen (lines 73–74). Do you agree or disagree? Explain.

_____
_____
_____
_____
_____
_____

"I know what it is," said he. "It's a whale. Whales are big fish, they shoot water up through their noses, and it falls down on them behind."

At this news, the little alligators began to scream at the top of their lungs, "It's a whale! It's a whale! It's a whale!" and they made for the water intending to duck out of sight.

But the big alligator cuffed with his tail a little alligator that was screaming nearby with his mouth open wide. "Dry up!" said 50 he. "There's nothing to be afraid of! I know all about whales! Whales are the afraidest people there are!" And the little alligators stopped their noise.

But they grew frightened again a moment afterward. The gray smoke suddenly turned to an inky black, and the *Chush! Chush! Chush!* was now so loud that all the alligators took to the water, with only their eyes and the tips of their noses showing at the surface.

Cho-ash-h-h! Cho-ash-h-h! Cho-ash-h-h! The strange monster came rapidly up the stream. The alligators saw it go crashing 60 past them, belching great clouds of smoke from the middle of its back and splashing into the water heavily with the big revolving things it had on either side.

It was a steamer, the first steamer that had ever made its way up to the Paraná.[1] *Chush! Chush! Chush!* It seemed to be getting farther away again. *Chug! Chug! Chug!* It had disappeared from view.

One by one, the alligators climbed up out of the water onto the bank again. They were all quite cross with the old alligator who had told them wrongly that it was a whale.

70 "It was not a whale!" they shouted in his ear—for he was rather hard of hearing. "Well, what was it that just went by?"

The old alligator then explained that it was a steamboat full of fire and that the alligators would all die if the boat continued to go up and down the river.

---

1. **Paraná:** river in South America that originates in Brazil, forms a border between Paraguay and Argentina, and continues through Argentina to the Atlantic Ocean.

The other alligators only laughed, however. Why would the alligators die if the boat kept going up and down the river? It had passed by without so much as speaking to them! That old alligator didn't really know so much as he pretended to! And since they were very hungry they all went fishing in the stream. But alas! There was not a fish to be found! The steamboat had frightened every single one of them away.

"Well, what did I tell you?" said the old alligator. "You see, we haven't anything left to eat! All the fish have been frightened away! However—let's just wait till tomorrow. Perhaps the boat won't come back again. In that case, the fish will get over their fright and come back so that we can eat them." But the next day the steamboat came crashing by again on its way back down the river, spouting black smoke as it had done before, and setting the whole river boiling with its paddle wheels.

"Well!" exclaimed the alligators. "What do you think of that? The boat came yesterday. The boat came today. The boat will come tomorrow. The fish will stay away and nothing will come down here at night to drink. We are done for!"

But an idea occurred to one of the brighter alligators: "Let's dam the river!" he proposed. "The steamboat won't be able to climb a dam!"

"That's the talk! That's the talk! A dam. A dam! Let's build a dam!" And the alligators all made for the shore as fast as they could.

They went up into the woods along the bank and began to cut down trees of the hardest wood they could find—walnut and mahogany, mostly. They felled more than ten thousand of them altogether, sawing the trunks through with the kind of saw that alligators have on the tops of their tails. They dragged the trees down into the water and stood them up about a yard apart, all the way across the river, driving the pointed ends deep into the mud and weaving the branches together. No steamboat, big or little, would ever be able to pass that dam! No one would frighten

WORD STUDY

Notice all the sound effects in lines 112–113. Say the lines aloud, and see if you sound like a steamboat.

VOCABULARY

obstruction (əb·struk′shən) *n.*: something blocking the way; obstacle.

IDENTIFY RELATIONSHIPS

Pause at line 142. What kind of relationship do the alligators have with the men in the boat?

---

the fish away again! They would have a good dinner the following day and every day! And since it was late at night by the time the dam was done, they all fell sound asleep on the riverbank.

Chug! Chug! Chug! Chush! Chush! Chush! Cho-ash-h-h-h! Cho-ash-h-h-h! Cho-ash-h-h-h!

They were still asleep, the next day, when the boat came up; but the alligators barely opened their eyes and then tried to go to sleep again. What did they care about the boat? It could make all the noise it wanted, but it would never get by the dam!

And that is what happened. Soon the noise from the boat stopped. The men who were steering on the bridge took out their spyglasses and began to study the strange **obstruction** that had been thrown up across the river. Finally a small boat was sent to look into it more closely. Only then did the alligators get up from where they were sleeping, run down into the water, and swim out behind the dam, where they lay floating and looking downstream between the piles. They could not help laughing, nevertheless, at the joke they had played on the steamboat!

The small boat came up, and the men in it saw how the alligators had made a dam across the river. They went back to the steamer but soon after came rowing up toward the dam again.

"Hey, you alligators!"

"What can we do for you?" answered the alligators, sticking their heads through between the piles in the dam.

"That dam is in our way!" said the men.

"Tell us something we don't know!" answered the alligators.

"But we can't get by!"

"I'll say so!"

"Well, take the old thing out of the way!"

"Nosireesir!"

The men in the boat talked it over for a while and then they called: "Alligators!"

"What can we do for you?"

"Will you take the dam away?"

"No!"

"No?"

"No!"

"Very well! See you later!"

"The later the better," said the alligators.

The rowboat went back to the steamer, while the alligators, as happy as could be, clapped their tails as loud as they could on the water. No boat could ever get by that dam and drive the fish away again!

But the next day the steamboat returned; and when the alligators looked at it, they could not say a word from their surprise: it was not the same boat at all but a larger one, painted gray like a mouse! How many steamboats were there, anyway? And this one probably would want to pass the dam! Well, just let it try! No, sir! No steamboat, little or big, would ever get through that dam!

"They shall not pass!" said the alligators, each taking up his station behind the piles in the dam.

The new boat, like the other one, stopped some distance below the dam; and again a little boat came rowing toward them. This time there were eight sailors in it, with one officer.

The officer shouted: "Hey, you alligators!"

"What's the matter?" answered the alligators.

"Going to get that dam out of there?"

"No!"

"No?"

"No!"

"Very well!" said the officer. "In that case, we shall have to shoot it down!"

"Shoot it up if you want to!" said the alligators.

And the boat returned to the steamer.

But now, this mouse-gray steamboat was not an ordinary steamboat: it was a warship with armor plate and terribly powerful guns. The old alligator who had made the trip to the

---

IDENTIFY RELATIONSHIPS

Pause at line 158. The alligators are confident that they have won their conflict with the men. Who do you think really has more power? Explain.

_____
_____
_____
_____

ALLEGORY

Notice that the alligators have provoked a war without even realizing it. How is this event similar to events in human wars?

_____
_____
_____
_____
_____
_____
_____
_____

The Alligator War 155

IDENTIFY RELATIONSHIPS

What role does the old alligator now play in the story?

_____
_____
_____
_____

VOCABULARY

derision (di·rizh'ən) *n.*: ridicule; scorn.

WORD STUDY

The word *sound* appears again in line 199 in its adverb form, *soundly*. What does it mean this time?

_____
_____

INFER

Why do the alligators jeer at the officer (line 203)?

_____
_____
_____
_____
_____
_____

river mouth suddenly remembered, and just in time to shout to the other alligators: "Duck for your lives! Duck! She's going to shoot! Keep down deep under water."

The alligators dived all at the same time and headed for the shore, where they halted, keeping all their bodies out of sight except for their noses and their eyes. A great cloud of flame and smoke burst from the vessel's side, followed by a deafening report. An immense solid shot hurtled through the air and struck the dam exactly in the middle. Two or three tree trunks were cut away into splinters and drifted off downstream. Another shot, a third, and finally a fourth, each tearing a great hole in the dam. Finally the piles were entirely destroyed; not a tree, not a splinter, not a piece of bark was left; and the alligators, still sitting with their eyes and noses just out of water, saw the warship come steaming by and blowing its whistle in **derision** at them.

Then the alligators came out on the bank and held a council of war. "Our dam was not strong enough," said they; "we must make a new and much thicker one."

So they worked again all that afternoon and night, cutting down the very biggest trees they could find and making a much better dam than they had built before. When the gunboat appeared the next day, they were sleeping soundly and had to hurry to get behind the piles of the dam by the time the rowboat arrived there.

"Hey, alligators!" called the same officer.

"See who's here again!" said the alligators, jeeringly.

"Get that new dam out of there!"

"Never in the world!"

"Well, we'll blow it up, the way we did the other!"

"Blaze away, and good luck to you!"

You see, the alligators talked so big because they were sure the dam they had made this time would hold up against the most terrible cannonballs in the world. And the sailors must have thought so, too; for after they had fired the first shot a tremendous explosion occurred in the dam. The gunboat was using shells, which burst among the timbers of the dam and broke the thickest trees into tiny, tiny bits. A second shell exploded right near the first, and a third near the second. So the shots went all along the dam, each tearing away a long strip of it till nothing, nothing, nothing was left. Again the warship came steaming by, closer in toward shore on this occasion, so that the sailors could make fun of the alligators by putting their hands to their mouths and holloing.

"So that's it!" said the alligators, climbing up out of the water. "We must all die, because the steamboats will keep coming and going, up and down, and leaving us not a fish in the world to eat!"

Alligators.
© Farrell Grehan/CORBIS

ALLEGORY

The alligators and the sailors seem to be enjoying their battle until the alligators realize the consequences of their defeat (lines 221–224). What abstract idea is the story expressing?

WORD STUDY

A sturgeon (line 230) is a large fish and a source of caviar.

IDENTIFY RELATIONSHIPS

Pause at line 241. Why does the Sturgeon dislike alligators? Why does the old alligator think the Sturgeon might help them?

_____
_____
_____
_____

VISUALIZE

How do you picture the Sturgeon? Underline details that support your description.

_____
_____
_____
_____

FLUENCY

Read the boxed passage here and on the next page aloud once for practice. Then, read it aloud with a partner. One of you can be the Sturgeon, and one of you can be the old alligator. Practice reading together until your voices express the personalities of these two characters.

The littlest alligators were already whimpering, for they had had no dinner for three days; and it was a crowd of very sad alligators that gathered on the river shore to hear what the old alligator now had to say.

"We have only one hope left," he began. "We must go and see the Sturgeon! When I was a boy, I took that trip down to the sea along with him. He liked the salt water better than I did and went quite a way out into the ocean. There he saw a sea fight between two of these boats; and he brought home a torpedo that had failed to explode. Suppose we go and ask him to give it to us. It is true the Sturgeon has never liked us alligators; but I got along with him pretty well myself. He is a good fellow, at bottom, and surely he will not want to see us all starve!"

The fact was that some years before an alligator had eaten one of the Sturgeon's favorite grandchildren, and for that reason the Sturgeon had refused ever since to call on the alligators or receive visits from them. Nevertheless, the alligators now trouped off in a body to the big cave under the bank of the river where they knew the Sturgeon stayed, with his torpedo beside him. There are sturgeons as much as six feet long, you know, and this one with the torpedo was of that kind.

"Mr. Sturgeon! Mr. Sturgeon!" called the alligators at the entrance of the cave. No one of them dared go in, you see, on account of that matter of the Sturgeon's grandchild.

"Who is it?" answered the Sturgeon.

"We're the alligators," the latter replied in a chorus.

"I have nothing to do with alligators," grumbled the Sturgeon crossly.

But now the old alligator with the two teeth stepped forward and said: "Why, hello, Sturgy. Don't you remember Ally, your old friend that took that trip down the river when we were boys?"

"Well, well! Where have you been keeping yourself all these years?" said the Sturgeon, surprised and pleased to hear his old friend's voice. "Sorry I didn't know it was you! How goes it? What can I do for you?"

Collection 6: Symbolism and Allegory

"We've come to ask you for that torpedo you found, remember? You see, there's a warship keeps coming up and down our river scaring all the fish away. She's a whopper, I'll tell you, armor plate, guns, the whole thing! We made one dam and she knocked it down. We made another and she blew it up. The fish have all gone away and we haven't had a bite to eat in near onto a week. Now you give us your torpedo and we'll do the rest!"

The Sturgeon sat thinking for a long time, scratching his chin with one of his fins. At last he answered: "As for the torpedo, all right! You can have it in spite of what you did to my eldest son's first-born. But there's one trouble: who knows how to work the thing?"

The alligators were all silent. Not one of them had ever seen a torpedo.

"Well," said the Sturgeon proudly, "I can see I'll have to go with you myself. I've lived next to that torpedo a long time. I know all about torpedoes."

The first task was to bring the torpedo down to the dam. The alligators got into line, the one behind taking in his mouth the tail of the one in front. When the line was formed it was fully a quarter of a mile long. The Sturgeon pushed the torpedo out into the current and got under it so as to hold it up near the top of the water on his back. Then he took the tail of the last alligator in his teeth and gave the signal to go ahead. The Sturgeon kept the torpedo afloat, while the alligators towed him along. In this way they went so fast that a wide wake followed on after the torpedo, and by the next morning they were back at the place where the dam was made.

As the little alligators who had stayed at home reported, the warship had already gone by upstream. But this pleased the others all the more. Now they would build a new dam, stronger than ever before, and catch the steamer in a trap, so that it would never get home again.

They worked all that day and all the next night, making a thick, almost solid dike, with barely enough room between the

ALLEGORY

Pause at line 315. How has the conflict between the alligators and the men grown? What abstract or moral point is the story making?

IDENTIFY RELATIONSHIPS

Pause at line 325. What is the relationship between the old alligator and the naval officer? Who do you think has more power?

piles for the alligators to stick their heads through. They had just finished when the gunboat came into view.

Again the rowboat approached with the eight men and their officer. The alligators crowded behind the dam in great excitement, moving their paws to hold their own with the current, for this time they were downstream.

"Hey, alligators!" called the officer.

"Well?" answered the alligators.

"Still another dam?"

"If at first you don't succeed, try, try, again!"

"Get that dam out of there!"

"No, sir!"

"You won't?"

"We won't!"

"Very well! Now you alligators just listen! If you won't be reasonable, we are going to knock this dam down, too. But to save you the trouble of building a fourth, we are going to shoot every blessed alligator around here. Yes, every single last alligator, women and children, big ones, little ones, fat ones, lean ones, and even that old codger sitting there with only two teeth left in his jaws!"

The old alligator understood that the officer was trying to insult him with that reference to his two teeth, and he answered: "Young man, what you say is true. I have only two teeth left, not counting one or two others that are broken off. But do you know what those two teeth are going to eat for dinner?" As he said this the old alligator opened his mouth wide, wide, wide.

"Well, what are they going to eat?" asked one of the sailors.

"A little dude of a naval officer I see in a boat over there!"— and the old alligator dived under water and disappeared from view.

Meantime the Sturgeon had brought the torpedo to the very center of the dam, where four alligators were holding it fast to the river bottom waiting for orders to bring it up to the top of

Sturgeon.
© blickwinkel/Alamy

330 the water. The other alligators had gathered along the shore, with their noses and eyes alone in sight as usual.

The rowboat went back to the ship. When he saw the men climbing aboard, the Sturgeon went down to his torpedo.

Suddenly there was a loud **detonation.** The warship had begun firing, and the first shell struck and exploded in the middle of the dam. A great gap opened in it.

"Now! Now!" called the Sturgeon sharply, on seeing that there was room for the torpedo to go through. "Let her go! Let her go!"

340 As the torpedo came to the surface, the Sturgeon steered it to the opening in the dam, took aim hurriedly with one eye closed, and pulled at the trigger of the torpedo with his teeth. The propeller of the torpedo began to revolve, and it started off upstream toward the gunboat.

> **VOCABULARY**
>
> **detonation** (det″n·ā′shən) *n.:* explosion.
>
> **PREDICT**
>
> Who do you predict will win this war—the men in the warship or the alligators with their torpedo?
>
> _____
> _____
> _____
> _____
> _____
> _____

The Alligator War 161

SUMMARIZE

Pause at line 353. Summarize what happens at the battle of the third dam.

_____
_____
_____
_____
_____
_____
_____

INTERPRET

Irony is the contrast between what is expected and what actually happens. How is the decision of the alligators not to eat the sailors (lines 359–361) ironic?

_____
_____
_____
_____

IDENTIFY RELATIONSHIPS

The old alligator has kept his word and eaten the officer. Why did the old alligator want to eat the officer?

_____
_____
_____

And it was high time. At that instant a second shot exploded in the dam, tearing away another large section.

From the wake the torpedo left behind it in the water the men on the vessel saw the danger they were in, but it was too late to do anything about it. The torpedo struck the ship in the middle, and went off.

350 You can never guess the terrible noise that torpedo made. It blew the warship into fifteen thousand million pieces, tossing guns and smokestacks and shells and rowboats—everything—hundreds and hundreds of yards away.

The alligators all screamed with triumph and made as fast as they could for the dam. Down through the opening bits of wood came floating, with a number of sailors swimming as hard as they could for the shore. As the men passed through, the alligators put their paws to their mouths and holloed, as the men had done to them three days before. They decided not to eat a 360 single one of the sailors, though some of them deserved it without a doubt. Except that when a man dressed in a blue uniform with gold braid came by, the old alligator jumped into the water off the dam and snap! snap! ate him in two mouthfuls.

"Who was that man?" asked an ignorant young alligator, who never learned his lessons in school and never knew what was going on.

"It's the officer of the boat," answered the Sturgeon. "My old friend, Ally, said he was going to eat him, and eaten him he has!"

The alligators tore down the rest of the dam, because they 370 knew that no boats would be coming by that way again.

The Sturgeon, who had quite fallen in love with the gold lace of the officer, asked that it be given him in payment for the use of his torpedo. The alligators said he might have it for the trouble of picking it out of the old alligator's mouth, where it had caught on the two teeth. They also gave him the officer's belt and sword. The Sturgeon put the belt on just behind his front fins and buckled the sword to it. Thus togged out, he swam up and down for more than an hour in front of the assembled alligators, who admired his beautiful spotted skin as something almost as pretty as the coral snake's, and who opened their mouths wide at the splendor of his uniform. Finally they escorted him in honor back to his cave under the riverbank, thanking him over and over again and giving him three cheers as they went off.

When they returned to their usual place they found the fish had already returned. The next day another steamboat came by; but the alligators did not care, because the fish were getting used to it by this time and seemed not to be afraid. Since then the boats have been going back and forth all the time, carrying oranges. And the alligators open their eyes when they hear the *chug! chug! chug!* of a steamboat and laugh at the thought of how scared they were the first time and of how they sank the warship.

But no warship has ever gone up the river since the old alligator ate the officer.

MEET THE WRITER

Horacio Quiroga (1878–1937) seems to have been stalked by tragedy throughout his life. Shortly after his birth his father, an Argentine diplomat, was killed in a hunting accident. His mother remarried, but his stepfather, depressed and sick, took his own life. Quiroga spent most of his youth in Uruguay, where he was born, but moved to Argentina in later life. He is considered one of Latin America's greatest short story writers. His writing often includes macabre and grotesque themes, showing the influence of Edgar Allan Poe.

ALLEGORY

Re-read the description of the Sturgeon's and alligators' actions in lines 371–381. What point is the story making here?

ALLEGORY

Re-read lines 385–395. What has changed since the beginning of the story? What has not changed? What abstract idea does this story illustrate?

The Alligator War 163

SKILLS PRACTICE

The Alligator War

Skills Focus: Literature Skills — Analyze an allegory.

Allegory Chart An **allegory** can be enjoyed for the literal story it tells and also for the allegorical, or symbolic, meaning behind the events. The chart below lists some literal events from the story in the left-hand column. Fill in their allegorical meaning in the right-hand column. Then, list the overall idea or lesson of the story.

Event from the Story	Allegorical Meaning
1. The alligators are cheerful and confident that a dam will solve their problem.	
2. The conflict between the alligators and the sailors grows from building and blowing up dams to making death threats.	
3. The alligators form an alliance with the Sturgeon.	
4. The Sturgeon enjoys parading about in military trappings.	
5. After the battle, the fish return and steamboats go up and down the river.	

Overall idea or lesson:

Skills Review

The Alligator War

VOCABULARY AND COMPREHENSION

A. Identifying Greek and Latin Roots Fill in the chart below with the related Word Box words and their meanings.

Word Box

obstruction
derision
detonation

Root and Meaning	Related Word	Word Bank Word	Meaning
–rid–, "laugh"	ridicule		
–ton–, "thunder"	thunderous		
–struct–, "build"	construction		

B. Reading Comprehension Answer each question below.

1. Why do the alligators decide to build a dam? _____
_____

2. How do the sailors get past the first dam? _____
_____

3. How do the alligators defeat the warship? _____
_____

4. What is the resolution of the story? _____
_____

SKILLS FOCUS

Vocabulary Skills
Identify Latin and Greek roots.

The Alligator War 165

Collection 7

Poetry

Academic Vocabulary for Collection 7

These are the terms you should know
as you read and analyze the selections in this collection.

Imagery Language that appeals to one or more of the senses—sight, hearing, taste, touch, smell—and that creates **images**, or pictures, in our minds. The image of a porcupine's prickly armor appeals to the senses of sight and touch.

Figurative Language Language in which one thing is compared to something that seems to be entirely different. A **figure of speech** is not literally true, but a good one suggests a powerful truth in its comparison.

- A **simile** is a comparison containing the word *like* or *as*: "His eyes were like laser beams."

- A **metaphor** is a comparison without a connecting word. In a **direct metaphor**, two parts of the comparison are generally linked by a form of the verb *to be*: "The old man was a dinosaur." In an **implied metaphor**, the comparison is suggested: "The leftover cereal had all the crunch of wet cardboard." An **extended metaphor** continues through several lines of a work.

- A special kind of metaphor, in which an object, animal, or idea is described as if it were a person, is called **personification**: "After the rain, the flowers hung their heads."

• • •

Rhyme The repetition of the accented vowel sound and all following sounds in a word *(lime / time; mixture / fixture)*.

- Most rhymes occur at the ends of lines and are called **end rhymes**.

- Rhymes that occur within a line or lines close together are called **internal rhymes**, as in this example by Alfred, Lord Tennyson: "The long light *shakes* across the *lakes*."

- In **approximate rhyme**, the repetition of sound is not exact, as in *now / know*.

Rhythm A musical quality in poetry that comes from stressed and unstressed sounds that make the voice rise and fall. **Meter** is a regular pattern formed by stressed and unstressed sounds.

Academic Vocabulary

Repetition Repeating words, parts of words, phrases, or clauses for dramatic or rhythmic effect.

- **Parallel Structure** Repeating phrase or sentence structure. The words are different, but the parts of speech and the rhythm are matched and repeated.
- **Alliteration** (ə·lit′ər·ā′shən) Repetition of initial consonant sounds in words that appear close together. The line on page 167 by Tennyson has alliteration: *long / light / lakes*.
- **Assonance** (as′ə·nəns) Repetition of similar vowel sounds that are followed by different consonant sounds, especially in words that are close together in a poem *(base / fade; young / love)*.

Onomatopoeia (än′ō·mat′ō·pē′ə) The use of words that sound like what they mean—for instance, the *buzzing* of bees and *croaking* of frogs.

• • •

Free Verse Poetry that does not follow a regular pattern of rhyme and meter.

Lyric A form of poetry that does not tell a story but rather is aimed at expressing the speaker's emotions or thoughts. Most lyrics are short, and they usually imply, rather than state, a single strong emotion.

Before You Read

POEM

Magic Island by Cathy Song

Have you ever heard that the best things in life are free? Here is a poem about that very subject.

LITERARY FOCUS: SOUND DEVICES IN FREE-VERSE POETRY

Free-verse poems sound more like everyday conversation than do other forms of poetry, in part because they lack a regular rhyme scheme. The **sound devices** used in free verse are harder to spot, but they make important contributions to the "music" of the lines. Here are some devices often found in free-verse poems:

rhyme	Free-verse poems seldom have exact rhymes or rhymes at the ends of lines, but they may have **approximate rhymes** (*now / know; solace / palace*) or **internal rhymes**—rhymes within a line or in nearby lines.
alliteration	Repetition of consonant sound in nearby words (as in Kipling's "great grey-green, greasy Limpopo River"). Alliteration can come at the end or the middle of words as well as at the beginning (*class assessment*).
assonance	Repetition of vowel sounds in nearby words. (The Kipling example above offers assonance in the pairings *great / grey* and *green / greasy* as well as *Lim– / River.*)

- As you read "Magic Island," listen for the sound devices. How do they contribute to the poem's **mood,** or atmosphere?

READING SKILLS: READING A POEM

When you're reading a poem, keep the following strategies in mind:
1. **Look for punctuation in the poem telling you where sentences begin and end.** Many poems—though not all—are written in full sentences.
2. **Do not pause at the end of a line if there is no period, comma, colon, semicolon, or dash.** If there is no punctuation at the end of a line of poetry, read right on to the next line to complete the sense of the sentence.
3. **If a passage of a poem is difficult to understand, look for the subject, verb, and complement of each sentence.** Try to identify the words the clauses and phrases relate to.
4. **Be alert for comparisons—figures of speech.** Try to visualize what the poet is describing for you.
5. **Read the poem aloud.** Poems are not usually meant to be read silently. The sound of a poem is very important.

SKILLS FOCUS

Literary Skills Understand sound devices in free-verse poetry.

Magic Island 169

Magic Island

Cathy Song

> **SOUND DEVICES**
>
> Find at least one example of each sound device—**internal rhyme, alliteration,** and **assonance**—in the first two stanzas of the poem (lines 1–22). Circle and connect the words. Then, write the name of the device next to the words.

> **FLUENCY**
>
> Read the first stanza (lines 1–12) aloud, following the tips for reading a poem on the previous page. Take your time when reading aloud to savor the sounds.

Three kites flying.
© Andy Bishop/Alamy

A collar of water
surrounds the park peninsula
at noon.
Voices are lost
5   in waves of wind
that catches a kite
and keeps it there
in the air above the trees.
If the day has one color,
10   it is this:
the blue immersion of horizons,
the sea taking the sky like a swimmer.

"Magic Island" by Cathy Song from *Making Waves* by Asian Women United. Copyright © 1989 by Asian Women United. Reproduced by permission of **Beacon Press**.

The picknickers have come
to rest their bicycles
15   in the sprawling shade.
Under each tree, a stillness
of small pleasures:
a boy, half in sunlight,
naps with his dog;
20   a woman of forty
squints up from her book
to bite into an apple.

It is a day an immigrant
and his family might remember,
25   the husband taking off his shirt
to sit like an Indian
before the hot grill.
He would not in his own language
call it work, to cook
30   the sticks of marinated meat
for his son circling a yarn
of joy around the chosen tree.
A bit of luck has made him generous.
At this moment in his life,
35   with the sun sifting through
the leaves in panes of light,
he can easily say he loves his wife.
She lifts an infant
onto her left shoulder
40   as if the child
were a treasured sack of rice.
He cannot see her happiness,
hidden in a thicket of blanket
and shining hair.

(continued)

SOUND DEVICES

Find another example of each sound device—**approximate rhyme**, **alliteration**, and **assonance**—in this final stanza of the poem (lines 23–50). Again, circle and connect the words, and write the name of the device next to the words.

INTERPRET

The first two stanzas set the scene in the park. This third stanza focuses on a family. Pause at line 44, and describe the family and what they are doing. How is the scene in the park affecting them?

Magic Island   171

ANALYZE

What does the black umbrella (line 46) **symbolize**, or represent?

45 On the grass beside their straw mat,
    a black umbrella,
    blooming like an ancient flower,
    betrays their recent arrival.
    Suspicious of so much sunshine,
50 they keep expecting rain.

MEET THE WRITER

Cathy Song (1955–   ) was born in Honolulu, Hawaii, of Chinese American and Korean American parents. She received a bachelor's degree from Wellesley College and a master's degree in creative writing from Boston University. In 1983, Song published her first volume of poetry, *Picture Bride,* which won the Yale Younger Poets Award. This book was followed by *Frameless Windows, Squares of Light* (1988) and *School Figures* (1994). Song lives in Hawaii with her husband and two children. She teaches at the University of Hawaii at Manoa and works as an editor for the Bamboo Ridge Press, which publishes Hawaiian literature.

Skills Practice and Review

Magic Island

Sound Devices Chart   Poets use sounds in special ways to give their work a musical quality or to emphasize ideas. For each example from the poem listed in the chart below, identify the sound device it illustrates: **alliteration, assonance, approximate rhyme,** or **internal rhyme.** Underline the letters, words, or phrases that show the sound device.

Example from Poem	Type of Sound Device
1. "A collar of water" (line 1)	
2. "in waves of wind / that catches a kite" (lines 5–6)	
3. "and keeps it there / in the air above the trees" (lines 7–8)	

Reading Comprehension   Answer each question below.

1. Describe the setting of the poem.
   _____
   _____
   _____

2. How does the setting affect the family?
   _____
   _____
   _____

3. What detail indicates the family members are not yet used to their environment?
   _____
   _____
   _____

SKILLS FOCUS

Literature Skills
Identify sound devices.

Magic Island   173

Before You Read

POEMS

Legal Alien by Pat Mora
Child of the Americas by Aurora Levins Morales

When a form asks you to check a box for your ethnicity, how many boxes do you need to check? Here are two poems that speak to the experience of having more than one heritage.

LITERARY FOCUS: RHYTHM IN FREE-VERSE POETRY

You have learned that **free-verse** poems sound like everyday conversations, in part because they don't have a regular rhyme scheme. Another reason is that they lack the **rhythm** of the regular pattern of stressed and unstressed syllables called **meter**. This does not mean that free-verse poems are without rhythm, however. Rather, the free-verse poet pays close attention to the rhythm of each line—to the rise and fall of the voice, to pauses, to the balance of short and long phrases, and to the repetition of certain sounds, words, phrases, or structures. In doing so, poets can make words ooze like melting ice cream or strike the ear like the clicking of castanets.

rhythm	Musical quality produced by the repetition of stressed and unstressed syllables or by the repetition of other sound patterns.
repetition	Use of repeated word parts, words, phrases, or whole sentences for rhythmic effect.
parallel structure	Repetition of grammatical forms. The words change, but the structure remains the same.

- As you read "Legal Alien" and "Child of the Americas," pay attention to the poems' rhythms. See if you can spot the poets' use of repetition and parallel structure. Then, ask yourself what these patterns contribute to the poems.

READING SKILLS: COMPARISON AND CONTRAST

When you read two poems on a similar subject, you naturally want to compare and contrast them. When you **compare** them, you discuss how they are similar. When you **contrast** them, you discuss how they are different.

- As you read "Legal Alien" and "Child of the Americas," think about the style and message of each poem. How does each poem create its rhythms? What **theme,** or message about life, does each poem reveal?

SKILLS FOCUS

Literary Skills
Understand rhythm in free-verse poetry.

Legal Alien

Pat Mora

Bi-lingual, Bi-cultural,
able to slip from "How's life?"
to *"Me'stan volviendo loca,"*°
able to sit in a paneled office
5   drafting memos in smooth English,
able to order in fluent Spanish
at a Mexican restaurant,

---

3. *Me'stan volviendo loca* (mā·stän′ vôl′vē·en′dô lô′kä): Spanish for "They're driving me crazy."

WORD STUDY

The prefix *bi–* means "two." In line 1, what do "bi-lingual" and "bi-cultural" mean?

CLARIFY

In lines 4–7, what does the speaker say she can do that shows she is "bi-lingual"?

RHYTHM

Underline three examples of **parallel structure**—the repetition of grammatical patterns—in lines 9–11, 14–15, and 19–20. What does this repetition add to the poem?

_____
_____
_____
_____
_____
_____

EVALUATE

What do you think are the advantages of being bilingual and bicultural? What are the disadvantages?

_____
_____
_____
_____
_____
_____
_____
_____

American but hyphenated,
viewed by Anglos as perhaps exotic,
10   perhaps inferior, definitely different,
viewed by Mexicans as alien,
(their eyes say, "You may speak
Spanish but you're not like me"),
an American to Mexicans
15   a Mexican to Americans
a handy token
sliding back and forth
between the fringes of both worlds
by smiling
20   by masking the discomfort
of being pre-judged
Bi-laterally.

MEET THE WRITER

Pat Mora (1942–) takes pride in being a Chicana writer and enjoys traveling to schools to inspire young people and teach writing. She was born in El Paso, Texas, the city her grandparents immigrated to during the Mexican Revolution. She grew up in a bilingual home in which she enjoyed reading many kinds of books. Mora writes poetry, nonfiction, and children's books in both English and Spanish. Many of her writing ideas come from the desert where she grew up and from her Mexican American family. Mora lives in both Santa Fe, New Mexico, and Cincinnati, Ohio.

Child of the Americas

Aurora Levins Morales

Aurora Levins Morales.
Photo copyright by Barry Kleider, Minneapolis

I am a child of the Americas,
a light-skinned mestiza° of the Caribbean,
a child of many diaspora,° born into this continent at a crossroads.

I am a U.S. Puerto Rican Jew,
5   a product of the ghettos of New York I have never known.
An immigrant and the daughter and granddaughter of
    immigrants.

---

2. **mestiza** (me·stē′zə) *n.:* woman or girl of mixed heritage.
3. **diaspora** (dī·as′pə·rə) *n.:* scattering of people who share a common origin.

"Child of the Americas" from *Getting Home Alive* by Aurora Levins Morales and Rosario Morales. Copyright © 1986 by Aurora Levins Morales and Rosario Morales. Reproduced by permission of **Firebrand Books**.

> **RHYTHM**
>
> In lines 1–7, circle the examples of **repetition**, and underline the **parallel structures**.

> **WORD STUDY**
>
> The word *ghetto* (line 5) derives from the Venetian Jewish quarter in Italy. The island of Ghetto was used to confine Jews. It now refers to any section of a city where members of a minority group live or to which they are confined by discrimination.

Child of the Americas   177

COMPARE & CONTRAST

Pause at line 14. What does English mean to the speaker of the poem? What does Spanish mean?

I speak English with passion: it's the tongue of my consciousness,
a flashing knife blade of crystal, my tool, my craft.

I am Caribeña,° island grown. Spanish is in my flesh,
10   ripples from my tongue, lodges in my hips:
the language of garlic and mangoes,
the singing in my poetry, the flying gestures of my hands.
I am of Latinoamerica, rooted in the history of my continent:
I speak from that body.

15   I am not african. Africa is in me, but I cannot return.
I am not taína.° Taíno is in me, but there is no way back.
I am not european. Europe lives in me, but I have no home there.

I am new. History made me. My first language was spanglish.
I was born at the crossroads
20   and I am whole.

---

9. **Caribeña** (kä′rē·bän′yä) *n.:* woman from the Caribbean.
16. **taína** (tī′nə) *n.:* woman of a West Indian people who lived in the Caribbean before Columbus arrived.

INFER

How does the speaker feel about her multiple ethnicity?

MEET THE WRITER

Aurora Levins Morales (1954–   ) was born in Puerto Rico of an American Jewish father and a Puerto Rican mother. When she was thirteen, her family moved to Chicago, Illinois. She later lived in Ann Arbor, Michigan; Rochester, New York; New York City; Minneapolis, Minnesota; and San Francisco, California, among other places. Many people imagine that her mixed heritage makes her feel confused about her identity—they want to know if she is more Jewish or more Puerto Rican—but Levins Morales argues that people are made up of the history of all their ancestors.

SKILLS PRACTICE

Legal Alien / Child of the Americas

Comparison-and-Contrast Chart The two poems you have just read address similar subjects. Compare and contrast the subject matter, aspects of **rhythm**—repetition and parallel structure—line length, and **theme**, or message about life, in the two poems.

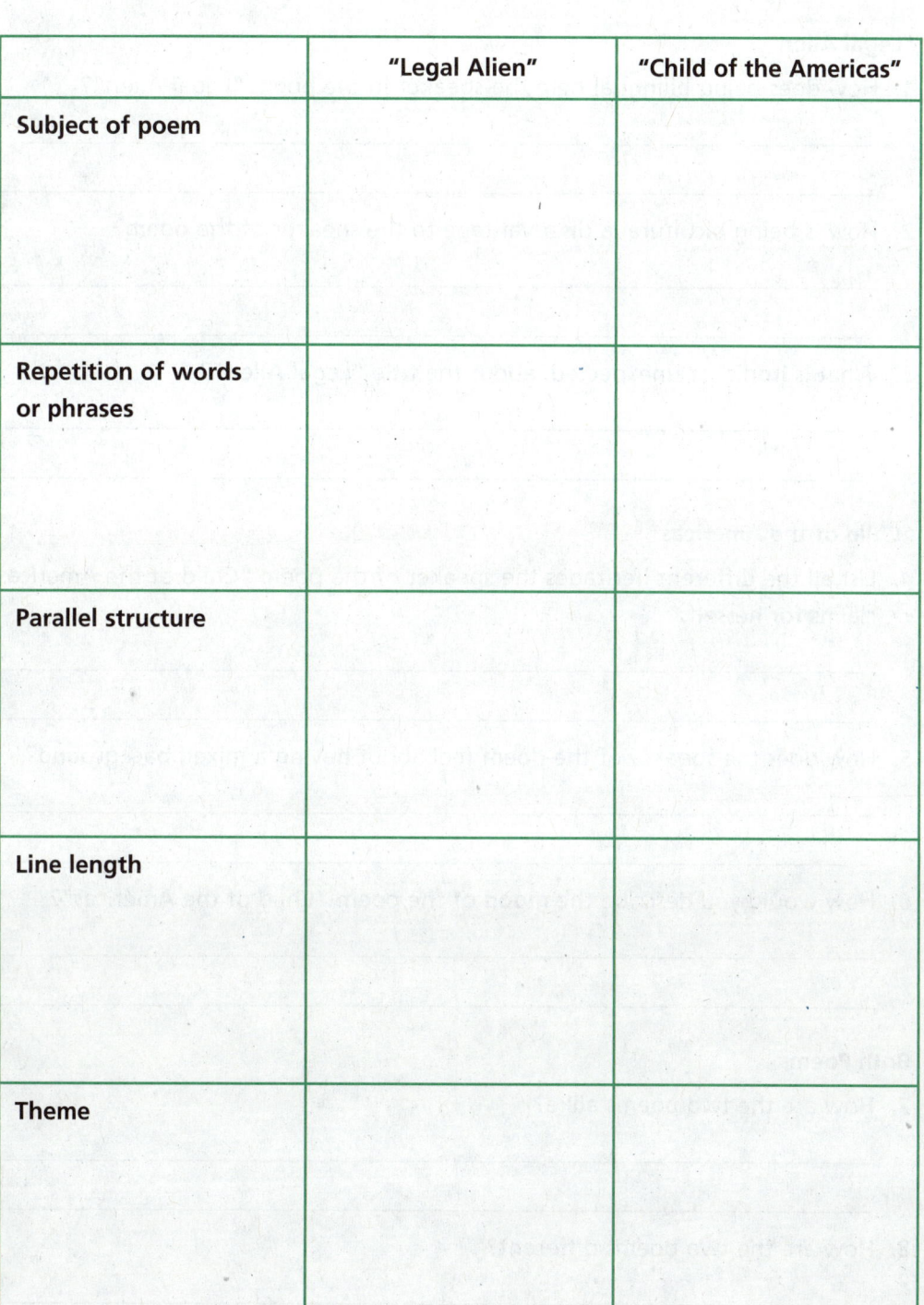

SKILLS FOCUS

Literary Skills
Analyze rhythm in free-verse poems.

Reading Skills
Compare and contrast poems.

	"Legal Alien"	"Child of the Americas"
Subject of poem		
Repetition of words or phrases		
Parallel structure		
Line length		
Theme		

Legal Alien / Child of the Americas 179

Skills Review

Legal Alien / Child of the Americas

Reading Comprehension Answer each question below.

"Legal Alien"

1. How does being bilingual help the speaker in the poem "Legal Alien"?
   _____
   _____

2. How is being bicultural a disadvantage to the speaker of the poem?
   _____
   _____

3. What is **ironic,** or unexpected, about the title "Legal Alien"?
   _____
   _____

"Child of the Americas"

4. List all the different heritages the speaker of the poem "Child of the Americas" claims for herself.
   _____
   _____

5. How does the speaker of the poem feel about having a mixed background?
   _____
   _____

6. How would you describe the **mood** of the poem "Child of the Americas"?
   _____
   _____

Both Poems

7. How are the two poems alike?
   _____
   _____

8. How are the two poems different?
   _____
   _____

Before You Read

Without Title by Diane Glancy

Times change, and people must change with them, but the memories of what once was still haunt us.

LITERARY FOCUS: FIGURATIVE LANGUAGE

An important element of poetry is **figurative language**—language based on imaginative comparisons that are not literally true. Figures of speech compare unlike things to reveal truths in surprising ways. Here are some examples of **figures of speech:**

Metaphor—a figure of speech in which two things are compared without using a connecting word. In a **direct metaphor,** the two items being compared are linked by a form of the verb *to be (is, are, was, were):* "The moon was a ghostly galleon." Other metaphors are **implied;** the comparison is suggested rather than stated: "The moon sailed away on the clouds." An **extended metaphor** is one that is carried throughout a poem or a section of a poem.

Simile—a figure of speech that compares two things using a connecting word such as *like, as,* or *resembles.* If in his famous poem, "The Highwayman," Alfred Noyes had written, "The moon was *like* a ghostly galleon," he would have created a simile instead of the metaphor above.

Personification—a special type of metaphor in which objects, animals, or ideas are given human qualities or abilities: "The moon smiled down upon us."

- As you read "Without Title," look for the various forms of figurative language.
- How does the author's use of an extended metaphor help you understand the poem?

SKILLS FOCUS

Literary Skills
Understand figurative language.

Without Title   **181**

Without Title

for my Father who lived without ceremony

Diane Glancy

Medicine man of the Mandan tribe in the costume of the Dog Dance (1834) by Karl Bodmer (1809–1893). Color lithograph.
© Private Collection, Peter Newark American Pictures/Bridgeman Art Library

It's hard you know without the buffalo,

the shaman,° the arrow,

but my father went out each day to hunt

as though he had them.

5   He worked in the stockyards.

---

2. **shaman** (shä′mən) *n.*: medicine man or priest in some American Indian cultures.

"Without Title" from *Iron Woman* by Diane Glancy. Copyright © 1990 by Diane Glancy. Reproduced by permission of **New Rivers Press**.

WORD STUDY

The word *title* has many meanings. It can mean "name of a piece of writing," "name given as a sign of rank," or "claim or right." What meaning (or meanings) do you think it has in the title of this poem?

METAPHOR

What is the speaker of the poem comparing her father's work in the stockyards to?

All his life he brought us meat.
No one marked his first kill,
no one sang his buffalo song.
Without a vision he had migrated to the city
10 and went to work in the packing house.
When he brought home his horns and hides
my mother said
get rid of them.
I remember the animal tracks of his car
15 out the drive in snow and mud,
the aerial on his old car waving
like a bow string.
I remember the silence of his lost power,
the red buffalo painted on his chest.
20 Oh, I couldn't see it
but it was there, and in the night I heard
his buffalo grunts like a snore.

FIGURES OF SPEECH

Underline the **metaphor** in line 14 and the **simile** in lines 16–17. Why does the poet use these figures of speech?

METAPHOR

The speaker compares her father's life to the traditional American Indian way of life. What does this **extended metaphor** tell you about the speaker's feelings for her father?

MEET THE WRITER

Diane Glancy (1941–   ) advises her students to do what they believe in no matter what others say. Her own children laughed at her for believing that writing poetry was a real job, but Glancy stuck with it—with great success. She has won numerous awards for her many books of poetry as well as for her plays, novels, and other prose works. One of Glancy's themes is the tensions and differences between her Cherokee, English, and German heritages.

SKILLS PRACTICE

Without Title

Figurative Language Chart Figurative language compares two unlike things to uncover a truth. Fill in the chart below to analyze the use of figurative language in "Without Title." For each passage listed from the poem, identify the type of figurative language—**simile** or **metaphor**—and its meaning. The first set has been completed for you. Finally, describe the overall **extended metaphor** of the poem and its meaning.

SKILLS FOCUS

Literary Skills Analyze figurative language.

Passage	Figure of Speech and Meaning
1. "It's hard you know without the buffalo, the shaman, the arrow, but my father went out each day to hunt as though he had them."	**Figure of speech:** metaphor **Meaning:** The author is saying that even though her father was cut off from the life of his ancestors, he was still a warrior.
2. "I remember the animal tracks of his car out the drive in snow and mud"	**Figure of speech:** **Meaning:**
3. "the aerial on his old car waving like a bow string"	**Figure of speech:** **Meaning:**
4. "I remember the silence of his lost power, the red buffalo painted on his chest. Oh, I couldn't see it but it was there, and in the night I heard his buffalo grunts like a snore."	**Figure of speech:** **Meaning:**
5. Overall extended metaphor:	**Meaning:**

Part 1   Collection 7: Poetry

Skills Review

Without Title

COMPREHENSION

Reading Comprehension   Answer each question below.

1. In this poem, traditional American Indian life is compared with contemporary life. What was the traditional life like?

2. How is the speaker's father's life similar to these traditional ways?

3. How is the father's life different from the traditional ways?

4. What did horns and hides represent to the father?

5. What did horns and hides represent to the speaker's mother?

Before You Read

POEM

Offspring by Naomi Long Madgett

Mothers may have dreams for their daughters, but what happens when daughters have their own dreams?

LITERARY FOCUS: EXTENDED METAPHOR

An **extended metaphor** is a metaphor that continues throughout a poem or a section of a poem. "Offspring" uses an extended metaphor to convey its message.
- The first line begins, "I tried to tell her." Ask yourself who the speaker is, keeping in mind the title of the poem.
- Line 2 offers the first clue to the extended metaphor. Read the indented section carefully, and then consider its meaning in the context of line 1.
- Continue in this way to the end of the poem.

READING SKILLS: SUMMARIZING

A **summary** is a short restatement of the important ideas in a work. When you summarize a poem, you retell the main events or ideas. Summarizing can help you understand meanings that at first glance may be unclear.

It may be helpful to make notes on each line or group of lines in a chart like the one below. Bear in mind that as your understanding of the poem changes, so may your interpretations.

Line	What It May Mean
Line 1	Taking the title into account, this line sounds like a parent attempting to offer guidance. The word "tried" may suggest rejection.

SKILLS FOCUS

Literary Skills Understand extended metaphor.

Reading Skills Summarize a poem.

OFFSPRING

Naomi Long Madgett

I tried to tell her:
    This way the twig is bent.
    Born of my trunk and strengthened by my roots,
    You must stretch newgrown branches
5   Closer to the sun
    Than I can reach.
I wanted to say:
    Extend my self to that far atmosphere
    Only my dreams allow.

(continued)

ANALYZE

How can you tell that the speaker of the poem is a mother addressing her daughter?

METAPHOR

Explain the **extended metaphor** in lines 2–6. What advice is the speaker giving her daughter?

INFER

In lines 7–9, what does the mother want her daughter to do for her?

"Offspring" from *Pink Ladies in the Afternoon* by Naomi Long Madgett. Copyright © 1972, 1990 by Naomi Long Madgett. Reproduced by permission of **Lotus Press**.

Offspring   187

METAPHOR

The **extended metaphor** ends at line 10. What does "But the twig broke" mean?

_____
_____
_____
_____
_____
_____
_____

INFER

The word *unpliable* (line 20) means "not bendable." Refer back to line 2 and what the mother claimed to want in the beginning of the poem. Do you think she is happy with the way her daughter turned out? Why or why not?

_____
_____
_____
_____
_____
_____
_____
_____

10 But the twig broke,
    And yesterday I saw her
    Walking down an unfamiliar street,
        Feet confident,
        Face slanted upward toward a threatening sky,
15 And
    She was smiling
    And she was
    Her very free,
    Her very individual,
20 Unpliable
    Own.

MEET THE WRITER

Naomi Long Madgett (1923–   ) began writing poetry at a young age, but it wasn't until her family moved to St. Louis, Missouri, and she attended an all-black high school that her writing was encouraged in school. She was only seventeen and a few days out of high school when her first book of poems was published. Her poetry is known for celebrating the experiences of African Americans. Madgett has also been a teacher and editor. She taught first in the Detroit public schools and later at Eastern Michigan University. At Lotus Press she encouraged and published a generation of black poets.

Skills Practice and Review

Offspring

Summary Chart   Use the chart below to summarize the poem. The first row has been done for you.

Lines	Summary
Lines 1–6	A mother wants to see her daughter reach for the same dreams the mother has cherished, but also to get closer to them than she has been able to do.
Lines 7–9	
Line 10	
Lines 11–21	

Reading Comprehension   Answer each question below.

1. In lines 1–9, how does the mother see her daughter?
   _____
   _____

2. What does the mother want the daughter to achieve?
   _____
   _____

3. What is the daughter like in lines 10–21?
   _____
   _____

SKILLS FOCUS

Reading Skills
Summarize a poem.

Offspring   189

Before You Read

POEM

There Is No Word for Goodbye by Mary TallMountain

What do you say when you must leave someone you love? Are there words to say what you are feeling?

LITERARY FOCUS: IMAGERY AND FIGURATIVE LANGUAGE IN LYRIC POETRY

A **lyric poem** expresses an emotion or thought. The term *lyric* comes from ancient Greece, where such poems were recited to the accompaniment of a stringed instrument called a lyre. Lyric poems are usually short, and they imply, rather than state directly, a strong emotion. To express emotion, lyric poets rely on imagery and figurative language.

Imagery is language that appeals to the senses. Sight is the sense many people rely on most, so it is not surprising that the most common form of imagery in poetry is visual. But images can also appeal to our senses of hearing, touch, smell, and taste.

Figurative language describes one thing in terms of another and is not meant to be understood in a literal sense. A **simile** makes a comparison using a connecting word such as *like* or *as*. A **metaphor** makes a comparison without a connecting word. In **personification,** something nonhuman is talked about as if it were human.

- As you read "There Is No Word for Goodbye," look for figures of speech and images that appeal to the senses. You will find strong images within figures of speech. Think about how these images help you share the speaker's experience.

SKILLS FOCUS

Literary Skills Understand imagery and figurative language in lyric poetry.

There Is No Word for Goodbye

Mary TallMountain

Sokoya,° I said, looking through
    the net of wrinkles into
    wise black pools
    of her eyes.

5 What do you say in Athabaskan°
    when you leave each other?
    What is the word
    for goodbye?

A shade of feeling rippled
10   the wind-tanned skin.
    Ah, nothing, she said,
    watching the river flash.

She looked at me close.
    We just say, Tlaa. That means,
15   See you.
    We never leave each other.
    When does your mouth
    say goodbye to your heart?

(continued)

---

1. **sokoya:** Athabaskan for "aunt, the sister of one's mother."
5. **Athabaskan:** North American Indian language.

"There Is No Word for Goodbye" from *The Light on the Tent Wall* by Mary TallMountain. Copyright © 1990 by Mary TallMountain. Published by University of California American Indian Studies Center, 1990. Reproduced by permission of M. Catherine Costello, Literary Executor for Mary TallMountain Circle.

IMAGERY/METAPHOR

Underline the **imagery** in lines 1–4 and 9–12 that describes the speaker's aunt. What senses do these images appeal to? Each of these stanzas also contains a **metaphor**. What comparisons are made in each metaphor?

PERSONIFICATION

Underline the personification in lines 17–18. How does this figure of speech make you feel?

Notes

IMAGERY/SIMILE

Lines 19–20 contain a **simile** that is also an **image.** What senses does the image appeal to? How do you imagine the aunt's touch?

IDENTIFY

What is the sorrow at the heart of this poem?

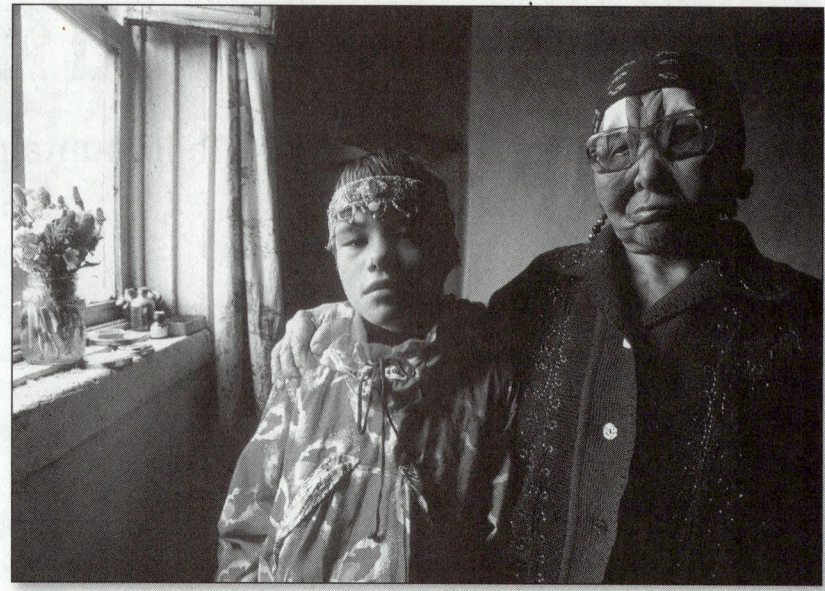

Yupik grandmother and granddaughter.
© Natalie Fobes/CORBIS

    She touched me light
20   as a bluebell.
        You forget when you leave us,
        You're so small then.
        We don't use that word.

    We always think you're coming back,
25   but if you don't,
        we'll see you some place else.
        You understand.
        There is no word for goodbye.

192   Part 1   Collection 7: Poetry

MEET THE WRITER

Mary TallMountain (1918–1994) was born in Nulato, a village on the Yukon River in Alaska. Her mother was Koyukon-Athabaskan, and her father was Scots-Irish. When she was six years old and her mother was dying of tuberculosis, she was adopted by a non-Indian couple and taken from her village. She eventually settled in San Francisco and worked as a public stenographer. Though she read voraciously from the age of three and quoted Wordsworth's poetry with her adoptive mother, TallMountain didn't begin writing until after a trip back to Alaska when she was about fifty-five. She became an important voice in the Native American literary renaissance, publishing poems, short stories, and essays. In her writing she tried to be a connection between American Indian and Western cultures.

Notes

There Is No Word for Goodbye   193

SKILLS PRACTICE

There Is No Word for Goodbye

SKILLS FOCUS

Literary Skills Analyze imagery and figurative language.

Imagery and Figurative Language Chart Imagery is language that appeals to the senses of sight, hearing, smell, taste, or touch. **Figurative language** creatively compares two unlike things. The chart below lists quotations from "There Is No Word for Goodbye." Analyze the imagery and figurative language in the poem by filling in the chart. First, identify the figure of speech—**metaphor, simile,** or **personification**—and then state what senses the images appeal to.

Quotation from Poem	Imagery and Figurative Language
1. "looking through the net of wrinkles into wise black pools of her eyes"	Figure of speech: Senses appealed to:
2. "A shade of feeling rippled the wind-tanned skin."	Figure of speech: Senses appealed to:
3. "Ah, nothing, she said, watching the river flash."	Figure of speech: Senses appealed to:
4. "When does your mouth say goodbye to your heart?"	Figure of speech: Senses appealed to:
5. "She touched me light as a bluebell."	Figure of speech: Senses appealed to:

Part 1   Collection 7: Poetry

Skills Review

There Is No Word for Goodbye

COMPREHENSION

Reading Comprehension Answer each question below.

1. What two people are having a conversation in the poem?

2. What do you learn about the speaker from the poem?

3. How do the two people in the poem feel about each other?

4. What do you think is the **theme**, or insight about life, revealed in this poem?

Collection 8

Literary Criticism: Evaluating Style

Maya Angelou.
© GARY HERSHORN/Reuters/CORBIS

Academic Vocabulary for Collection 8

These are the terms you should know
as you read and analyze the selections in this collection.

Style The special way a writer uses language. A writer's style may be described as plain, complex, ornate, simple, poetic, conversational, formal, informal, and so on.

Diction The words a writer chooses. Diction contributes to a writer's style.

Sentence structure The way words are put together to form sentences. Sentences may be long and complex, plain and direct, or short and punchy. Some writers deliberately use sentence fragments for certain effects.

Tone The attitude a writer takes toward a work's subject, characters, or audience. Tone is also an important contributor to a writer's style.

• • •

Figures of speech Expressions that are based on unusual comparisons and that are not literally true. Some writers avoid using figures of speech; other writers use them frequently.

Mood The atmosphere or feeling a writer creates in a work.

Theme The revelation or truth about the human experience expressed in a story or poem.

Before You Read

Late-Night Chitlins with Momma
by Audrey Petty

Do you have a favorite food that others think is weird or unusual? In the following essay, Audrey Petty describes a favorite treat of hers and her mother's—chitlins, the cooked small intestines of pigs.

LITERARY FOCUS: STYLE, DICTION, AND TONE

Style is an author's individual way of writing. In the same way that people dress differently or speak differently, people write differently. Word choice and sentence length have an important effect on style. When you evaluate style, look at how extensively the writer uses figurative language, dialogue, and description.

Diction, or word choice, is another element of style. Writers choose words to help communicate their feelings and thoughts—and to create an overall effect. Informal diction includes streetwise or casual language, such as "Get it?" instead of "Do you understand?" If a writer changes the phrase "a charging elephant" to "a swiftly approaching pachyderm," the style changes from matter-of-fact to pointedly elevated.

Diction also has a strong effect on **tone,** the attitude a writer takes toward his or her subject, characters, or life in general. The tone of a work can be playful, sarcastic, affectionate, ironic. Adjusting a word or two can change tone; if a writer changes the phrase "he took the biggest piece" to "he served himself generously," the tone changes.

- As you read "Late-Night Chitlins with Momma," notice how Petty varies the sentence structure to create her unique style.
- Also, pay close attention to Petty's diction. Is it formal or informal?
- Finally, think about Petty's attitude in this story. What tone does she use as she tells her tale?

READING SKILLS: DRAWING CONCLUSIONS

A **conclusion** is a judgment that you draw, or come to, after you have considered all the evidence. In literature, evidence is based on details you are given about the setting, the action, the characters, and the events.

- As you read this essay, pay careful attention to the details in the text in order to draw a conclusion about the symbolic meaning of chitlins to each of the main characters.

SKILLS FOCUS

Literary Skills Understand style, diction, and tone.

Reading Skills Draw conclusions.

Vocabulary Skills Understand words in context.

VOCABULARY DEVELOPMENT

PREVIEW SELECTION VOCABULARY

The following words appear in "Late-Night Chitlins with Momma." Look them over before you begin the story.

dissent (di·sent′) *n.:* difference of opinion; disagreement.

*I did not like **dissent** between my sisters; I much preferred that we all get along.*

pervasive (pər·vā′siv) *adj.:* spreading everywhere.

*Even adding a potato to the pot cannot erase the **pervasive** odor of chitlins cooking.*

furtive (fur′tiv) *adj.:* hidden; secret.

*Eating chitlins is a **furtive** treat for Petty and her mother.*

assimilated (ə·sim′ə·lāt′ed) *v.* used as *adj.:* blending with the dominant culture.

*Mr. and Mrs. Petty worried that their children's **assimilated** ways would cause them to lose their own heritage.*

CONTEXT CLUES

Don't let unfamiliar words be a stumbling block to your reading progress. Look at a word's **context**—the words, phrases, and sentences that surround it—for clues to its meaning. In the examples below, the italicized context clues will help you figure out the meaning of the boldface words.

DEFINITION: People say one of two things about **chitlins,** which are *cooked hog intestines:* They're to die for, or they're to die from.

EXAMPLE: Audrey Petty calls chitlins "precious, strange, **furtive** food"; *she and her mother savor them alone, never admitting to others that they eat them.*

COMPARISON: Some say chitlins are as **malodorous** as a *yard full of angry skunks.*

CONTRAST: Chitlins have a **potent** smell; their aroma is *not delicate or subtle.*

Late-Night Chitlins with Momma   199

Late-Night Chitlins with Momma

It's a little bit country but has a whole lot of soul

Audrey Petty

Ours came frozen solid in a red plastic bucket. Butchered and packaged by Armour. Ten pounds in all. Cleaned, they'd reduce to much less, not even filling my mother's cast-iron pot.

We usually ate them in the wintertime, Momma and I. Negotiations regarding their appearance began weeks in advance, usually around the dinner table. My mother would tell my father she was considering fixing chitlins for the holidays. My father would groan, twist his mouth, and complain in vain.

"Why you got to be cooking them?"

My two sisters backed him up with exaggerated whimpers, calls for gas masks, threats to run away from home.

"I'll cook them next Saturday," Momma would say, suddenly matter-of-fact. Daddy would plan that next Saturday accordingly: out of the house for hours, in protest, then coming back with the Sunday papers, opening the living-room windows wide before heading upstairs to read and watch football in his La-Z-Boy behind a closed door.

My mother would turn to me, smiling and winking. "You'll help me eat them, won't you?"

I was a pleaser, plagued by the classic middle-child complex. With the exception of fierce bickering and the occasional smack-down match with my sisters, **dissent** tended to make me nervous. Maybe my love of chitlins all began with my feeling sorry for my mother. In terms of labor and attention, cooking proper chitlins is as involved as cooking paella or fufu or risotto milanese.[1] Cleaning them took hours. Hours. So I'd keep Momma company while she rinsed the tangles of pig intestines

---

1. **paella . . . milanese:** Paella is a Spanish dish consisting of rice and seafood or vegetables. Fufu is a West African food made from root vegetables, similar to mashed potatoes. Risotto milanese is an Italian dish made by slowly stirring hot broth into rice flavored with saffron.

DRAW CONCLUSIONS

What **conclusion** can you reach about the father's attitude toward chitlins (lines 8–17)?

INFER

Circle the word in line 20 that Petty uses to sum up her personality. How do you think she'll answer her mother's request to help her eat the chitlins?

VOCABULARY

dissent (di·sent′) n.: difference of opinion; disagreement.

in the basement sink. And I'd sit with her in the kitchen since they'd simmered down to something that needed watching. By that time, the house was filled with their sharp scent. Despite the addition of a potato to the pot to help absorb some of the odor, the smell was **pervasive**—vinegary and slightly farmy. When one of my sisters would storm in holding her nose and proclaiming her disgust, I'd puff out my bony chest and call her stupid.

I'd stay up late with Momma, and we'd eat the chitlins off of small saucers as a bedtime snack. For all their potent smell, their flavor was calm and subtle. They had a distinct taste; they didn't remind me of anything. Their texture was pleasing, tender but not soft. My mother's were never greasy, though I marveled at how the leftovers emerged from the fridge congealed[2] in a murky gelatin. Momma would warm up a few in a frying pan, and we'd douse them with hot sauce and put some corn bread on the side. They never failed to build a craving after the first bite. Precious, strange, and **furtive** food; I longed for them even as I consumed them.

I am a first-generation Northerner. My mother was reared in a middle-class family in El Dorado, a boomtown in southern Arkansas; my father, in a coal-mining camp in Alabama. The two met and fell in love in the late '50s while students at Talladega (a historically black college in Alabama), married, and then moved to Chicago. My sisters and I came of age in Hyde Park, at the time one of the city's few intentionally racially integrated neighborhoods. My dearest friend was Jewish (and white). We shared Sasson jeans, Jolly Ranchers, Judy Blume books, and plenty of secrets. My mother grew to love Karyn, but in the first days of our acquaintance, her anxiety about our closeness showed itself. She had lots of questions about how I was treated by the Levins. Were they kind? Had they *made* me eat the matzo ball soup? Did Karyn have other black friends? Gradually it emerged: Momma was trying to prepare me for the

---

2. **congealed** (kən·jēld′): thickened; jelled.

CONNECT
Re-read the description of chitlins in lines 30–45. Do you think you would enjoy eating them? Why or why not?

VOCABULARY
pervasive (pər·vā′siv) *adj.*: spreading everywhere.

furtive (fur′tiv) *adj.*: hidden; secret.

STYLE
The phrase "first-generation Northerner" (line 46) means that Petty is in the first generation of her family to be born in the northern United States. Where were her parents born? Why might this detail be important in an essay about chitlins?

Notes

INFER

Re-read lines 53–64. Why did Petty's mother seem nervous about her friendship with Karen?

VOCABULARY

assimilated (ə·sim′ə·lāt′ed) v. used as adj.: blending with the dominant culture.

DRAW CONCLUSIONS

Re-read lines 71–76. Given that Petty's father disliked chitlins, why would she say she ate them to please him?

Audrey Petty.
Maurice Rabb/Courtesy of Audrey Petty

prospect of rejection, once recalling to me how little white girls in El Dorado customarily grew out of their friendships with little black girls. At the time, my only response was confused irritation. Karyn was my best friend.

As my sisters and I reached adolescence, my parents became more visibly concerned about our **assimilated** ways. While the Jackson 5's *ABC* had been our very first album and we still crowded around the television to watch *Soul Train*,[3] we also knew all the words to "Bohemian Rhapsody."[4] And at 17 I fell for a boy with blond hair and blue eyes. He also fell for me. On more than one occasion, my sisters and I were summoned to a dialogue that began with my father's question "Do you all know that you're black?" As adults, my sisters and I laugh about it now. My parents do, too. But their uneasiness was real and deadly serious, and I'd sensed it for years. Maybe I ate chitlins to please Momma *and* Daddy.

3. *Soul Train:* television series that features rhythm-and-blues, soul, and rap musicians.
4. **"Bohemian Rhapsody":** a song made famous by the rock group Queen. *Bohemian* refers to a person living an unconventional lifestyle.

My grandfathers died before I was born; my grandmothers, when I was quite young. I have missed their embraces, their indulgence, and seeing my face in theirs. I have especially missed their stories. The down-South tales my parents passed on to me and my sisters were rather limited. We'd hear about my uncle Booker T.'s setting the mean goat after my father or how my mother's father was a high-school principal and an avid fisherman and how my mother's mother taught piano and Latin. What we didn't hear were the bloody details, the chronicles of Jim Crow.[5] My parents gave us their South as best they could: in their politesse[6] and their hymns and verses. In their ways with words. They gave us only what they hoped would be nourishing: a sip of pot liquor[7] for our growing bodies and black-eyed peas for good luck at New Year's dinner.

DRAW CONCLUSIONS

Re-read lines 77–90. How does Petty feel about her heritage?

INFER

Why do you think Petty's parents did not tell her and her sisters about negative racial aspects of the South?

The Petty family.
Courtesy of Audrey Petty

---

5. **Jim Crow:** laws discriminating against African Americans, especially in the South.
6. **politesse** (päl′i·tes′) *n.:* politeness.
7. **pot liquor:** liquid left over from cooking meat and vegetables.

Late-Night Chitlins with Momma

STYLE

Re-read lines 97–106 aloud. How does Petty's **diction** change in this paragraph?

_____
_____
_____

DRAW CONCLUSIONS

In lines 107–116, Petty explains that before she began writing this essay, she had come to the conclusion that her father did not like chitlins because he considered them "suffering food." How was she wrong?

_____
_____
_____
_____

STYLE

In lines 117–125, notice how Petty uses dialogue to make her mother's voice come alive. How would you describer her **tone** in this paragraph?

_____
_____
_____
_____

I never saw anyone's chitlins but my family's when I was coming up. At least a few of my classmates must have eaten chitlins at home, but I, for one, never raised the subject. Chicago was a Great Migration city, where a wave of black folks had begun arriving in the early 1900s and been red-lined to black belts on the South and West sides. That was my story and the story of so many of my childhood friends. We all had roots and people down South. And we ate like it, too. I remember red beans and rice at Kim Odoms's house, fried gizzards at LaTonya Mott's, and my junior-high business teacher Miss Rice's eating take-out rib tips from Ribs n' Bibs during our fourth-period typing class. I remember hot sauce on everything. But chitlins were their own category of soul food. Chitlins were straight-up country. If you called someone country, you were calling that someone out. Country meant backwoods, backwards, barefoot, 'Bama-fied. K-U-N-T-R-E-E.

I once believed that my father didn't like chitlins because of how they smelled, but as I got older, I began to contemplate my father's childhood and I formulated a more complex theory. My father had seven brothers and sisters; his father was a miner and a preacher and his mother was a domestic worker (a fact I discovered only this year). I assumed that Daddy rejected chitlins as suffering food—a struggling people's inheritance. It wasn't until I began brainstorming for this essay that I finally learned the truth. "He had a bad plate of chitlins as a boy," my mother recently told me. "He never got over it."

When my mother cleaned our chitlins, she never failed to stress how important it was to clean them well. That meant washing them, one section of intestine at a time, with a mild saltwater solution. "You don't just eat any old body's chitlins." I knew that rule by heart. When a cafeteria called Soul by the Pound opened and quickly closed down on State Street, my mother was not at all surprised. "Black people don't live that way. Risk taking for no reason at all. Flying from bungee cords or buying all-you-can-eat chitlins made by God knows who."

My mother has not cooked a pot of chitlins in fifteen years. Perhaps the ritual ended the year I lived in France and sorely missed Christmas with my family. My mother and I shared a good laugh when I told her about chitlins in France, how they called them andouillette de Lyon and topped them with dijon mustard. I smelled them before I saw them, in a Left Bank bistro. *Et voilà!*[8]—there they were, on a nearby plate. I trusted the chef at Les Fontaines, but I couldn't imagine eating his chitlins. Not without my mother's company. And not without Louisiana-style hot sauce as generous seasoning.

As my mother has gotten used to the idea of my going public with our chitlins habit, she's reminded me that she cooked hers with onion and a green bell pepper or two, and she also splashed in cider vinegar to taste. I've learned how some people add white bread instead of potatoes for the odor. And I've shared Momma's excitement about the new technology in chitlin processing. "They really clean them now. More expensive, but you don't have to do all that work."

She didn't have to ask me twice; we have a date for chitlins this December.

---

8. ***Et voila!:*** French for "And there!"

DRAW CONCLUSIONS

Re-read lines 126–145. What role do chitlins now play in the lives of Petty and her mother?

Recipe for Chitlins

SERVES 4–6

Simmering the chitlins with a potato is said to help reduce their aroma.

9–10 lbs. frozen cleaned chitlins (sometimes labeled "chitterlings"); thawed and drained
Salt
1 large onion, peeled
1 russet potato, peeled
1 green bell pepper
4 cloves garlic, peeled
½ cup cider vinegar
¾ tsp. crushed red pepper flakes
2 bay leaves
Freshly ground black pepper
Hot sauce, preferably Frank's brand

1. Put chitlins into a large colander and rinse under tepid running water in the sink. Transfer chitlins to a very large bowl or pot. Cover chitlins by at least 2 inches with tepid mildly salty water (dissolve 1–2 tbsp. salt in every 2 gallons of water needed) and wash, one section at a time. Drain in a colander set in the sink, rinsing them again under tepid running water. Set colander over a bowl and let chitlins drain well.

2. Put chitlins into a large pot and cover with cold water. Add onion, potato, bell pepper, garlic, vinegar, red pepper flakes, bay leaves, and salt and pepper to taste. Partially cover pot and bring to a boil over high heat. Reduce heat to medium-low and cook, partially covered, until chitlins are very tender, about 6 hours.

3. Pour off most of the cooking water from the pot, leaving enough to keep chitlins moist. Discard potato and bay leaves. Cut chitlins on a cutting board into 1-inch pieces, return them to the pot, and bring to a simmer.

4. Using a slotted spoon, serve chitlins (drained fairly well and apart from the vegetables) in bowls and douse with hot sauce to taste.

MEET THE WRITER

Born and raised in Chicago, Illinois, **Audrey Petty** (1967–   ) graduated from Knox College with a degree in French literature. For her graduate work she studied creative writing and literature at the University of Massachusetts at Amherst. Petty writes both fiction and nonfiction. Her essay "Late-Night Chitlins with Momma" was featured in *Saveur* magazine.

SKILLS PRACTICE

Late-Night Chitlins with Momma

Style Chart Use the chart below to record examples of Petty's style in "Late-Night Chitlins with Momma." Then, describe her use of each element.

Literary Skills Analyze an author's style.

Style Element	Text Examples	Description
Sentence length		
Diction		
Figurative language		
Tone		

Late-Night Chitlins with Momma

Skills Review

Late-Night Chitlins with Momma

VOCABULARY AND COMPREHENSION

Word Box
- dissent
- pervasive
- furtive
- assimilated

A. Identifying Context Clues For each sentence below, underline the context clue to the meaning of the boldface word. Then, write a definition for the boldface word on the blank following the sentence.

1. The **pervasive** smell of chitlins crept into every corner of the house. _____

2. Felipe quickly **assimilated** into his new school, joining both the baseball team and the debate club. _____

3. The old-fashioned teacher allowed no **dissent** in her classroom; students were not allowed to challenge her lessons. _____

4. The team made **furtive** plans to hold a surprise retirement party for their coach. _____

B. Reading Comprehension Answer each question below.

1. What is the relationship between Petty and her mother?
   _____
   _____

2. Why can't Petty eat anyone's chitlins besides her mother's?
   _____
   _____

3. Why does Momma claim that black people don't take unnecessary risks?
   _____
   _____

SKILLS FOCUS

Vocabulary Skills
Identify context clues.

Before You Read

My Two Lives by Jhumpa Lahiri

If you are a hyphenated American, which side of the hyphen are you really? Sometimes it takes a lifetime to decide.

LITERARY FOCUS: STYLE

Style is the way individual writers express themselves. Some writers have a very distinctive style. You can probably instantly recognize a Dr. Seuss poem, for example, with it strong rhythm, made-up words, and humorous rhymes. An E. E. Cummings poem is also easily recognized for its unusual punctuation and lack of capital letters. Most writers' styles are less distinctive, but every written work has a particular style.

Some adjectives that can define a writer's style:	conversational, street smart, dark, gritty, highly descriptive, succinct, casual, funny, witty, serious, formal, poetic, lyrical, long-winded

The most important element of a writer's style is **diction**, or word choice. Mark Twain wrote, "The difference between the almost right word and the right word is really a large matter—it's the difference between the lightning bug and the lightning."

To understand a writer's style, ask yourself these questions:
- Are the words long or short, formal or slang?
- Are the sentences long or short, complex or simple?
- Does the writer include vivid **images** or **figures of speech**?
- Does the writer include facts or opinions?
- What is the writer's **tone**, or attitude toward the subject?

READING SKILLS: CAUSE AND EFFECT

A **cause** is a person, event, or thing that makes something happen. An **effect** is what happens as a result of a cause. A cause-and-effect relationship exists between two things when one thing makes something else happen.
- As you read Jhumpa Lahiri's "My Two Lives," you'll notice that the assumptions she and her parents had as people from India living in America had different effects on their lives.

SKILLS FOCUS

Literary Skills
Understand style.

Reading Skills
Understand cause and effect.

Vocabulary Skills
Understand synonyms: shades of meaning.

ESSAY

VOCABULARY DEVELOPMENT

PREVIEW SELECTION VOCABULARY

Preview the following words from "My Two Lives" before you begin the essay:

outmoded (out·mōd´id) *adj.*: old-fashioned; obsolete.

*Jhumpa Lahiri found her parents' customs to be as worthless in her American life as **outmoded** money.*

ineffectually (in´e·fek´chōō·ə·lē) *adv.*: without producing the desired effect.

*As a teenager, Lahiri tried **ineffectually** to explain who she was.*

intertwined (in´tər·twīnd´) *v.* used as *adj.*: twisted together, inseparable.

*The traditions of her two cultures have become **intertwined** in Lahiri's life.*

proficiency (prō·fish´ən·sē) *n.*: skill; expertise.

*Lahiri speaks to her children in Bengali but does not have the **proficiency** to teach them to read and write it.*

ascendancy (ə·sen´dən·sē) *n.*: dominance

*At times, one side of her background gains **ascendancy** over the other.*

SYNONYMS: SHADES OF MEANING

Synonyms are words with similar or identical meanings. Sometimes synonyms can be used interchangeably, but often the **shades of meaning** of the words influence a writer's choice. For example, *baby* and *infant* are synonyms meaning a very young child, but the choice of which word to use would depend on the tone the writer wanted to convey. "The baby cried" has a conversational tone; "the infant cried" sounds more formal.

Synonyms / Shades of Meaning

Sentence	Synonyms for *quick*
She has a *quick* mind.	agile, apt, fast, fleet, perceptive, ready, swift, speedy

- Replace *quick* with each of the synonyms to see how the meaning and impact of the original sentence change.

210   Part 1   Collection 8: Literary Criticism: Evaluating Style

My Two Lives

Jhumpa Lahiri

I have lived in the United States for almost thirty-seven years and anticipate growing old in this country. Therefore, with the exception of my first two years in London, "Indian-American" has been a constant way to describe me. Less constant is my relationship to the term. When I was growing up in Rhode Island in the 1970s I felt neither Indian nor American. Like many immigrant offspring I felt intense pressure to be two things, loyal to the old world and fluent in the new, approved of on either side of the hyphen. Looking back, I see that this was generally the case. But my perception as a young girl was that I fell short at both ends, shuttling between two dimensions that had nothing to do with one another.

At home I followed the customs of my parents, speaking Bengali and eating rice and dal[1] with my fingers. These ordinary facts seemed part of a secret, utterly alien way of life, and I took pains to hide them from my American friends. For my parents, home was not our house in Rhode Island but Calcutta, where they were raised. I was aware that the things they lived for—the Nazrul[2] songs they listened to on the reel-to-reel, the family they missed, the clothes my mother wore that were not available in any store in any mall—were at once as precious and as worthless as an **outmoded** currency.

I also entered a world my parents had little knowledge or control of: school, books, music, television, things that seeped in

---

1. **dal** (däl) *n.:* Indian dish made using peas or beans, cooked to a smooth consistency.
2. **Nazrul:** Kazi Nazrul Islam (1899–1976), Bengali musician and poet who modernized the two art forms by combining North Indian classical music with Bengali folk tunes.

"My Two Lives" by Jhumpa Lahiri from *Newsweek*, March 6, 2006. Copyright © 2006 by Newsweek, Inc. Reproduced by permission of the publisher.

IDENTIFY

What two cultures does Jhumpa Lahiri identify with?

_____

_____

WORD STUDY

Some synonyms for *shuttling* (line 11) are *oscillating, alternating,* or *zigzagging.* Although all of these words are defined in terms of movement, *shuttling* in particular suggests the social forces being exerted on the narrator, like a commuter train endlessly traveling between fixed destinations.

COMPARE & CONTRAST

How are the customs of Lahiri's parents different from those of her American friends?

_____

_____

_____

_____

_____

VOCABULARY

outmoded (out'mōd'id) *adj.:* old-fashioned; obsolete.

Notes

INTERPRET

Why do you think the author finds the process of immigration to be "frequently humiliating" (line 33)?

Jhumpa Lahiri.
© Nancy Kaszerman/ZUMA/CORBIS

and became a fundamental aspect of who I am. I spoke English without an accent, comprehending the language in a way my parents still do not. And yet there was evidence that I was not entirely American. In addition to my distinguishing name and looks, I did not attend Sunday school, did not know how to ice-
30 skate, and disappeared to India for months at a time. Many of these friends proudly called themselves Irish-American or Italian-American. But they were several generations removed from the frequently humiliating process of immigration, so that

the ethnic roots they claimed had descended underground whereas mine were still tangled and green. According to my parents I was not American, nor would I ever be no matter how hard I tried. I felt doomed by their pronouncement, misunderstood and gradually defiant. In spite of the first lessons of arithmetic, one plus one did not equal two but zero, my conflicting selves always canceling each other out.

When I first started writing I was not conscious that my subject was the Indian-American experience. What drew me to my craft was the desire to force the two worlds I occupied to mingle on the page as I was not brave enough, or mature enough, to allow in life. My first book was published in 1999, and around then, on the cusp[3] of a new century, the term "Indian-American" has become part of this country's vocabulary. I've heard it so often that these days, if asked about my background, I use the term myself, pleasantly surprised that I do not have to explain further. What a difference from my early life, when there was no such way to describe me, when the most I could do was to clumsily and **ineffectually** explain.

As I approach middle age, one plus one equals two, both in my work and in my daily existence. The traditions on either side of the hyphen dwell in me like siblings, still occasionally sparring, one outshining the other depending on the day. But like siblings they are intimately familiar with one another, forgiving and **intertwined**. When my husband and I were married five years ago in Calcutta we invited friends who had never been to India, and they came full of enthusiasm for a place I avoided talking about in my childhood, fearful of what people might say. Around non-Indian friends, I no longer feel compelled to hide the fact that I speak another language. I speak Bengali to my children, even though I lack the **proficiency** to teach them to read or write the language. As a child I sought perfection and so

---

3. **cusp** (kusp) *n.*: point of transition.

IDENTIFY CAUSE & EFFECT

Re-read lines 41–45. What **caused** Lahiri to write about the "Indian-American experience"?

STYLE

In lines 54–58, underline the **extended simile** that describes Lahiri's two traditions. What does this figure of speech add to the writer's style?

VOCABULARY

ineffectually (in′e·fek′chōō·ə·lē) *adv.*: without producing the desired effect.

intertwined (in′tər·twīnd′) *v.* used as *adj.*: twisted together; inseparable.

proficiency (prō·fish′ən·sē) *n.*: skill; expertise.

© Jack Hollingsworth/Getty Images

IDENTIFY CAUSE & EFFECT

What **causes** Lahiri to be American? What causes her to be Indian?

_____
_____
_____
_____
_____
_____
_____

denied myself the claim to any identity. As an adult I accept that a bicultural upbringing is a rich but imperfect thing.

While I am American by virtue of the fact that I was raised in this country, I am Indian thanks to the efforts of two individuals. I feel Indian not because of the time I've spent in India or because of my genetic composition but rather because of my parents' steadfast presence in my life. They live three hours from my home; I speak to them daily and see them about once a month. Everything will change once they die. They will take certain things with them—conversations in another tongue, and perceptions about the difficulties of being foreign. Without them, the back-and-forth life my family leads, both literally and figuratively, will at last approach stillness. An anchor will drop, and a line of connection will be severed.

> I have always believed that I lack the authority my parents bring to being Indian. But as long as they live they protect me from feeling like an impostor. Their passing will mark not only the loss of the people who created me but the loss of a singular way of life, a singular struggle. The immigrant's journey, no matter how ultimately rewarding, is founded on departure and deprivation, but it secures for the subsequent generation a sense of arrival and advantage. I can see a day coming when my American side, lacking the counterpoint India has until now maintained, begins to gain **ascendancy** and weight. It is in fiction that I will continue to interpret the term "Indian-American," calculating that shifting equation, whatever answers it may yield.

FLUENCY
Read aloud the boxed passage, initially for smoothness and then to convey the author's meanings and feelings.

VOCABULARY
ascendancy (ə·sen′dən·sē) *n.*: dominance.

STYLE
In lines 80–92, underline examples of **parallel structure** using *and*. Circle examples of **alliteration,** the repetition of consonants in words close together. Notice how these choices add elegance and eloquence to the author's style.

MEET THE WRITER

Although she lives in the United States, **Jhumpa Lahiri** (1967–) has traveled often to India and feels strong ties to both countries. Born in London to Bengali parents, she was a child when she moved with her family to Rhode Island, where she grew up. Her first book, a collection of short stories titled *Interpreter of Maladies,* won the Pulitzer Prize for fiction in 2000 and has been translated into twenty-nine languages. In 2002, Lahiri was also awarded a Guggenheim Fellowship. The following year she published her first novel, *The Namesake.* She now lives with her husband and son in New York City.

SKILLS PRACTICE

My Two Lives

SKILLS FOCUS

Reading Skills
Identify causes and effects.

Cause-and-Effect Chart A **cause** is the reason an action takes place. An **effect** is the result or consequence of the cause. Fill in the chart below with causes and effects from "My Two Lives." Sometimes you are asked to identify a cause, and sometimes an effect. Fill in whichever one is missing. The first cause and effect are identified for you.

Cause	Effect
1. To fit into the American culture, Lahiri . . .	. . . keeps the Indian customs of her home a secret from her American friends.
2. Because she has an Indian name and appearance, Lahiri . . .	
3.	. . . Lahiri feels misunderstood and gradually defiant.
4. Because her two traditions dwell in Lahiri like siblings . . .	
5. The difficulties of the immigrant's journey secure for the subsequent generation . . .	

Skills Review

My Two Lives

VOCABULARY AND COMPREHENSION

A. Synonyms/Shades of Meaning   For each boldface word, circle the letter of the synonym that more closely matches the author's meaning.

Word Box
- outmoded
- ineffectually
- intertwined
- proficiency
- ascendancy

1. Lahiri is aware that the things her parents love are to her "at once as precious and as worthless as an **outmoded** currency."
   a. outdated   b. unfashionable

2. Before the term *Indian American* was commonly understood in the United States, Lahiri tried **ineffectually** to explain who she was.
   a. incompetently   b. fruitlessly

3. The two traditions in Lahiri's life dwell within her "like siblings"—familiar, forgiving, and **intertwined**.
   a. enmeshed   b. mixed up

4. Lahiri lacks the **proficiency** to teach her children to read or write Bengali, although she speaks to them in that language.
   a. ability   b. expertise

5. Lahiri predicts that her American side will begin "to gain **ascendancy** and weight" when her parents are no longer here to represent her Indian side.
   a. dominance   b. prestige

B. Reading Comprehension   Answer each question below.

1. Except for Native Americans, all citizens of the United States descend from immigrants. What makes the experience of recent immigrants different from that of people whose families have been here a long time?

   _____
   _____

2. How have Lahiri's perceptions of her identity changed over time?

   _____
   _____

SKILLS FOCUS

Vocabulary Skills
Evaluate shades of meaning.

Collection 9

Literary Criticism: Biographical and Historical Approach

President John F. Kennedy and Jacqueline Kennedy, Dallas, Texas, November 22, 1963.
© Bettmann/CORBIS

Academic Vocabulary for Collection 9

These are the terms you should know
as you read and analyze the selections in this collection.

Biographical knowledge Information about a writer's experiences. Understanding a writer's life—including his or her attitudes, heritage, and traditions—adds meaning to what we are reading.

Biographical approach The use of a writer's life experiences to help analyze and respond to text.

● ● ●

Historical setting or historical context The historical period that shapes a work of literature. Understanding the historical setting helps us grasp the issues that were important in a given time period.

Historical approach The use of historical context to help analyze and respond to a text.

Academic Vocabulary 219

Before You Read

POEM

Theme for English B
by Langston Hughes

The seventeenth-century poet John Donne wrote, "No man is an island." The twentieth-century poet Langston Hughes reflects on this idea in his composition for an English class.

LITERARY FOCUS: BIOGRAPHICAL APPROACH

When you take a **biographical approach** to literary criticism, you look for ways that the writer's personal experiences are revealed in a text. Writers often set their works in places they have lived. Their characters may be based, at least in part, on themselves or on people they know. The feelings or ideas a character expresses may belong to the writer. Such biographical details are generally included not for their own sake but as a means of revealing the **theme,** or message about life, the writer hopes to reveal.

- As you read "Theme for English B," think about how Hughes's personal experiences are revealed in the poem.

READING SKILLS: MAKING INFERENCES ABOUT BIOGRAPHICAL DETAILS

When you read a work of fiction told from the first-person point of view (using the pronouns *I, me, we,* and *us*), how can you tell if the details come from the writer's experience or are the made-up experiences of a fictional speaker or narrator? Without reading an authoritative biography of the writer, you can't be sure, but when you know a few biographical details, you can make **inferences,** or educated guesses.

- Once you know that Langston Hughes attended Columbia University, the "college on the hill," for two semesters and that he lived in Harlem, a neighborhood in New York City near the university, you might infer that he is writing about his own experiences in "Theme for English B."

SKILLS FOCUS

Literary Skills
Understand a biographical approach to literary criticism.

Reading Skills
Make inferences about biographical details.

Collection 9: Literary Criticism: Biographical and Historical Approach

Theme for English B

Langston Hughes

The instructor said,

    Go home and write
    a page tonight.
    And let that page come out of you—
5   *then, it will be true.*

I wonder if it's that simple?
I am twenty-two, colored, born in Winston-Salem.
I went to school there, then Durham, then here
to this college on the hill above Harlem.
10 I am the only colored student in my class.
The steps from the hill lead down into Harlem,
through a park, then I cross St. Nicholas,
Eighth Avenue, Seventh, and I come to the Y,
the Harlem Branch Y, where I take the elevator
15 up to my room, sit down, and write this page:

It's not easy to know what is true for you or me
at twenty-two, my age. But I guess I'm what
I feel and see and hear. Harlem, I hear you:
hear you, hear me—we two—you, me, talk on this page.
20 (I hear New York, too.) Me—who?
Well, I like to eat, sleep, drink, and be in love.
I like to work, read, learn, and understand life.
I like a pipe for a Christmas present,
or records—Bessie,° bop, or Bach.

---

24. Bessie: Bessie Smith (1898–1937), a jazz and blues singer.

"Theme for English B" from *Montage of a Dream Deferred* by Langston Hughes. Copyright © 1994 by the Estate of Langston Hughes. Reproduced by permission of **Alfred A. Knopf**, a division of **Random House, Inc.**

BIOGRAPHICAL APPROACH

Underline the details in lines 1–15 that describe the speaker. Do you think these details also describe the writer? Why or why not?

INFER

Whom is the speaker addressing in lines 16–20? Why is he exploring "what is true"?

BIOGRAPHICAL APPROACH

Underline the things mentioned in lines 21–24 that you think most people like. Circle the things you think the speaker—or writer—particularly likes.

Harlem (1942) by Jacob Lawrence (1917–2000). Gouache on composition board.
© The Jacob and Gwendolyn Lawrence Foundation/Art Resource, NY

EVALUATE

Underline what Hughes says is American (lines 29–33). Do you agree with him? Why or why not?

_____
_____
_____
_____
_____

25   I guess being colored doesn't make me *not* like
     the same things other folks like who are other races.
     So will my page be colored that I write?
     Being me, it will not be white.
     But it will be
30   a part of you, instructor.
     You are white—
     yet a part of me, as I am a part of you.
     That's American.
     Sometimes perhaps you don't want to be a part of me.
35   Nor do I often want to be a part of you.

But we are, that's true!
As I learn from you,
I guess you learn from me—
although you're older—and white—
40 and somewhat more free.

This is my page for English B.

ANALYZE

What do you learn from this poem? What is its **theme,** or truth about life?

MEET THE WRITER

Langston Hughes (1902–1967) was born into an accomplished family. His grandmother was the first African American woman to graduate from Oberlin College. Her first husband, an abolitionist, was killed in John Brown's raid at Harpers Ferry. Her second husband was a conductor on the Underground Railroad and also founded schools for African American children in the Midwest. Hughes's parents divorced when he was young, and he was brought up by his grandmother. His father, a businessman and lawyer living in Mexico City, agreed to pay Hughes's college tuition at Columbia University, but only if he studied engineering. Hughes gave it a try, but he preferred the pleasures of poetry and of Harlem. He eventually dropped out of college and signed on as a sailor, traveling to Africa and later to Paris, where he lived for a time before returning to New York. There he settled in as a writer, publishing numerous books of poetry as well as short stories, novels, essays, autobiographies, plays, children's poetry, musicals, operas, radio and television scripts, and magazine articles. Hughes was an important member of the Harlem Renaissance, an outpouring of African American art—literature, painting, music, dance, theater—in the 1920s and 1930s.

Skills Practice and Review

Theme for English B

Biographical Details Chart   In his poem "Theme for English B," Langston Hughes includes biographical details that are personal and biographical details that are common to humanity. In the chart below, cite some of the details from the poem, and then explain the purpose they serve in helping reveal Hughes's meaning.

Kind of Detail	Examples	Purpose
Biographical details that are unique to Langston Hughes		
Biographical details that Hughes shares with most people		

Reading Comprehension   Answer each question below.

1. What was Hughes's motivation for writing this poem?
   _____
   _____
   _____

2. What subject or issue is explored in the poem?
   _____
   _____
   _____

3. What does being American mean to the speaker of the poem?
   _____
   _____
   _____

SKILLS FOCUS

Literary Skills
Analyze biographical detail.

Collection 9: Literary Criticism: Biographical and Historical Approach

Before You Read

The Disappearances by Vijay Seshadri

Some events in history are so momentous that almost everyone remembers where they were, whom they were with, and what they were doing when they first heard about them. The poem you are about to read concerns itself with such an occasion.

LITERARY FOCUS: HISTORICAL CONTEXT

Historical context is the time and place that shape a piece of literature. In some works the time and place are made very clear. In others they may be a pretext for exploring deeper issues.

- The historical context for the poem "The Disappearances" is the assassination of President John F. Kennedy on November 22, 1963.
- As you read the poem, you will see that the writer uses this important event from his childhood to explore issues of memory and loss.
- Another historical context for the poem came with its publication. Although written before the events, it was published in the *New Yorker* in the weeks following the attacks on the World Trade Center in New York City and the Pentagon in Washington, D.C., on September 11, 2001. For many readers the loss associated with these attacks became the context for the poem.

READING SKILLS: RE-READING

Successful readers read and re-read and re-read some more. They know that it's nearly impossible to come to a full understanding of any piece of literature in a single reading. There are many good reasons for re-reading. You may re-read to

- refresh your memory about details, characters, events, ideas
- clear up any misunderstandings or confusion
- deepen your understanding of a work's symbols or theme
- enjoy the richness of the language and style of the work

As you read "The Disappearances," stop every time you come to a period. Think of questions you have about what you have just read. Then, re-read to find answers to your questions.

SKILLS FOCUS

Literary Skills
Understand historical context.

Reading Skills
Re-read a poem.

The Disappearances 225

The Disappearances

Vijay Seshadri

"Where was it one first heard of the truth?"

> On a day like any other day,
> like "yesterday or centuries before,"
> in a town with the one remembered street,
> shaded by the buckeye and the sycamore—
> 5 the street long and true as a theorem,
> the day like yesterday or the day before,
> the street you walked down centuries before—
> the story the same as the others flooding in
> from the cardinal points° is
> 10 turning to take a good look at you.
> Every creature, intelligent or not, has disappeared—
> the humans, phosphorescent,
> the duplicating pets, the guppies and spaniels,
> the Woolworth's turtle that cost forty-nine cents
> 15 (with the soiled price tag half peeled on its shell)—
> but, from the look of things, it only just happened.
> The wheels of the upside-down tricycle are spinning.
> The swings are empty but swinging.
> And the shadow is still there, and there
> 20 is the object that made it,
> riding the proximate atmosphere,
> oblong and illustrious above
> the dispeopled bedroom community,
> venting the memories of those it took,
> 25 their corrosive human element.

---

9. **cardinal points:** north, south, east, and west, the principal points on a compass.

"The Disappearances" from *The Long Meadow* by Vijay Seshadri. Copyright © 2004 by Vijay Seshadri. Reproduced by permission of **Graywolf Press, Saint Paul, MN.**

INTERPRET

Pause at line 10. What is the setting of this poem? What are some clues that it will be about a remembered event?

HISTORICAL CONTEXT

Pause at the end of the page, and think about what you have just read. Poems are often meant to be interpreted on many different levels. What do you think has caused the disappearances? What are the "shadow" (line 19) and "the object that made it" (line 20)? Might the speaker be referring to one or more specific historical events? If so, which one(s)? Explain your interpretation.

This is what you have to walk through to escape,
transparent but alive as coal dust.
This is what you have to hack through,
bamboo-tough and thickly clustered.
30　The myths are somewhere else, but here are the meanings,
and you have to breathe them in
until they burn your throat
and peck at your brain with their intoxicated teeth.
This is you as seen by them, from the corner of an eye
35　(was that the way you were always seen?).

INTERPRET

How do the details and the figures of speech in lines 26–35 contribute to a sense that the memory of a great tragedy or loss is both hurtful and confusing?

The Disappearances

HISTORICAL CONTEXT

Re-read lines 36-50. What does the speaker remember about the day that President Kennedy was shot?

___

This is you when the President died°
(the day is brilliant and cold).
This is you poking a ground-wasps' nest.
This is you at the doorway, unobserved,
40 while your aunts and uncles keen over the body.
This is your first river, your first planetarium, your first Popsicle.
The cold and brilliant day in six-color prints—
but the people on the screen are black and white.
Your friend's mother is saying,
45 *Hush, children! Don't you understand history is being made?*
You do, and you still do. Made and made again.
This is you as seen by them, and them as seen by you,
and you as seen by you, in five dimensions,
in seven, in three again, then two,
50 then reduced to a dimensionless point
in a universe where the only constant is the speed of light.
This is you at the speed of light.

---

36. **when the President died:** November 22, 1963, the day President John F. Kennedy was assassinated.

ANALYZE

In lines 51–57, the poet uses **metaphors** based in physics to describe how our views of ourselves, formed from our experiences and memories, are constantly changing. What **theme,** or truth about life, do you think is revealed by this complex, many-layered poem? Remember that a poem can contain many themes.

MEET THE WRITER

Vijay Seshadri (1954–   ) has moved a great deal. He was born in Bangalore, India, and moved with his family when he was five to Columbus, Ohio, where they were often the only Indian family. As an adult, he worked in the fishing and logging industries in the Pacific Northwest and as a truck driver in San Francisco. He eventually moved to New York City, where he earned a master's degree at Columbia University. Seshadri was inspired to write poetry when he was sixteen, after hearing the poet Galway Kinnell read at Oberlin College. Seshadri now teaches at Sarah Lawrence College and lives in Brooklyn, New York.

Skills Practice and Review

The Disappearances

Historical Context Chart   In "The Disappearances," the speaker remembers the day in 1963 that President John F. Kennedy was assassinated. Fill in details from the poem about that historic day.

	Details from the Poem
What the day is like	
What the speaker does that day	
What the adults do	

Reading Comprehension   Answer each question below.

1. Describe the setting of the town as the speaker remembers it.
   _____
   _____

2. What memories does the speaker have of the day President Kennedy was shot?
   _____
   _____

3. For you, the assassination of President Kennedy is an event from history to be studied rather than an event from life to be assimilated. However, you have experienced other moments when history was being made. What historic events have caused you to remember where you were, whom you were with, and what you were doing when you heard what happened?
   _____
   _____
   _____

SKILLS FOCUS

Literary Skills
Analyze historical context.

The Disappearances   229

Before You Read

How It Feels to Be Colored Me
by Zora Neale Hurston

Zora Neale Hurston tells how she feels about being an African American woman, all the while poking fun at stereotypes held by both whites and blacks.

LITERARY FOCUS: BIOGRAPHICAL AND HISTORICAL APPROACH

When you take a **biographical approach** to literature, you consider how the writer's experiences affect the work. "How It Feels to Be Colored Me" is a **personal essay,** a nonfiction genre in which writers describe their experiences, emotions, and thoughts. Therefore, you know before you begin reading that the information will be biographical.

When you take a **historical approach** to literature, you consider how the historical context affects the work. In this essay, Hurston describes experiences from the early 1900s, so you know the historical context will be different from today. During the period Hurston is writing about, segregation was the norm in the South, and racial bigotry was common across the United States.

- Hurston's first historical setting is the all-black town of Eatonville, Florida, a place where Hurston was accepted as herself.
- Her next setting is a racially mixed community in which she is changed in the eyes of the world from her own self, Zora, to a racial stereotype of "a little colored girl."
- Next, Hurston moves to New York City, where she stands out in the white world of Barnard College.
- Finally, in a Harlem nightclub Hurston feels a connection to her African ancestry through the rhythms of jazz while her white companion sits unmoved.

READING SKILLS: COMPARE AND CONTRAST

When you **compare** two things, you look for *similarities,* or ways the things are alike. When you **contrast** two things, you look for *differences* between them.

- As you read "How It Feels to Be Colored Me," compare and contrast Zora Neale Hurston's experience of being an African American in the various settings she describes.

SKILLS FOCUS

Literary Skills
Understand biographical and historical approaches to literary criticism.

Reading Skills
Compare and contrast.

Vocabulary Skills
Understand figurative language.

Collection 9: Literary Criticism: Biographical and Historical Approach

ESSAY

VOCABULARY DEVELOPMENT

PREVIEW SELECTION VOCABULARY
The following words appear in "How It Feels to Be Colored Me." Look them over before you begin the selection.

extenuating (ek·sten′yo͞o·āt′iŋ) *v.* used as *adj.*: making seem less serious by serving as an excuse or justification.

*Hurston is African American and offers no **extenuating** information that would make her seem other than what she is.*

deplored (dē·plôrd′) *v.*: strongly disapproved of; condemned.

*The adults **deplored** any showing off before the visitors.*

circumlocutions (sʉr′kəm·lō·kyo͞o′shənz) *n.*: roundabout ways of expressing something.

*The music started without any fancy riffs or other **circumlocutions** on the way to its heart.*

rambunctious (ram·buŋk′shəs) *adj.*: wild; disorderly.

*As the music became more upbeat, the orchestra became downright **rambunctious**.*

exultingly (eg·zult′iŋ·lē) *adv.*: triumphantly.

*The dancers snaked across the floor, following each other **exultingly**.*

veneer (və·nir′) *n.*: superficially attractive surface or appearance.

*Polite behavior and customs form a **veneer** we call civilization.*

UNDERSTANDING FIGURATIVE LANGUAGE

Figurative language compares one thing to another, very different thing and is not meant to be understood literally. Here are some common figures of speech:

- A **simile** is a comparison that uses a connecting word such as *like, as, than,* or *resembles.* For example: *Her wit was as sharp as a tack.*
- A **metaphor** makes a comparison without a connecting word. Some metaphors say that something *is* something else: *His heart was a glowing ember.* Others imply the comparison: *His heart smoldered and burned.* An **extended metaphor** is one that is continued for several sentences.
- **Personification** gives human qualities to inanimate objects, ideas, animals, machines—in other words, to anything *not* human—to make its comparison: *The sky cried in pity for the parched land below.*
- An **idiom** is an expression common to a particular language that means something different from the literal meaning of the words. For example: *My heart is broken.*

As you read "How It Feels to Be Colored Me," look for the many ways in which Hurston uses figurative language to bring her message to the reader.

How It Feels to Be Colored Me   231

HOW IT FEELS TO BE COLORED ME

Zora Neale Hurston

VOCABULARY

extenuating (ek·sten′yoo·āt′iŋ) v. used as *adj.*: making seem less serious by serving as an excuse or justification.

INFER

Re-read lines 5–16. Why do you think Hurston did not feel "colored" while growing up in Eatonville, Florida?

INTERPRET

Underline the **extended metaphor** in lines 19–21. What does this figure of speech tell you about Hurston's character?

I am colored but I offer nothing in the way of **extenuating** circumstances except the fact that I am the only Negro in the United States whose grandfather on the mother's side was *not* an Indian chief.

I remember the very day that I became colored. Up to my thirteenth year I lived in the little Negro town of Eatonville, Florida. It is exclusively a colored town. The only white people I knew passed through the town going to or coming from Orlando. The native whites rode dusty horses; the Northern tourists chugged down the sandy village road in automobiles. The town knew the Southerners and never stopped cane chewing when they passed. But the Northerners were something else again. They were peered at cautiously from behind curtains by the timid. The more venturesome would come out on the porch to watch them go past and got just as much pleasure out of the tourists as the tourists got out of the village.

The front porch might seem a daring place for the rest of the town, but it was a gallery seat for me. My favorite place was atop the gatepost. Proscenium[1] box for a born first-nighter. Not only did I enjoy the show, but I didn't mind the actors knowing that I liked it. I usually spoke to them in passing. I'd wave at them and when they returned my salute, I would say something like this: "Howdy-do-well-I-thank-you-where-you-goin'?" Usually the automobile or the horse paused at this, and after a queer exchange of compliments, I would probably "go a piece of the way" with them, as we say in farthest Florida. If one of my

---

1. **proscenium** (prō·sē′nē·əm) *n.* used as *adj.*: area separating the stage from the audience. A proscenium box is a good theater seat close to the stage.

family happened to come to the front in time to see me, of course negotiations would be rudely broken off. But even so, it is clear that I was the first "welcome-to-our-state" Floridian, and I hope the Miami Chamber of Commerce will please take notice.

During this period, white people differed from colored to me only in that they rode through town and never lived there. They liked to hear me "speak pieces" and sing and wanted to see me dance the parse-me-la, and gave me generously of their small silver for doing these things, which seemed strange to me, for I wanted to do them so much that I needed bribing to stop. Only they didn't know it. The colored people gave no dimes. They **deplored** any joyful tendencies in me, but I was their Zora nevertheless. I belonged to them, to the nearby hotels, to the county—everybody's Zora.

But changes came in the family when I was thirteen, and I was sent to school in Jacksonville. I left Eatonville, the town of the oleanders,[2] as Zora. When I disembarked from the riverboat at Jacksonville, she was no more. It seemed that I had suffered a sea change. I was not Zora of Orange County any more, I was now a little colored girl. I found it out in certain ways. In my heart as well as in the mirror, I became a fast brown—warranted not to rub nor run.

But I am not tragically colored. There is no great sorrow dammed up in my soul, nor lurking behind my eyes. I do not mind at all. I do not belong to the sobbing school of Negrohood who hold that nature somehow has given them a lowdown dirty deal and whose feelings are all hurt about it. Even in the helter-skelter skirmish that is my life, I have seen that the world is to the strong regardless of a little pigmentation more or less. No, I do not weep at the world—I am too busy sharpening my oyster knife.

Someone is always at my elbow reminding me that I am the granddaughter of slaves. It fails to register depression with me. Slavery is sixty years in the past.[3] The operation was successful

---

2. **oleanders** (ō'lē·an'dərz) n.: shrubs with fragrant flowers.
3. **Slavery . . . past:** Hurston wrote this essay as an adult in the mid-1920s. Slavery officially ended in the South in 1863, with the signing of the Emancipation Proclamation, although it did not end in fact until the Civil War concluded in 1865.

VOCABULARY

deplored (dē·plôrd') v.: strongly disapproved of; condemned.

HISTORICAL CONTEXT

Why does Hurston become a racial stereotype—"a little colored girl"—when she goes to the city of Jacksonville?

WORD STUDY

The word *fast* (line 46) is a multiple-meaning word. Here it means "that won't fade."

INTERPRET

In line 55, Hurston uses a **metaphor** that alludes to a famous quote from Shakespeare's *The Merry Wives of Windsor:* "Why then, the world's mine oyster." What does Hurston mean by her figure of speech?

HISTORICAL CONTEXT

At the time Hurston wrote this, her first essay, the social question aimed at African Americans was essentially, "How does it feel to be a problem?" Hurston rejects this way of seeing herself. She claims her identity despite racism. In this essay she also seeks to resolve the incongruities between *colored me* and *real me*, much as all people seek to resolve the differences between other people's ideas of who they are and who they really are.

HISTORICAL CONTEXT

Re-read lines 60–75. Why does Hurston consider the time she is living in a great time to be an African American? Why does she think that it is more exciting to be black than white?

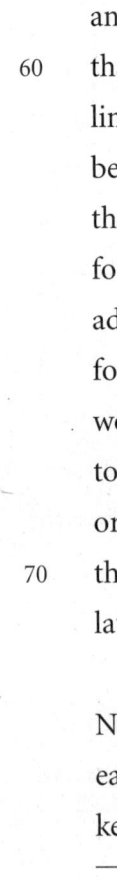

_____
_____
_____
_____
_____
_____
_____
_____

Zora Neale Hurston.
© CORBIS

and the patient is doing well, thank you. The terrible struggle that made me an American out of a potential slave said, "On the line!" The Reconstruction[4] said, "Get set!" and the generation before said, "Go!" I am off to a flying start and I must not halt in the stretch to look behind and weep. Slavery is the price I paid for civilization, and the choice was not with me. It is a bully[5] adventure and worth all that I have paid through my ancestors for it. No one on earth ever had a greater chance for glory. The world to be won and nothing to be lost. It is thrilling to think— to know that for any act of mine, I shall get twice as much praise or twice as much blame. It is quite exciting to hold the center of the national stage, with the spectators not knowing whether to laugh or to weep.

The position of my white neighbor is much more difficult. No brown specter[6] pulls up a chair beside me when I sit down to eat. No dark ghost thrusts its leg against mine in bed. The game of keeping what one has is never so exciting as the game of getting.

---
4. **Reconstruction:** period after the Civil War when the South was being rebuilt.
5. **bully** (bool′ē) *adj.*: (informal) excellent.
6. **specter** (spek′tər) *n.*: ghost.

I do not always feel colored. Even now I often achieve the unconscious Zora of Eatonville before the Hegira.[7] I feel most colored when I am thrown against a sharp white background.

For instance at Barnard.[8] "Beside the waters of the Hudson" I feel my race. Among the thousand white persons, I am a dark rock surged upon, and overswept, but through it all, I remain myself. When covered by the waters, I am; and the ebb but reveals me again.

Sometimes it is the other way around. A white person is set down in our midst, but the contrast is just as sharp for me. For instance, when I sit in the drafty basement that is The New World Cabaret with a white person, my color comes. We enter chatting about any little nothing that we have in common and are seated by the jazz waiters. In the abrupt way that jazz orchestras have, this one plunges into a number. It loses no time in **circumlocutions,** but gets right down to business. It constricts the thorax and splits the heart with its tempo and narcotic harmonies. This orchestra grows **rambunctious,** rears on its hind legs and attacks the tonal veil with primitive fury, rending it, clawing it until it breaks through to the jungle beyond. I follow those heathen—follow them **exultingly.** I dance wildly inside myself; I yell within, I whoop; I shake my assegai[9] above my head, I hurl it true to the mark *yeeeeooww!* I am in the jungle and living in the jungle way. My face is painted red and yellow and my body is painted blue. My pulse is throbbing like a war drum. I want to slaughter something—give pain, give death to what, I do not know. But the piece ends. The men of the orchestra wipe their lips and rest their fingers. I creep back slowly to the **veneer** we call civilization with the last tone and find the white friend sitting motionless in his seat, smoking calmly.

---

7. **Hegira** (hi·jī′rə) *n.:* journey, especially one taken to escape danger. The word comes from Arabic, referring to Muhammad's flight from Mecca.
8. **Barnard:** liberal arts college for women in New York City, associated with Columbia University. Hurston studied anthropology there on scholarship and got her bachelor's degree in 1928.
9. **assegai** (as′ə·gī′) *n.:* slender iron-tipped spear used in South Africa.

INFER

Re-read lines 76–83. How does Hurston show that color consciousness is a socially constructed phenomenon?

INTERPRET

Why do you think Hurston uses stereotyped images of Africans to describe her reaction to the music in the night club (lines 91–102)?

VOCABULARY

circumlocutions (sur′kəm·lō·kyōō′shənz) *n.:* roundabout ways of expressing something.

rambunctious (ram·bunk′shəs) *adj.:* wild; disorderly.

exultingly (eg·zult′in·lē) *adv.:* triumphantly.

veneer (və·nir′) *n.:* superficially attractive surface or appearance.

Zora Neale Hurston sitting on a porch in Eatonville, Florida, with musicians Rochelle French and Gabriel Brown.
© CORBIS

COMPARE & CONTRAST

Compare and contrast Hurston's reaction to the music with that of her companion.

"Good music they have here," he remarks, drumming the table with his fingertips.

Music. The great blobs of purple and red emotion have not touched him. He has only heard what I felt. He is far away and I see him but dimly across the ocean and the continent that have fallen between us. He is so pale with his whiteness then and I am *so* colored.

At certain times I have no race. I am *me*. When I set my hat at a certain angle and saunter down Seventh Avenue, Harlem City, feeling as snooty as the lions in front of the Forty-Second Street Library, for instance. So far as my feelings are concerned, Peggy Hopkins Joyce on the Boule Mich[10] with her gorgeous raiment, stately carriage, knees knocking together in a most aristocratic manner, has nothing on me. The cosmic Zora emerges. I belong to no race nor time. I am the eternal feminine[11] with its string of beads.

10. **Peggy . . . Mich:** Peggy Hopkins Joyce (1893–1957), flamboyant actress who appeared on stage and in silent films. *Boule Mich* is short for *Boulevard St. Michel,* a famous avenue in Paris.
11. **eternal feminine:** from the last lines of the eighteenth-century German writer Goethe's play *Faust:* "The eternal feminine leads us upward."

I have no separate feeling about being an American citizen and colored. I am merely a fragment of the Great Soul that surges within the boundaries. My country, right or wrong.

Sometimes, I feel discriminated against, but it does not make me angry. It merely astonishes me. How *can* any deny themselves the pleasure of my company? It's beyond me.

But in the main, I feel like a brown bag of miscellany propped against a wall. Against a wall in company with other bags, white, red, and yellow. Pour out the contents, and there is discovered a jumble of small things priceless and worthless. A first-water diamond,[12] an empty spool, bits of broken glass, lengths of string, a key to a door long since crumbled away, a rusty knife blade, old shoes saved for a road that never was and never will be, a nail bent under the weight of things too heavy for any nail, a dried flower or two still a little fragrant. In your hand is the brown bag. On the ground before you is the jumble it held—so much like the jumble in the bags, could they be emptied, that all might be dumped in a single heap and the bags refilled without altering the content of any greatly. A bit of colored glass more or less would not matter. Perhaps that is how the Great Stuffer of Bags filled them in the first place—who knows?

---

12. **first-water diamond:** diamond of the highest quality.

MEET THE WRITER

Zora Neale Hurston (1891–1960) grew up in Eatonville, Florida, where her father was a carpenter, preacher, and sometime mayor. Her mother died in 1904. Hurston did not get along with her new stepmother, so she left home with a traveling theater company. She completed high school at Morgan Academy in Baltimore and attended Howard University. After having a story published in a New York magazine, she moved to that city, where she studied anthropology at Barnard College and became an acclaimed member of the Harlem Renaissance. Hurston published short stories, novels, essays, an autobiography, and books based on her anthropological research in the South and in the Caribbean. Her work later fell out of favor, and Hurston died in poverty. In 1973, the writer Alice Walker erected a gravestone for her.

FLUENCY

Read the boxed passage aloud, first for smoothness and then to characterize the feelings behind the text. Hurston's voice in this passage is different from her voice when she is making fun. Try, with your own voice, to illustrate that difference.

INTERPRET

Notice the **extended metaphor** of people as bags of different colors in lines 128–142 and the individual metaphors of the different bits of jumble. What do these metaphors tell you about the human condition? What is the **theme** of Hurston's essay?

SKILLS PRACTICE

How It Feels to Be Colored Me

SKILLS FOCUS

Literary Skills
Analyze historical context. Take a historical approach to literary criticism.

Historical Context Chart   The chart below lists the settings from "How It Feels to Be Colored Me." For each setting, describe the historical context and its influence on Zora Neale Hurston's essay.

Setting	Historical Context
Eatonville, Florida	
Jacksonville, Florida	
Barnard College, New York City	
New World Cabaret, Harlem, New York City	

Skills Review

How It Feels to Be Colored Me

VOCABULARY AND COMPREHENSION

A. Analyzing Figurative Language For each item below, fill in the blank with the appropriate word from the Word Box. Then, circle the figure of speech, and identify it as a **simile**, a **metaphor**, an **idiom**, or **personification**.

1. Everyone in town _____ the dirty lowdown deal Harry got from the slick salesman. **Figure of speech:** _____

2. Massie's _____ meandered like a butterfly in a flower garden. **Figure of speech:** _____

3. There were no _____ circumstances to excuse her for driving them all out of their minds. **Figure of speech:** _____

4. The _____ students were a herd of buffalo stampeding into the classroom. **Figure of speech:** _____

5. The _____ of new paint turned the ugly old house into a palace. **Figure of speech:** _____

6. The painted house thought to itself _____, "I am now the best-looking house on the block." **Figure of speech:** _____

Word Box

extenuating
deplored
circumlocutions
rambunctious
exultingly
veneer

B. Reading Comprehension Answer each question below.

1. Why did Hurston think she was living at a great time to be an African American?
   _____
   _____

2. What point is Hurston making with her extended metaphor in the last paragraph of the essay?
   _____
   _____

SKILLS FOCUS

Vocabulary Skills
Identify figurative language.

Collection 10

Drama

Ruby Dee, Sidney Poitier, and Diana Sands in *A Raisin in the Sun* (1954).
© Bettmann/CORBIS

Academic Vocabulary for Collection 10

These are the terms you should know
as you read and analyze the selection in this collection.

Drama A story written to be acted out live for an audience. A drama, also called a **play,** uses dialogue and action. Elements of dramatic plot include **exposition,** in which we learn who the characters are and what they want; **complications; climax,** and **resolution.** Types of drama include tragedy and comedy, but the term *drama* can also mean a play that combines elements of both tragedy and comedy.

- **Tragedy** A play that presents serious and important actions and ends unhappily for the main character.
- **Comedy** An amusing play that ends happily, with the main character usually getting what he or she wants.

• • •

Characters Individuals in a story, poem, or play.

- **Dynamic characters** change and grow as a result of their experiences.
- **Static characters** remain essentially the same from beginning to end.
- **Character foil** is a character who contrasts dramatically with another character. A foil serves to highlight the qualities of the character(s) he or she is contrasted with.

Dialogue A conversation between characters in a play.

Monologue A long speech made by one character to one or more characters onstage.

Stage directions Stage directions for setting may be elaborate or spare; they are usually found at the beginning of each scene and describe the playwright's vision of the set and perhaps the mood and characterization as well. Stage directions for characters follow the characters' names and describe the way the characters are to move onstage and speak their lines.

Props The portable items that actors carry or handle onstage. Props add verisimilitude to a production by more closely mirroring life. When placed at the center of the action, props can serve as symbols or metaphors for larger ideas.

Before You Read

from A Raisin in the Sun

by Lorraine Hansberry

Langston Hughes's poem "Dream Deferred," from which the play *A Raisin in the Sun* takes its title, asks, "What happens to a dream deferred? / Does it dry up / like a raisin in the sun?" The excerpt from the play that you are about to read follows one family as its members pursue their dreams—and struggle with what they are willing to do to have their dreams fulfilled.

LITERARY FOCUS: DRAMA

A **drama,** or play, is a story that is written to be acted out by people for a live audience. Like other stories, dramas are about characters who want something and who take steps to get it. A dramatic plot usually includes an **exposition,** in which the characters and their **conflicts** are introduced; **complications;** a **climax;** and a **resolution.** Modern dramas are generally concerned with the personal and domestic struggles of ordinary people rather than the gods, kings, and heroes that often took the starring roles in ancient Greek and Elizabethan theater. Their endings may be happy, tragic, or bittersweet, but the stories have their roots in the life around us. The term *drama* can also mean a serious play that is neither a comedy nor a tragedy.

- As you read this excerpt from *A Raisin in the Sun,* consider why this acclaimed drama remains so powerful half a century after it was first performed.

READING SKILLS: CAUSES AND EFFECTS

Most of our actions have cause-and-effect relationships. When Langston Hughes asks, "What happens to a dream deferred?" he is asking what the effect is of a dream deferred—a dream that is given up or that is not fulfilled. A **cause** is the *reason* an action takes place. An **effect** is the *result* of the action. Every human being is born into a web of causes and effects that influence his or her choices.

- As you read this excerpt from *A Raisin in the Sun,* notice how the characters' dreams cause them to take certain actions, which then have dramatic effects.

SKILLS FOCUS

Literary Skills
Understand characteristics of drama.

Reading Skills
Understand cause and effect.

Vocabulary Skills
Understand dialect.

242 Part 1 Collection 10: Drama

DRAMA

VOCABULARY DEVELOPMENT

PREVIEW SELECTION VOCABULARY

The following words appear in the excerpt from *A Raisin in the Sun.* Get to know them before you begin to read.

exuberant (eg·zoo′bər·ənt) *adj.:* in good spirits; full of life.

*Ruth is **exuberant** about the long-hoped-for move to a new house.*

agitation (aj′ə·tā′shən) *n.:* act of stirring up people's interest to produce change.

***Agitation** is useful in raising people's consciousness of a social wrong.*

oblivious (ə·bliv′ē·əs) *adj.:* completely unaware.

*At first Walter and Ruth are **oblivious** of Lindner's presence.*

epitaph (ep′ə·taf′) *n.:* words on a tombstone.

*Mama accuses Beneatha of wanting to write Walter's **epitaph.***

precariously (pri·ker′ē·əs·lē) *adv.:* in an unstable manner.

*Mama scolds the moving men for lifting a chair **precariously.***

raucously (rô′kəs·lē) *adv.:* loudly and roughly.

*Impatient to leave, Walter calls out **raucously** for Mama and Ruth.*

UNDERSTANDING DIALECT

Dialect is a way of speaking that is characteristic of a particular region or group of people. In the United States the dialect used in formal writing and spoken by most radio and TV announcers is called standard English. This is also the dialect you are taught to speak and write in school, but you probably have more than one way of speaking. For instance, you may speak one dialect at school, another with your friends, and yet another with your family.

To bring characters to life, writers often use the dialect spoken in the setting of the story. Thus, characters would speak one way in a story set in Maine and another way in a story set in Texas. *A Raisin in the Sun* is set in an African American neighborhood in Chicago sometime in the 1950s. This was a period soon after World War II, when many blacks had migrated from the South to work in northern factories.

- As you read the excerpts from the play, notice when characters use the regional dialect of the setting and when they use standard English.

from A Raisin in the Sun

from *A Raisin in the Sun*

Lorraine Hansberry

> The title of the play comes from a line in Langston Hughes's poem "Dream Deferred." Set in 1950s Chicago, the play explores an African American family's struggle to achieve their dreams. The five Youngers are living in a cramped Southside apartment. In Act I, Mama is waiting to receive a $10,000 check from her husband's life insurance policy. The family is torn over what to use the money for: Mama wants a house with a yard; her daughter, Beneatha, wants to go to medical school; her son, Walter, wants to open a liquor store with two friends, Willie and Bobo; and his wife, Ruth, wants more opportunities for their son.
>
> In Act II, Mama puts a down payment on a roomy house in an all-white suburb, even though moving there will not be easy. Walter is enraged that Mama has "butchered up" his dream. Later, in order not to hurt his pride, she gives him responsibility for $6,500. Mama intends for $3,000 to go toward Beneatha's education and the rest to be put away for the family's future.
>
> The following scene takes place in the apartment a week later, on moving day.

IDENTIFY

Where are the Youngers living as the play begins? Where are they moving?

_____
_____
_____
_____
_____

VOCABULARY

exuberant (eg·zōō′bər·ənt) *adj.:* in good spirits; full of life.

Act II, Scene 3

As the curtain rises we see that RUTH *is alone in the living room, finishing up the family's packing. She is nailing crates and tying cartons.* BENEATHA *enters, carrying a guitar case, and watches her* **exuberant** *sister-in-law.*

Ruth. Hey!

Beneatha (*putting away the case*). Hi.

Ruth (*pointing at a package*). Honey—look in that package there and see what I found on sale this morning at the South

10   Center. (RUTH *gets up and moves to the package and draws out some curtains.*) Lookahere—hand-turned hems!

Act 2, Scene 3, and Act 3 from *A Raisin in the Sun,* Expanded 25th Anniversary Edition by Lorraine Hansberry. Copyright © 1958 by Robert Nemiroff as an unpublished work; copyright © 1959, 1966, 1984, 1987 by Robert Nemiroff. Reproduced by permission of **Random House, Inc.**

Beneatha. How do you know the window size out there?

Ruth (*who hadn't thought of that*). Oh— Well, they bound to fit something in the whole house. Anyhow, they was too good a bargain to pass up. (RUTH *slaps her head, suddenly remembering something.*) Oh, Bennie—I meant to put a special note on that carton over there. That's your mama's good china and she wants 'em to be very careful with it.

Beneatha. I'll do it.

[BENEATHA *finds a piece of paper and starts to draw large letters on it.*]

Ruth. You know what I'm going to do soon as I get in that new house?

Beneatha. What?

Ruth. Honey—I'm going to run me a tub of water up to here . . . (*With her fingers practically up to her nostrils*) And I'm going to get in it—and I am going to sit . . . and sit . . . and sit in that hot water and the first person who knocks to tell *me* to hurry up and come out—

Beneatha. Gets shot at sunrise.

Ruth (*laughing happily*). You said it, sister! (*Noticing how large* BENEATHA *is absent-mindedly making the note*) Honey, they ain't going to read that from no airplane.

Beneatha (*laughing herself*). I guess I always think things have more emphasis if they are big, somehow.

Ruth (*looking up at her and smiling*). You and your brother seem to have that as a philosophy of life. Lord, that man—done changed so 'round here. You know—you know what we did last night? Me and Walter Lee?

Beneatha. What?

Ruth (*smiling to herself*). We went to the movies. (*Looking at* BENEATHA *to see if she understands*) We went to the movies.

INFER

Re-read Ruth's speech in lines 25–29. What does it suggest about their present living conditions?

IDENTIFY

Look at lines 34–37. Underline the description of Walter and Beneatha's "philosophy of life."

IDENTIFY CAUSE & EFFECT

Pause at line 55. After reading what Ruth, Walter's wife, says about him, describe the ways in which Walter has changed. What might be the cause of these changes?

_____

INTERPRET

Circle in the **stage directions** in lines 57–66 four of Walter's actions that indicate his mood. What do they suggest about his current state of mind?

_____

You know the last time me and Walter went to the movies together?

Beneatha. No.

Ruth. Me neither. That's how long it been. (*Smiling again*) But we went last night. The picture wasn't much good, but that didn't seem to matter. We went—and we held hands.

Beneatha. Oh, Lord!

50 **Ruth.** We held hands—and you know what?

Beneatha. What?

Ruth. When we come out of the show it was late and dark and all the stores and things was closed up . . . and it was kind of chilly and there wasn't many people on the streets . . . and we was still holding hands, me and Walter.

Beneatha. You're killing me.

[WALTER *enters with a large package. His happiness is deep in him; he cannot keep still with his newfound exuberance. He is singing and wiggling and snapping his fingers. He puts his pack-*
60 *age in a corner and puts a phonograph record, which he has brought in with him, on the record player. As the music, soulful and sensuous, comes up he dances over to* RUTH *and tries to get her to dance with him. She gives in at last to his raunchiness and in a fit of giggling allows herself to be drawn into his mood. They dip and she melts into his arms in a classic, body-melding "slow drag."*]

Beneatha (*regarding them a long time as they dance, then drawing in her breath for a deeply exaggerated comment which she does not particularly mean*). Talk about—olddddddddddd-
70 fashionedddddddd—Negroes!

Walter (*stopping momentarily*). What kind of Negroes? (*He says this in fun. He is not angry with her today, nor with anyone. He starts to dance with his wife again.*)

Beneatha. Old-fashioned.

Walter (*as he dances with* RUTH). You know, when these *New Negroes* have their convention—(*pointing at his sister*)—that is

Sean "P. Diddy" Combs, holding a photograph of Lorraine Hansberry, and fellow cast members, taking a bow at the end of the opening-night performance of *A Raisin in the Sun* in 2004.
© Scott Eells/Getty Images

going to be the chairman of the Committee on Unending **Agitation.** (*He goes on dancing, then stops.*) Race, race, race! . . . Girl, I do believe you are the first person in the history of the entire human race to successfully brainwash yourself. (BENEATHA *breaks up and he goes on dancing. He stops again, enjoying his tease.*) Shoot, even the N double A C P[1] takes a holiday sometimes! (BENEATHA *and* RUTH *laugh. He dances with* RUTH *some more and starts to laugh and stops and pantomimes someone over an operating table.*) I can just see that chick someday looking down at some poor cat on an operating table and before she starts to slice him, she says . . .

---

1. **NAACP:** National Association for the Advancement of Colored People, a civil rights organization founded in 1909.

> **VOCABULARY**
>
> **agitation** (aj'ə·tā'shən) *n.*: act of stirring up people's interest to produce change.
>
> **INTERPRET**
>
> Walter and Beneatha are brother and sister. Re-read lines 67–92, and describe how their relationship reminds you of other sibling relationships.

from A Raisin in the Sun   247

VOCABULARY

oblivious (ə·bliv′ē·əs) *adj.:* completely unaware.

INTERPRET

What does the **stage direction** in line 111 imply about how Ruth and Beneatha view Walter?

_____
_____
_____
_____
_____
_____
_____

ANALYZE

Consider Walter's lines on pages 247–248. In what ways does Walter's manner of speaking change from *before* Lindner's entrance to *after* it? Why do you think this happens?

_____
_____
_____
_____
_____
_____

(*Pulling his sleeves back maliciously*) "By the way, what are your views on civil rights down there? . . ." (*He laughs at her again and starts to dance happily. The bell sounds.*)

Beneatha. Sticks and stones may break my bones but . . . words will never hurt me!

[BENEATHA *goes to the door and opens it as* WALTER *and* RUTH *go on with the clowning.* BENEATHA *is somewhat surprised to see a quiet-looking middle-aged white man in a business suit holding his hat and a briefcase in his hand and consulting a small piece of paper.*]

Man. Uh—how do you do, miss. I am looking for a Mrs.—(*He looks at the slip of paper.*) Mrs. Lena Younger? (*He stops short, struck dumb at the sight of the* **oblivious** WALTER *and* RUTH.)

Beneatha (*smoothing her hair with slight embarrassment*). Oh—yes, that's my mother. Excuse me. (*She closes the door and turns to quiet the other two.*) Ruth! Brother! Somebody's here. (*Then she opens the door. The man casts a curious quick glance at all of them.*) Uh—come in please.

Man (*coming in*). Thank you.

Beneatha. My mother isn't here just now. Is it business?

Man. Yes . . . well, of a sort.

Walter (*freely, the Man of the House*). Have a seat. I'm Mrs. Younger's son. I look after most of her business matters.

[RUTH *and* BENEATHA *exchange amused glances.*]

Man (*regarding* WALTER, *and sitting*). Well—My name is Karl Lindner . . .

Walter (*stretching out his hand*). Walter Younger. This is my wife—(RUTH *nods politely.*)—and my sister.

Lindner. How do you do.

Walter (*amiably, as he sits himself easily on a chair, leaning forward on his knees with interest and looking expectantly into the newcomer's face*). What can we do for you, Mr. Lindner!

120 **Lindner** (*some minor shuffling of the hat and briefcase on his knees*). Well—I am a representative of the Clybourne Park Improvement Association—

Walter (*pointing*). Why don't you sit your things on the floor?

Lindner. Oh—yes. Thank you. (*He slides the briefcase and hat under the chair.*) And as I was saying—I am from the Clybourne Park Improvement Association and we have had it brought to our attention at the last meeting that you people— or at least your mother—has bought a piece of residential property at—(*He digs for the slip of paper again.*)—four o six
130 Clybourne Street . . .

Walter. That's right. Care for something to drink? Ruth, get Mr. Lindner a beer.

Lindner (*upset for some reason*). Oh—no, really. I mean thank you very much, but no thank you.

Ruth (*innocently*). Some coffee?

Lindner. Thank you, nothing at all.

[BENEATHA *is watching the man carefully.*]

Lindner. Well, I don't know how much you folks know about our organization. (*He is a gentle man; thoughtful and some-*
140 *what labored in his manner.*) It is one of these community organizations set up to look after—oh, you know, things like block upkeep and special projects and we also have what we call our New Neighbors Orientation Committee . . .

Beneatha (*drily*). Yes—and what do they do?

Lindner (*turning a little to her and then returning the main force to* WALTER). Well—it's what you might call a sort of welcoming committee, I guess. I mean they, we—I'm the chairman of the committee—go around and see the new people who move into the neighborhood and sort of give them the lowdown on
150 the way we do things out in Clybourne Park.

Beneatha (*with appreciation of the two meanings, which escape* RUTH *and* WALTER). Un-huh.

INFER

Look at lines 120–130. What is the Clybourne Park Improvement Association, and why might it be important to the Youngers?

PREDICT

In lines 131–136, Lindner turns down any refreshments. From his behavior, what might you predict about his visit?

IDENTIFY

Underline in lines 146–150 what the New Neighbors Orientation Committee is and what it does.

from A Raisin in the Sun

DRAMA

Re-read the **stage directions** for Beneatha in Lindner's monologue (lines 169–185). Based on these directions, what might Beneatha be thinking?

_____
_____
_____
_____

WORD STUDY

Look at the word *quizzical* in line 179. What is its root word? Describe what "quizzical interest" might be.

_____
_____
_____
_____
_____

CLARIFY

Re-read lines 180–190. Lindner is encouraged when Ruth shows approval. What remark of Lindner's does Ruth affirm?

_____
_____
_____
_____
_____

Lindner. And we also have the category of what the association calls—(*He looks elsewhere.*)—uh—special community problems . . .

Beneatha. Yes—and what are some of those?

Walter. Girl, let the man talk.

Lindner (*with understated relief*). Thank you. I would sort of like to explain this thing in my own way. I mean I want to explain to you in a certain way.

Walter. Go ahead.

Lindner. Yes. Well. I'm going to try to get right to the point. I'm sure we'll all appreciate that in the long run.

Beneatha. Yes.

Walter. Be still now!

Lindner. Well—

Ruth (*still innocently*). Would you like another chair—you don't look comfortable.

Lindner (*more frustrated than annoyed*). No, thank you very much. Please. Well—to get right to the point I—(*A great breath, and he is off at last.*) I am sure you people must be aware of some of the incidents which have happened in various parts of the city when colored people have moved into certain areas—(BENEATHA *exhales heavily and starts tossing a piece of fruit up and down in the air.*) Well—because we have what I think is going to be a unique type of organization in American community life—not only do we deplore that kind of thing—but we are trying to do something about it. (BENEATHA *stops tossing and turns with a new and quizzical interest to the man.*) We feel—(*gaining confidence in his mission because of the interest in the faces of the people he is talking to*)—we feel that most of the trouble in this world, when you come right down to it—(*He hits his knee for emphasis.*)—most of the trouble exists because people just don't sit down and talk to each other.

Ruth (*nodding as she might in church, pleased with the remark*). You can say that again, mister.

Lindner (*more encouraged by such affirmation*). That we don't try hard enough in this world to understand the other fellow's problem. The other guy's point of view.

Ruth. Now that's right.

[BENEATHA *and* WALTER *merely watch and listen with genuine interest.*]

Lindner. Yes—that's the way we feel out in Clybourne Park. And that's why I was elected to come here this afternoon and talk to you people. Friendly like, you know, the way people should talk to each other and see if we couldn't find some way to work this thing out. As I say, the whole business is a matter of *caring* about the other fellow. Anybody can see that you are a nice family of folks, hard working and honest I'm sure. (BENEATHA *frowns slightly, quizzically, her head tilted regarding him.*) Today everybody knows what it means to be on the outside of *something*. And of course, there is always somebody who is out to take advantage of people who don't always understand.

Walter. What do you mean?

Lindner. Well—you see our community is made up of people who've worked hard as the dickens for years to build up that little community. They're not rich and fancy people; just hardworking, honest people who don't really have much but those little homes and a dream of the kind of community they want to raise their children in. Now, I don't say we are perfect and there is a lot wrong in some of the things they want. But you've got to admit that a man, right or wrong, has the right to want to have the neighborhood he lives in a certain kind of way. And at the moment the overwhelming majority of our people out there feel that people get along better, take more of a common interest in the life of the community, when they share a common background. I want you

---

PREDICT

Pause at line 205. Where do you think Lindner's speech is going? What does he mean? What is the true purpose of his visit?

_____
_____
_____
_____
_____
_____
_____

INFER

Pause at line 219. What do you think Lindner means by the phrase "share a common background"? Explain.

_____
_____
_____
_____
_____
_____
_____
_____

from A Raisin in the Sun

SUMMARIZE

Write a brief summary in your own words of Lindner's monologue (lines 207–224).

INTERPRET

Considering what you know now, what is ironic about Lindner's describing his association as "a sort of welcoming committee"? Explain.

DRAMA

What **complication** does Lindner's visit add to the family's goal of moving?

---

220 to believe me when I tell you that race prejudice simply doesn't enter into it. It is a matter of the people of Clybourne Park believing, rightly or wrongly, as I say, that for the happiness of all concerned that our Negro families are happier when they live in their *own* communities.

Beneatha (*with a grand and bitter gesture*). This, friends, is the Welcoming Committee!

Walter (*dumbfounded, looking at* LINDNER). Is this what you came marching all the way over here to tell us?

Lindner. Well, now we've been having a fine conversation. I
230 hope you'll hear me all the way through.

Walter (*tightly*). Go ahead, man.

Lindner. You see—in the face of all the things I have said, we are prepared to make your family a very generous offer . . .

Beneatha. Thirty pieces and not a coin less![2]

Walter. Yeah?

Lindner (*putting on his glasses and drawing a form out of the briefcase*). Our association is prepared, through the collective effort of our people, to buy the house from you at a financial gain to your family.

240 **Ruth.** Lord have mercy, ain't this the living gall!

Walter. All right, you through?

Lindner. Well, I want to give you the exact terms of the financial arrangement—

Walter. We don't want to hear no exact terms of no arrangements. I want to know if you got any more to tell us 'bout getting together?

Lindner (*taking off his glasses*). Well—I don't suppose that you feel . . .

Walter. Never mind how I feel—you got any more to say 'bout
250 how people ought to sit down and talk to each other? . . . Get out of my house, man. (*He turns his back and walks to the door.*)

Lindner (*looking around at the hostile faces and reaching and assembling his hat and briefcase*). Well—I don't understand

---

2. **Thirty . . . less:** reference to the thirty pieces of silver Judas Iscariot received for betraying Jesus (Matthew 26:14–15).

why you people are reacting this way. What do you think you are going to gain by moving into a neighborhood where you just aren't wanted and where some elements—well—people can get awful worked up when they feel that their whole way of life and everything they've ever worked for is threatened.

Walter. Get out.

Lindner (*at the door, holding a small card*). Well— I'm sorry it went like this.

Walter. Get out.

Lindner (*almost sadly regarding* WALTER). You just can't force people to change their hearts, son.

[*He turns and puts his card on a table and exits.* WALTER *pushes the door to with stinging hatred, and stands looking at it.* RUTH *just sits and* BENEATHA *just stands. They say nothing.* MAMA *and* TRAVIS *enter.*]

Mama. Well—this all the packing got done since I left out of here this morning. I testify before God that my children got all the energy of the *dead*! What time the moving men due?

Beneatha. Four o'clock. You had a caller, Mama. (*She is smiling, teasingly.*)

Mama. Sure enough—who?

Beneatha (*her arms folded saucily*). The Welcoming Committee.

[WALTER *and* RUTH *giggle.*]

Mama (*innocently*). Who?

Beneatha. The Welcoming Committee. They said they're sure going to be glad to see you when you get there.

Walter (*devilishly*). Yeah, they said they can't hardly wait to see your face.

[*Laughter*]

Mama (*sensing their facetiousness*).[3] What's the matter with you all?

---

3. **facetiousness** (fə·sē′shəs·nis) *n.*: humor; playfulness.

> **INFER**
>
> Pause at line 268. How do Walter's feelings about Lindner change from his entrance to the time he leaves? What details tell you so? Explain.

> **INTERPRET**
>
> Pause at line 282. Why do you think Walter, Ruth, and Beneatha are laughing?

INTERPRET

Pause at line 295. What tone are Walter, Ruth, and Beneatha using when telling Mama about Lindner's visit? Is this tone surprising to you? Explain.

_____
_____
_____
_____
_____

DRAMA

What do the **stage directions** in lines 296–298 imply?

_____
_____
_____
_____
_____
_____

INTERPRET

Pause at line 310. How would you describe Mama's reaction to Lindner's visit? Underline the dialogue on which you base your description.

_____
_____
_____
_____

Walter. Ain't nothing the matter with us. We just telling you 'bout the gentleman who came to see you this afternoon. From the Clybourne Park Improvement Association.

Mama. What he want?

Ruth (*in the same mood as* BENEATHA *and* WALTER). To welcome you, honey.

290   **Walter.** He said they can't hardly wait. He said the one thing they don't have, that they just *dying* to have out there is a fine family of fine colored people! (*To* RUTH *and* BENEATHA) Ain't that right!

Ruth (*mockingly*). Yeah! He left his card—

Beneatha (*handing card to* MAMA). In case.

[MAMA *reads and throws it on the floor—understanding and looking off as she draws her chair up to the table on which she has put her plant and some sticks and some cord.*]

Mama. Father, give us strength. (*Knowingly—and without fun*)
300   Did he threaten us?

Beneatha. Oh—Mama—they don't do it like that anymore. He talked Brotherhood. He said everybody ought to learn how to sit down and hate each other with good Christian fellowship.

[*She and* WALTER *shake hands to ridicule the remark.*]

Mama (*sadly*). Lord, protect us . . .

Ruth. You should hear the money those folks raised to buy the house from us. All we paid and then some.

Beneatha. What they think we going to do—eat 'em?

Ruth. No, honey, marry 'em.

310   **Mama** (*shaking her head*). Lord, Lord, Lord . . .

Ruth. Well—that's the way the crackers crumble. (*A beat*) Joke.

Beneatha (*laughingly noticing what her mother is doing*). Mama, what are you doing?

Mama. Fixing my plant so it won't get hurt none on the way . . .

Beneatha. Mama, you going to take *that* to the new house?

Mama. Un-huh—

Beneatha. That raggedy-looking old thing?

Mama (*stopping and looking at her*). It expresses ME!

Later, a distraught Bobo arrives and reveals that Willie has disappeared with all the money for the liquor-store venture, including the $6,500 that Mama had entrusted to Walter, ending Act II. The last act begins in the apartment an hour later.

Act III

[MAMA *enters from her bedroom. She is lost, vague, trying to catch hold, to make some sense of her former command of the world, but it still eludes her. A sense of waste overwhelms her gait; a measure of apology rides on her shoulders. She goes to her plant, which has remained on the table, looks at it, picks it up, and takes it to the windowsill and sits it outside, and she stands and looks at it a long moment. Then she closes the window, straightens her body with effort, and turns around to her children.*]

Mama. Well—ain't it a mess in here, though? (*A false cheerfulness, a beginning of something*) I guess we all better stop moping around and get some work done. All this unpacking and everything we got to do. (RUTH *raises her head slowly in response to the sense of the line; and* BENEATHA *in similar manner turns very slowly to look at her mother.*) One of you all better call the moving people and tell 'em not to come.

Ruth. Tell 'em not to come?

Mama. Of course, baby. Ain't no need in 'em coming all the way here and having to go back. They charges for that too. (*She sits down, fingers to her brow, thinking.*) Lord, ever since I was a little girl, I always remembers people saying, "Lena— Lena Eggleston, you aims too high all the time. You needs to

---

INTERPRET

What does Mama mean by saying of the plant "It expresses ME!" (line 318)?

INFER

In lines 327–331, Mama signals her resolve by restoring her plant to its place outside the kitchen window. What has she decided?

from **A Raisin in the Sun**

ANALYZE

In lines 347–348, underline the remark Mama says people used to make about her. How does this help explain the dreams of Walter and Beneatha?

INFER

Why does Ruth become frantic (lines 357–362)?

INFER

Pause at line 376. What decision has Mama made? Underline the details that tell you so.

slow down and see life a little more like it is. Just slow down some." That's what they always used to say down home—"Lord, that Lena Eggleston is a high-minded thing. She'll get her due one day!"

Ruth. No, Lena . . .

350 **Mama.** Me and Big Walter just didn't never learn right.

Ruth. Lena, no! We gotta go. Bennie—tell her . . . (*She rises and crosses to* BENEATHA *with her arms outstretched.* BENEATHA *doesn't respond.*) Tell her we can still move . . . the notes ain't but a hundred and twenty-five a month. We got four grown people in this house—we can work . . .

Mama (*to herself*). Just aimed too high all the time—

Ruth (*turning and going to* MAMA *fast—the words pouring out with urgency and desperation*). Lena—I'll work . . . I'll work twenty hours a day in all the kitchens in Chicago . . . I'll strap
360 my baby on my back if I have to and scrub all the floors in America and wash all the sheets in America if I have to—but we got to MOVE! We got to get OUT OF HERE!!

[MAMA *reaches out absently and pats* RUTH's *hand.*]

Mama. No—I sees things differently now. Been thinking 'bout some of the things we could do to fix this place up some. I seen a secondhand bureau over on Maxwell Street just the other day that could fit right there. (*She points to where the new furniture might go.* RUTH *wanders away from her.*) Would need some new handles on it and then a little varnish and it
370 look like something brand-new. And—we can put up them new curtains in the kitchen . . . Why this place be looking fine. Cheer us all up so that we forget trouble ever come . . . (*To* RUTH) And you could get some nice screens to put up in your room round the baby's bassinet . . . (*She looks at both of them, pleadingly.*) Sometimes you just got to know when to give up some things . . . and hold on to what you got. . . .

256   Part 1   Collection 10: Drama

[WALTER *enters from the outside, looking spent and leaning against the door, his coat hanging from him.*]

Mama. Where you been, son?

Walter (*breathing hard*). Made a call.

Mama. To who, son?

Walter. To The Man. (*He heads for his room.*)

Mama. What man, baby?

Walter (*stops in the door*). The Man, Mama. Don't you know who The Man is?

Ruth. Walter Lee?

Walter. *The Man.* Like the guys in the streets say—The Man. Captain Boss—Mistuh Charley . . . Old Cap'n Please Mr. Bossman . . .

Beneatha (*suddenly*). Lindner!

Walter. That's right! That's good. I told him to come right over.

Beneatha (*fiercely, understanding*). For what? What do you want to see him for!

Walter (*looking at his sister*). We going to do business with him.

Mama. What you talking 'bout, son?

Walter. Talking 'bout life, Mama. You all always telling me to see life like it is. Well—I laid in there on my back today . . . and I figured it out. Life just like it is. Who gets and who don't get. (*He sits down with his coat on and laughs.*) Mama, you know it's all divided up. Life is. Sure enough. Between the takers and the "tooken." (*He laughs.*) I've figured it out finally. (*He looks around at them.*) Yeah. Some of us always getting "tooken." (*He laughs.*) People like Willy Harris, they don't never get "tooken." And you know why the rest of us do? 'Cause we all mixed up. Mixed up bad. We get to looking 'round for the right and the wrong; and we worry about it and cry about it and stay up nights trying to figure out 'bout the wrong and the right of things all the time . . . And all the time, man, them takers is out there operating, just taking and taking. Willy Harris? Shoot—Willy Harris don't even count.

CLARIFY

Pause at line 394. What "business" does Walter want to do with Mr. Lindner? Do you think Mama will agree with this? Explain why or why not.

WORD STUDY

Why does Walter use the word "tooken" in lines 400–403? What does he mean by it? Who are the "takers" and who are the "tooken" that he refers to?

from A Raisin in the Sun

DRAMA

Pause at line 429. What decision has Walter made? What **conflicts** arise as a result of Walter's decision?

INTERPRET

Pause at line 431. Why is Beneatha horrified by Walter's plan? What does she mean by the "honest-to-God bottom"?

IDENTIFY CAUSE & EFFECT

Pause at line 447. What causes Walter to plan to accept Mr. Lindner's offer?

He don't even count in the big scheme of things. But I'll say one thing for old Willy Harris . . . he's taught me something. He's taught me to keep my eye on what counts in this world. Yeah—(*Shouting out a little*) Thanks, Willy!

Ruth. What did you call that man for, Walter Lee?

Walter. Called him to tell him to come on over to the show. Gonna put on a show for the man. Just what he wants to see. You see, Mama, the man came here today and he told us that them people out there where you want us to move—well they so upset they willing to pay us *not* to move! (*He laughs again.*) And—and oh, Mama—you would of been proud of the way me and Ruth and Bennie acted. We told him to get out . . . Lord have mercy! We told the man to get out! Oh, we was some proud folks this afternoon, yeah. (*He lights a cigarette.*) We were still full of that old-time stuff . . .

Ruth (*coming toward him slowly*). You talking 'bout taking them people's money to keep us from moving in that house?

Walter. I ain't just talking 'bout it, baby—I'm telling you that's what's going to happen!

Beneatha. Oh, God! Where is the bottom! Where is the real honest-to-God bottom so he can't go any farther!

Walter. See—that's the old stuff. You and that boy that was here today. You all want everybody to carry a flag and a spear and sing some marching songs, huh? You wanna spend your life looking into things and trying to find the right and the wrong part, huh? Yeah. You know what's going to happen to that boy someday—he'll find himself sitting in a dungeon, locked in forever—and the takers will have the key! Forget it, baby! There ain't no causes—there ain't nothing but taking in this world, and he who takes most is smartest—and it don't make a bit of difference *how*.

Mama. You making something inside me cry, son. Some awful pain inside me.

Walter. Don't cry, Mama. Understand. That white man is going to walk in that door able to write checks for more money than we ever had. It's important to him and I'm going to help him . . . I'm going to put on the show, Mama.

Mama. Son—I come from five generations of people who was slaves and sharecroppers—but ain't nobody in my family never let nobody pay 'em no money that was a way of telling us we wasn't fit to walk the earth. We ain't never been that poor. (*Raising her eyes and looking at him*) We ain't never been that—dead inside.

Beneatha. Well—we are dead now. All the talk about dreams and sunlight that goes on in this house. It's all dead now.

Walter. What's the matter with you all! I didn't make this world! It was give to me this way! Lord, yes, I want me some yachts someday! Yes, I want to hang some real pearls 'round my wife's neck. Ain't she supposed to wear no pearls? Somebody tell me—tell me, who decides which women is suppose to wear pearls in this world. I tell you I am a *man*—and I think my wife should wear some pearls in this world!

[*This last line hangs a good while and* WALTER *begins to move about the room. The word "Man" has penetrated his consciousness; he mumbles it to himself repeatedly between strange agitated pauses as he moves about.*]

Mama. Baby, how you going to feel on the inside?

Walter. Fine! . . . Going to feel fine . . . a man . . .

Mama. You won't have nothing left then, Walter Lee.

Walter (*coming to her*). I'm going to feel fine, Mama. I'm going to look that man in the eyes and say—(*He falters.*)—and say, "All right, Mr. Lindner—(*He falters even more.*)—that's *your* neighborhood out there! You got the right to keep it like you want! You got the right to have it like you want! Just write the check and—the house is yours." And—and I am going to say—(*His voice almost breaks.*) "And you—you people just put the money in my hand and you won't have to live next to this bunch of stinking . . ." (*He straightens up and moves away from his mother, walking around the room.*) And maybe—maybe I'll

> **CLARIFY**
>
> Pause at line 453. How do Mama's lines clarify Beneatha's reaction to Walter's plan?

> **INFER**
>
> Pause at line 469. What does Mama's reaction to Walter indicate about her **character**?

from A Raisin in the Sun

INFER

Why does Walter speak lines 481–487 in **dialect**? What is he implying?

DRAMA

Pause at line 510. How does Mama address the **conflict** between Beneatha and her brother?

VOCABULARY

epitaph (ep′ə·taf′) *n.:* words on a tombstone.

480 just get down on my black knees . . . (*He does so;* RUTH *and* BENNIE *and* MAMA *watch him in frozen horror.*) "Captain, Mistuh, Bossman—(*He starts crying.*) A-hee-hee-hee! (*Wringing his hands in profoundly anguished imitation of the slow-witted movie stereotype*) Yassssssuh! Great White Father, just gi' ussen de money, fo' God's sake, and we's— we's ain't gwine come out deh and dirty up yo' white folks neighborhood . . ." (*He breaks down completely.*) And I'll feel fine! Fine! FINE! (*He gets up and goes into the bedroom.*)

Beneatha. That is not a man. That is nothing but a toothless rat.

490 **Mama.** Yes—death done come in this here house. (*She is nodding, slowly, reflectively.*) Done come walking in my house on the lips of my children. You what supposed to be my beginning again. You—what supposed to be my harvest. (*To* BENEATHA) You—you mourning your brother?

Beneatha. He's no brother of mine.

Mama. What you say?

Beneatha. I said that that individual in that room is no brother of mine.

Mama. That's what I thought you said. You feeling like you better than he is today? (BENEATHA *does not answer.*) Yes? What 500 you tell him a minute ago? That he wasn't a man. Yes? You give him up for me? You done wrote his **epitaph** too—like the rest of the world? Well, who give you the privilege?

Beneatha. Be on my side for once! You saw what he just did, Mama! You saw him—down on his knees. Wasn't it you who taught me to despise any man who would do that? Do what he's going to do?

Mama. Yes—I taught you that. Me and your daddy. But I thought I taught you something else too . . . I thought I 510 taught you to love him.

Beneatha. Love him? There is nothing left to love.

Mama. There is *always* something left to love. And if you ain't learned that, you ain't learned nothing. (*Looking at her*) Have you cried for that boy today? I don't mean for yourself and

Opening-night cast of *A Raisin in the Sun,* New York City, April 26, 2004.
© Scott Eells/Getty Images

for the family 'cause we lost the money. I mean for him: what he been through and what it done to him. Child, when do you think is the time to love somebody the most? When they done good and made things easy for everybody? Well then, you ain't through learning—because that ain't the time at all. It's when he's at his lowest and can't believe in hisself 'cause the world done whipped him so! When you starts measuring somebody, measure him right, child, measure him right. Make sure you done taken into account what hills and valleys he come through before he got to wherever he is.

PARAPHRASE

Paraphrase lines 521–524 of Mama's speech.

_____
_____
_____
_____
_____

from A Raisin in the Sun 261

PREDICT

Pause at line 533. Both Mr. Lindner and the moving men have arrived. What do you think will happen next?

_____
_____
_____
_____
_____

IDENTIFY

Pause at line 551. Describe the **tone** Mr. Lindner takes when speaking with the Younger family. Underline the words and phrases that lead you to identify his tone in this way.

_____
_____
_____
_____
_____

INFER

Why do you think Mama tells Travis to stay?

_____
_____
_____
_____
_____

[TRAVIS *bursts into the room at the end of the speech, leaving the door open.*]

Travis. Grandmama—the moving men are downstairs! The truck just pulled up.

Mama (*turning and looking at him*). Are they, baby? They 530 downstairs?

[*She sighs and sits.* LINDNER *appears in the doorway. He peers in and knocks lightly, to gain attention, and comes in. All turn to look at him.*]

Lindner (*hat and briefcase in hand*). Uh—hello . . .

[RUTH *crosses mechanically to the bedroom door and opens it and lets it swing open freely and slowly as the lights come up on* WALTER *within, still in his coat, sitting at the far corner of the room. He looks up and out through the room to* LINDNER.]

Ruth. He's here.

540 [*A long minute passes and* WALTER *slowly gets up.*]

Lindner (*coming to the table with efficiency, putting his briefcase on the table and starting to unfold papers and unscrew fountain pens*). Well, I certainly was glad to hear from you people. (WALTER *has begun the trek out of the room, slowly and awkwardly, rather like a small boy, passing the back of his sleeve across his mouth from time to time.*) Life can really be so much simpler than people let it be most of the time. Well—with whom do I negotiate? You, Mrs. Younger, or your son here? (MAMA *sits with her hands folded on her lap and her eyes closed* 550 *as* WALTER *advances.* TRAVIS *goes closer to* LINDNER *and looks at the papers curiously.*) Just some official papers, sonny.

Ruth. Travis, you go downstairs—

Mama (*opening her eyes and looking into* WALTER'S). No. Travis, you stay right here. And you make him understand what you doing, Walter Lee. You teach him good. Like Willy Harris taught you. You show where our five generations done come to. (WALTER *looks from her to the boy, who grins at him innocently.*) Go ahead, son—(*She folds her hands and closes her eyes.*) Go ahead.

Walter (*looks down into his boy's eyes.* TRAVIS *grins at him merrily and* WALTER *draws him beside him with his arm lightly around his shoulders*). Well, Mr. Lindner. (BENEATHA *turns away.*) We called you—(*There is a profound, simple groping quality in his speech.*)—because, well, me and my family (*He looks around and shifts from one foot to the other.*) Well—we are very plain people . . .

Lindner. Yes—

Walter. I mean—I have worked as a chauffeur most of my life—and my wife here, she does domestic work in people's kitchens. So does my mother. I mean—we are plain people . . .

Lindner. Yes, Mr. Younger—

Walter (*really like a small boy, looking down at his shoes and then up at the man*). And—uh—well, my father, well, he was a laborer most of his life. . . .

Lindner (*absolutely confused*). Uh, yes—yes, I understand. (*He turns back to the contract.*)

Walter (*looking down at his toes once again*). My father almost beat a man to death once because this man called him a bad name or something, you know what I mean?

Lindner (*looking up, frozen*). No, no, I'm afraid I don't—

Walter (*finally straightening up*). Well—what I mean is that we come from people who had a lot of *pride*. I mean—we are very proud people. And that's my sister over there and she's going to be a doctor—and we are very proud—

Lindner. Well—I am sure that is very nice, but—

Walter. What I am telling you is that we called you over here to tell you that we are very proud and that this—(*Signaling to* TRAVIS) Travis, come here. (TRAVIS *crosses and* WALTER *draws him before him facing the man.*) This is my son, and he makes

---

DRAMA

Everyone is waiting to hear what Walter will say to Mr. Lindner. How do Walter's speeches on this page build **suspense**?

_____
_____
_____
_____
_____
_____
_____
_____
_____
_____
_____
_____
_____
_____
_____
_____

DRAMA

Underline the **stage directions** that show that Walter has reached a turning point.

from A Raisin in the Sun

DRAMA

The **climax** of a drama is the most exciting or emotional moment, when the outcome is decided. Underline Walter's statement that marks the play's climax.

IDENTIFY

Identify the **irony** in Beneatha's remark in line 602.

_____
_____
_____
_____
_____

INFER

In lines 611–616, Mr. Lindner wonders whether the Youngers know what they are getting into. Do you think the Youngers are prepared to live in their new community? Explain.

_____
_____
_____
_____
_____

590 the sixth generation our family in this country. And we have all thought about your offer and we have decided to move into our house because my father—my father—he earned it for us brick by brick. (MAMA *has her eyes closed and is rocking back and forth as though she were in church, with her head nodding the Amen yes.*) We don't want to make no trouble for nobody or fight no causes—but we will try to be good neighbors. And that's all we got to say. (*He looks the man absolutely in the eyes.*) We don't want your money. (*He turns and walks away from the man.*)

600 **Lindner** (*looking around at all of them*). I take it then—that you have decided to occupy . . .

Beneatha. That's what the man said.

Lindner (*to* MAMA *in her reverie*). Then I would like to appeal to you, Mrs. Younger. You are older and wiser and understand things better I am sure . . .

Mama (*rising*). I am afraid you don't understand. My son said we was going to move and there ain't nothing left for me to say. (*Shaking her head with double meaning*) You know how these young folks is nowadays, mister. Can't do a thing with 610 'em. Goodbye.

Lindner (*folding up his materials*). Well—if you are that final about it . . . there is nothing left for me to say. (*He finishes, almost ignored by the family, who are concentrating on* WALTER LEE. *At the door* LINDNER *halts and looks around.*) I sure hope you people know what you're getting into. (*He shakes his head and exits.*)

Ruth (*looking around and coming to life*). Well, for God's sake—if the moving men are here—LET'S GET THIS BLESSED FAMILY OUT OF HERE!

620 **Mama** (*into action*). Ain't it the truth! Look at all this here mess. Ruth, put Travis' good jacket on him . . . Walter Lee, fix your tie and tuck your shirt in, you look like somebody's hoodlum! Lord have mercy, where is my plant? (*She flies to get it amid the*

general bustling of the family, who are deliberately trying to ignore the nobility of the past moment.) You all start on down . . . Travis child, don't go empty-handed . . . Ruth, where did I put that box with my skillets in it? I want to be in charge of it myself . . . I'm going to make us the biggest dinner we ever ate tonight . . . Beneatha, what's the matter with them stockings? Pull them things up, girl . . .

[*The family starts to file out as two moving men appear and begin to carry out the heavier pieces of furniture, bumping into the family as they move about.*]

Beneatha. Mama, Asagai asked me to marry him today and go to Africa—

Mama (*in the middle of her getting-ready activity*). He did? You ain't old enough to marry nobody—(*Seeing the moving men lifting one of her chairs* **precariously**) Darling, that ain't no bale of cotton, please handle it so we can sit in it again! I had that chair twenty-five years . . .

[*The movers sigh with exasperation and go on with their work.*]

Beneatha (*girlishly and unreasonably trying to pursue the conversation*). To go to Africa, Mama—be a doctor in Africa . . .

Mama (*distracted*). Yes, baby—

Walter. *Africa!* What he want you to go to Africa for?

Beneatha. To practice there . . .

Walter. Girl, if you don't get all them silly ideas out your head! You better marry yourself a man with some loot . . .

Beneatha (*angrily, precisely as in the first scene of the play*). What have you got to do with who I marry!

Walter. Plenty. Now I think George Murchison—

[*He and* BENEATHA *go out yelling at each other vigorously and the anger is loud and real till their voices diminish.* RUTH *stands at the door and turns to* MAMA *and smiles knowingly.*]

INFER

Pause at line 630. Why do you think Mama is suddenly concerned about Beneatha's appearance?

VOCABULARY

precariously (pri·ker′ē·əs·lē) *adv.:* in an unstable manner.

IDENTIFY

Pause at line 651. How would you describe the **tone** at this point in the play? Explain how it has changed.

from A Raisin in the Sun

DRAMA

In this drama, is Walter a **static** (unchanging) or **dynamic** (changing, growing) **character**? What about Lindner? Explain.

_____
_____
_____
_____
_____
_____
_____

VOCABULARY

raucously (rô′kəs·lē) adv.: loudly and roughly.

INTERPRET

What does the plant **symbolize** to Mama? How is it **symbolic** of her character?

_____
_____
_____
_____
_____
_____
_____
_____

Mama (*fixing her hat at last*). Yeah—they something all right, my children . . .

Ruth. Yeah—they're something. Let's go, Lena.

Mama (*stalling, starting to look around at the house*). Yes—I'm coming. Ruth—

660 **Ruth.** Yes?

Mama (*quietly, woman to woman*). He finally come into his manhood today, didn't he? Kind of like a rainbow after the rain . . .

Ruth (*biting her lip lest her own pride explode in front of* MAMA). Yes, Lena.

[WALTER'S *voice calls for them* **raucously**.]

Walter (*offstage*). Y'all come on! These people charges by the hour, you know!

Mama (*waving* RUTH *out vaguely*). All right, honey—go on down. I be down directly.

670 [RUTH *hesitates, then exits.* MAMA *stands, at last alone in the living room, her plant on the table before her as the lights start to come down. She looks around at all the walls and ceilings and suddenly, despite herself, while the children call below, a great heaving thing rises in her and she puts her fist to her mouth to stifle it, takes a final desperate look, pulls her coat about her, pats her hat, and goes out. The lights dim down. The door opens and she comes back in, grabs her plant, and goes out for the last time.*]

[*Curtain.*]

MEET THE WRITER

Lorraine Hansberry (1930–1965) was the daughter of well-known Chicago intellectuals and activists. In their home she met some of the greatest African Americans of her parents' generation, including the poet Langston Hughes, the musician Duke Ellington, the athletes Joe Louis and Jesse Owens, the actor-singer-activist Paul Robeson, and the writer and civil rights leader W.E.B. Du Bois. In 1938, Hansberry's father purchased a house in an all-white neighborhood. The family was threatened by a white mob and was forced to leave by a court order. Hansberry's father took the case to the Supreme Court, before which he won a favorable decision. Despite the victory, the experience left him disillusioned and bitter.

A Raisin in the Sun, which resonates with these feelings, was written in 1957. In 1959, it became the first play by an African American woman to be produced on Broadway. It won the New York Drama Critics Circle Award, a first for any African American playwright, and was a great success with critics, activists, and artists as well with theatergoers of different ages and races.

Although her career was cut short by her death from cancer when she was still young, Hansberry left behind an important legacy. Before turning to drama, she wrote and edited articles for Paul Robeson's progressive magazine, *Freedom.* She also wrote several other plays in addition to *A Raisin in the Sun.* Much of Hansberry's work was collected and arranged by Robert Nemiroff in the "informal autobiography" *To Be Young, Gifted and Black.*

SKILLS PRACTICE

from *A Raisin in the Sun*

SKILLS FOCUS

Reading Skills
Infer causes and effects.

Cause-and-Effect Chart   Complete the following chart about the events in Act III of *A Raisin in the Sun*. Sometimes you have to infer a cause or effect. Fill in the blanks, and then identify the motivations, or reasons, behind the cause or effect.

Cause	Effect	Motivations/Reasons
1.	Ruth promises to work twenty hours a day to make extra money.	
2. Beneatha announces that Walter is no brother of hers.		
3.	Walter calls Lindner and announces that he will accept Lindner's offer.	
4. Mama tells Travis to stay and listen to his father when Lindner arrives.		
5.	Walter refuses Lindner's offer.	
6.	Mama understands that Walter has come into his manhood.	

268   Part 1   Collection 10: Drama

Skills Review

from A Raisin in the Sun

VOCABULARY AND COMPREHENSION

A. Recognizing Dialect   Fill in each blank below with the appropriate word from the Word Box. Circle all the examples of dialect that are not standard English.

1. Maria loves her first pair of high heels, but she teeters in them _____.

2. After scoring the winning touchdown, Ken was _____. He cried out, "This be the best day of my life!"

3. Jackie is so deeply involved in her art project that she is _____ of what is going on around her.

4. Howard said, "Don't write me an _____. I ain't dead just yet."

5. On the last day of school, all the students burst _____ from the building, loudly calling out, "Good-bye!"

6. When Paula was collecting signatures for a town park, she was surprised to hear a neighbor say, "We don't want no _____ around here."

> **Word Box**
> exuberant
> agitation
> oblivious
> epitaph
> precariously
> raucously

B. Reading Comprehension   Answer each question below.

1. *A Raisin in the Sun* takes place in a specific place and time: Chicago in the 1950s. What makes the play a classic, a work that is still relevant to today's audiences?

   _____
   _____
   _____

2. How does Hansberry answer the question "What happens to a dream deferred?" _____
   _____

SKILLS FOCUS

Vocabulary Skills
Identify dialect.

from A Raisin in the Sun   269

Part Two

Reading Informational Texts

Informational Articles

Academic Vocabulary

These are the terms you should know
as you read and analyze the selections.

Source A person, book, or document that provides information on a topic.

Elaboration The addition of details to support the ideas already presented in a work.

Synthesis The merging of information gathered from more than one source.

• • •

Argument A series of statements designed to persuade the reader to accept a claim, or opinion.

Claim An opinion on a topic or issue, often stated as a generalization, or broad statement that covers many situations.

Evidence Material presented as proof of a claim or an idea. Evidence includes facts, statistics, examples, anecdotes (brief stories about real people), and quotations.

Credibility The believability of an argument or statement.

Before You Read

Reign of the Reader by M. Freeman

In this informational article, you'll be reading about reading—that is, the long-ago practice of reading aloud to skilled workers in the cigar factories of Cuba and Florida. After you read, think of questions that you'd still like answered. You may want to do some additional research about this fascinating historical phenomenon.

INFORMATIONAL FOCUS: HOW TO GENERATE QUESTIONS

When you start to do a research project, your first step is to think of questions that will help you find the information you're looking for. Here are some guidelines for asking useful research questions:

- **Check the subheads** of an informational article to locate ideas for a limited topic to research.
- **Focus on one aspect** of your subject, and limit your questions to a narrow topic. Try to focus your questions on the main idea of your topic.
- **Ask the *5W-How?* questions**—*who? what? when? where? why?* and *how?*—about your topic. Be sure to ask reasonable questions that you will be able to answer.

READING SKILLS: MAKE A KWL CHART

Practice asking and answering questions by completing a KWL chart like the one below. Fill in the first two columns of the KWL chart *before* you read the article. In the first column, list what you know about cigar making, Cuba, or the labor movement and workers' rights. In the second column, list questions you would like answered as you read about the cigar-factory readers. Then, *after* you read the article, fill out the last column. Some sample items are given below.

What I Already KNOW	What I WANT to Find Out	What I LEARNED
Cuba is an island nation in the Caribbean near the southern tip of Florida.	Who hired the readers?	
Cuba is famous for its cigars.	What did the readers read?	

SKILLS FOCUS

Reading Skills
Generate research questions. Make a KWL chart.

Vocabulary Skills
Identify and understand synonyms.

ARTICLE

VOCABULARY DEVELOPMENT

PREVIEW SELECTION VOCABULARY

Preview these vocabulary words before you begin to read.

meticulous (mə·tik′yōō·ləs) *adj.:* very careful in the treatment of details.

Making cigars by hand required workers to be **meticulous**.

solidarity (säl′ə·dar′ə·tē) *n.:* unity of purpose, interests, and feelings among members of a class or group.

Cigar makers, like other skilled workers, felt a sense of **solidarity** *that gave them strength.*

agitating (aj′i·tāt′iŋ) *v.:* stirring up public interest in and support for a cause.

Cuban revolutionaries were **agitating** *for political and social changes.*

perennial (pə·ren′ē·əl) *adj.:* lasting; enduring.

The workers had **perennial** *favorites that the readers read again and again.*

whimsical (hwim′zi·kəl) *adj.:* full of fanciful humor.

The readers typically finished the day by reading something light and **whimsical**.

SYNONYMS

A **synonym** is a word that has the same meaning or close to the same meaning as another word. If you aren't satisfied with a certain word in your writing, you can try to replace it with a synonym. A **thesaurus** is the most useful tool for finding synonyms. Most thesauri list synonyms based on a word's different shades of meaning, or **connotations**. When using a thesaurus, you should look at all the synonyms given and follow the cross-references until you find the exact meaning you would like to convey.

Think about the following synonyms of the word *reign: rule, administration, command, dominion, supremacy, sway, tenure.* Would any of these words be a better choice in the title of the following article? *Rule* might sound good—similar to *reign. Rule* expresses the importance of the readers, but it also implies *law* or *regulation. Tenure* is the only word that conveys the time aspect of *reign,* but it wouldn't sound as good or express the same importance. None of the synonyms would work as well in the title as the original word, *reign.*

Reign of the Reader

Reign of the Reader

M. Freeman

> **BACKGROUND: Informational Text and Social Studies**
>
> In Cuba during the mid-1800s, readers were hired to read out loud to workers in cigar-making factories. For four hours each day, these *lectores* read great literature, news reports, and socially relevant stories. The workers controlled this practice, much to the annoyance of the factory owners.

GENERATE QUESTIONS

Ask at least two questions about the title of this article.

VOCABULARY

meticulous (mə·tik′yōō·ləs) *adj.*: extremely careful in the treatment of details.

IDENTIFY

Pause at line 16. In addition to providing entertainment, what did the readers do for the cigar workers?

No one is certain of the exact place it started. But somewhere in nineteenth-century Cuba, people started reading to help bored manual laborers pass the time. The idea caught on, and in the island's fabled tobacco industry, the role of *el lector*, the reader, took hold.

Fashioning fine cigars by hand was demanding, **meticulous** work, certainly, but once learned it could not have been mentally stimulating. Conversation helped, but the reading—*la lectura*—helped more.

Gary Mormino, professor of history at University of South Florida, Tampa, has studied and written extensively about *la lectura*, and he stresses that it represented far more than entertainment during a repetitive job. The readers broadened the intellectual scope and sharpened the political outlook of the workers they read to. And those workers appreciated, even revered them for it.

The readers even helped shape history at the turn of the twentieth century, when the institution was at its height. But even from its earliest beginnings, the practice was a threat to the status quo, and the factory owners knew it. But it took them half

"Reign of the Reader" by M. Freeman from *Reading Today*, December 1, 2001. Copyright © 2001 by International Reading Association, Inc. Reproduced by permission of the publisher.

Cigar workers listen to a reader while they work (c. 1900–1910).
©Hulton-Deutsch Collection/CORBIS

a century to stop it, because it was a practice that the workers themselves controlled from the beginning.

Self-Selected

From the beginning—readers were already well established in Cuban cigar factories by the 1860s—the workers decided what the readers would read and how much they would be paid. The workers paid the readers themselves, because from the beginning the factory owners were opposed to the idea, mostly because of the type of literature the workers wanted to hear.

30   The cigar makers were highly skilled and had a sense of **solidarity,** and could not be simply fired and replaced. The labor movement was a strong force in the late nineteenth century, and the cigar workers wanted to learn, as they worked, about the fore-

GENERATE QUESTIONS

What questions do you have about the photograph above?

_____
_____
_____
_____
_____

VOCABULARY

solidarity (säl′ə·dar′ə·tē) *n.:* unity of purpose, interests, and feelings among members of a class or group.

Reign of the Reader   275

IDENTIFY CAUSE & EFFECT

Pause at line 41. Why did cigar factories spring up in Florida?

_____
_____
_____

TEXT FEATURES

Underline the subhead in line 42. What do you think this tells you about the information to follow?

_____
_____
_____

CLARIFY

Re-read lines 51–62. Briefly explain what the readers did during their second hour of reading.

_____
_____
_____

VOCABULARY

agitating (aj′i·tāt′iŋ) v.: stirring up public interest in and support for a cause.

perennial (pə·ren′ē·əl) adj.: lasting; enduring.

whimsical (hwim′zi·kəl) adj.: full of fanciful humor.

---

most thinkers in progressive politics. This did not sit well with the factory owners, but there was little they could do about it.

At the same time, revolutionaries were **agitating** to throw the Spanish colonial overlords out of Cuba. This unrest eventually pushed many cigar makers out of the island, and cigar factories sprang up in Key West, Florida, and particularly in a section of the city of Tampa that came to be known as Ybor City, for the cigar manufacturer Vicente Martínez Ybor.

Prose and Politics

There were cigar factories and readers in other places, but the heyday of the reader was certainly in Ybor City from the late 1880s to about 1930. There were hundreds of them active at any one time.

The practice had a certain formal structure. In some factories, the reader sat in a plain chair, but at many they had a platform on which the reader sat and stood. They typically read for about four hours a day.

The first hour was devoted to reading newspapers, which would be translated into Spanish by the readers if necessary. During the second hour, the reader read a serialized novel. This was "always the most significant act of the day," Mormino says.

The readers would assume the voices of the characters, acting out the dialogue and injecting as much drama and emotion as possible into their reading. The better able they were to do this, the more respect they were accorded.

Cervantes' *Don Quixote* was a **perennial** favorite, but also popular were such novelists of the day as Victor Hugo and Emile Zola. The work of these French social realists represented, at the time, a progressive political outlook.

The edge sharpened in the third hour, with what the readers called "political economy"—radical social thinkers such as Bakunin and Marx. The fourth hour was devoted to something like Shakespeare or a short story with a **whimsical** theme, always something light to end the day with, often a story by Benito Pérez-Galdós, whom Mormino described as "the O. Henry of Spain."

End of an Era

The readers were the superstars of their day and place, Mormino says, not least because they helped the cigar workers attain a degree of intellectual sophistication few manual laborers could hope to equal. The opportunity was not limited to men—women were present in the factories as well as men, and at least two women were active as readers.

The institution furthered the Cuban revolution against Spanish rule, since the readers and workers were strong supporters of the revolutionary movement and gave its leader, the brilliant writer José Martí, a hero's welcome when he visited Ybor City in 1891.

But by 1931, unsuccessful strikes had weakened the power of the cigar workers, the Depression had hurt cigar sales, and the owners settled on the readers as scapegoats and banned them. The workers went on strike to save their beloved readers, but the strike was broken and the readers' podiums torn down. The radio replaced the reader, and increasingly machines replaced the workers.

But the institution of *la lectura* still stands, Mormino says, not just as an historical curiosity but as an "almost unique" example of how merely reading aloud could be so strongly loved, so fiercely defended, and how such a deep love of the life of the mind could be instilled in people who labored with their hands and empowered their intellects in those hot Florida factories in the days, gone forever, of *el lector*—the reader.

GENERATE QUESTIONS

Pause at line 69. What questions do you have about the texts that the readers read?

INTERPRET

Re-read lines 71–81. In what ways was the practice of reading in cigar factories socially significant?

GENERATE QUESTIONS

If you could ask Gary Mormino only one question about his research into *la lectura*, what question would you ask?

WORD STUDY

Lector comes from the Latin word *legere,* meaning "to read." What is a similar word in English that comes from the same root?

Reign of the Reader   277

SKILLS PRACTICE

Reign of the Reader

SKILLS FOCUS

Reading Skills
Generate research question.

5W-How? Chart   Imagine you are doing research on the cigar-factory readers. Think about the information you learned from the article. Then, use the investigation guide below to focus your research.

Ask *who? what? when? where? why?* and *how?*—the *5W-How?* questions—about your topic. Remember that you can ask more than one of each type of question.

Investigation Guide	
Who?	
What?	
When?	
Where?	
Why?	
How?	

Part 2   Reading Informational Texts

Skills Review

Reign of the Reader

VOCABULARY AND COMPREHENSION

A. Synonyms Write the word from the Word Box that is a synonym of each given word. Use a thesaurus for help if necessary.

1. cohesion _____

2. perpetual _____

3. painstaking _____

4. rousing _____

5. amusing _____

Word Box

meticulous
solidarity
agitating
perennial
whimsical

B. Reading Comprehension Answer each question below.

1. Why did it take factory owners so long to put an end to the reading?
   _____
   _____

2. Where and when did the heyday of the reader occur?
   _____
   _____

3. Which three novelists are mentioned as favorites of the workers?
   _____
   _____

4. What was typically read during the fourth hour?
   _____
   _____

SKILLS FOCUS

Vocabulary Skills Identify synonyms.

Before You Read

Matthew Henson's Polar Travails; National Geographic Society Honors Arctic Explorer; Matthew Henson

Robert Peary received sole credit for discovering the North Pole. But he did not do it alone. In the following articles, you will learn about Matthew Henson, a man who had as much impact on the expeditions as Peary himself.

INFORMATIONAL FOCUS: SYNTHESIZING SOURCES

When you research a topic, you collect information from several sources. After that, you need to synthesize what you've learned—put it together to better grasp the subject. Here are some guidelines for synthesizing sources:

- **Find the main idea** of each source.
- **Compare and contrast** the ideas presented in each source. What do they have in common? How are they different?
- **Connect the main ideas.** Now, consider all your sources as a group. What **conclusions** can you draw from your sources?

Source 1	Source 2	Source 3
Main Ideas	Main Ideas	Main Ideas
⬇	⬇	⬇
Synthesize: What I can conclude about issue or topic		

SKILLS FOCUS

Reading Skills
Synthesize information from several sources on a single topic. Understand elements of informational articles.

Vocabulary Skills
Create word maps.

READING SKILLS: INFORMATIONAL ARTICLES

Informational articles, such as those you find in magazines or on the World Wide Web, are meant to teach as well as to entertain. They deliver factual information, such as dates, quotations, and statistics. They also guide the reader in the subject matter through text features, such as photographs and headings.

The three informational articles you'll read are all on the same topic: the remarkable story of Matthew Henson. As you read, look for

- the **main idea** of each piece
- **details** that support the main idea
- **text features,** such as headings and visuals

VOCABULARY DEVELOPMENT

PREVIEW SELECTION VOCABULARY

Preview these vocabulary words before you begin to read.

indispensable (in′di·spen′sə·bəl) *adj.*: essential.

> Henson's range of knowledge proved **indispensable** to the other explorers.

abiding (ə·bīd′iŋ) *adj.* long-lasting; unchanging.

> Henson's **abiding** belief in his contributions ultimately led to his recognition for them.

interred (in·turd′) *v.*: buried.

> It is a great honor to be **interred** in Arlington National Cemetery.

sojourn (sō′jurn) *n.*: period of time away from home.

> Henson may have longed to return home after his **sojourn** at sea.

stevedore (stē′və·dôr′) *n.*: one who loads and unloads ships.

> Working on the ship as a **stevedore** was just one of many experiences that prepared Henson for his explorations.

WORD MAPPING

Sometimes you are able to figure out the meaning of a word from its context in a sentence, but at times you may need to refer to a dictionary. If you want to pin down the precise meaning of an unfamiliar word, create a **word map**, or semantic map. Ask yourself questions about the word. Then, use the answers to the questions to help you figure out the word's meaning. Here is a sample word map for *indispensable*:

What words mean the opposite of <u>indispensable</u>?
- disposable
- unnecessary

What makes something <u>indispensable</u>?
- usefulness
- uniqueness

indispensable

What things are often considered <u>indispensable</u>?
- advice
- family photographs

Make up two original sentences using the word <u>indispensable</u>.
- My experience on the yearbook will be <u>indispensable</u> as I work to become a photographer.
- My jazz compact discs are an <u>indispensable</u> part of my collection.

Matthew Henson's Polar Travails

from Land magazine

IDENTIFY

Pause at line 10. What was Matthew Henson's title when he signed on to his first expedition? Circle it.

INFER

The description of Henson's duties is vague. What kind of responsibilities might being a "body servant" entail?

_____

_____

_____

VOCABULARY

indispensable
(in′di·spen′sə·bəl)
adj.: essential.

DRAW CONCLUSIONS

Pause at line 26. The writer points out that Henson did a number of difficult tasks before building a shelter for himself. What **conclusion** can you draw about Henson from this detail?

_____

_____

_____

_____

In the race for the North Pole, perhaps the most accomplished of the explorers—certainly the most overlooked—was Matthew Henson, the son of a sharecropper, who had crewed on ships to China, Japan, North Africa and southern Russia before he turned 18. He met Peary at about that age and signed on as "body servant" for an expedition to Nicaragua. As he wrote in his 1912 autobiography, *A Negro Explorer at the North Pole,* Henson would travel with Peary for the next twenty-two years "in the capacity of assistant: a term that covers a multitude of
10   duties, abilities, and responsibilities."

Henson struggled every inch as far as Peary, while at the same time working to keep expedition members alive and on the move. According to 1908 team member Donald B. MacMillan, Henson, "with years of experience equal to that of Peary himself, was **indispensable** to Peary and of more real value than the combined services of all four white men. . . . He made all the sledges, he made all the camp equipment, he talked the [Eskimo] language like a native."

The Eskimos claimed that nobody drove dogs better than
20   Henson. They said he could fix a broken-down sledge as fast and as well as any of them. During the 1908–09 journey to the Pole, as Peary rode in a sledge, his frostbitten feet all but useless, Henson walked. When the team stopped for the day, Henson built Peary's igloo, took care of the dogs, repaired equipment, and hunted hares "with wolfish desperation." Only then did he build shelter for himself.

"After twenty-two long years of service with Peary we are now as strangers," he wrote in the *Boston American* on July 17,

"Matthew Henson's Polar Travails" by Matthew Henson from *Life: The Greatest Adventures of All Time*, with a Foreword by Will Steger. Copyright © 2000 by **Time, Inc.** Originally appeared in *Land*, 2000. Reproduced by permission of the publisher.

1910. What had happened between the two men? Plenty. Henson went on to say that Peary had intended to make his dash to the Pole without Henson. "I was sorely disappointed," he wrote, "but somehow I had an **abiding** faith that he was wrong in his calculations." Henson believed they were already at the Pole. After an hour, reported Henson, Peary returned with a "long and serious" face. "He would not speak to me," Henson wrote. "From the moment I declared to Commander Peary that I believed we stood upon the Pole he apparently ceased to be my friend."

Henson tried to mend the rift, attempting to contact Peary but receiving no response. Or hardly any response: After Henson gave a lecture about his adventures, Peary sent a telegram warning him not to use photographs of their expeditions. There was irony to this. Henson claimed that Peary had never returned some 110 images that he—Henson—had paid for, exposed, developed, and then lent to Peary.

For the most part ignored by organizations such as the National Geographic Society, which sponsored several of Peary's expeditions, Henson defiantly continued to tell his side of the story. Certainly some did believe him, and in 1937 he was made an honorary member of the Explorers Club.

Henson died in 1955 at age eighty-eight and was buried in New York's Woodlawn Cemetery. In 1988, after a tireless campaign by Harvard professor S. Allen Counter, Henson's remains were transferred to Arlington National Cemetery, where, sixty-eight years earlier, Peary had been **interred** with great ceremony. On Matthew Henson's headstone are engraved the last words from his memoir: "The lure of the Arctic is tugging at my heart, to me the trail is calling! The Old Trail! The Trail that is always New!"

VOCABULARY

abiding (ə·bīd′ĭng) *adj.* long-lasting; unchanging.

interred (ĭn·tûrd′) *v.:* buried.

DRAW CONCLUSIONS

Re-read lines 27–37. Describe the reason why Henson's relationship to Peary changed. What conclusions can you draw about Peary based on this detail?

Matthew Henson.
©Topham/The Image Works

Matthew Henson's Polar Travails 283

National Geographic Society Honors Arctic Explorer

Jennifer Mapes
from NationalGeographic.com

SYNTHESIZE SOURCES

Pause at line 9. What new information do you learn from the introduction of this article?

_____
_____
_____
_____
_____

IDENTIFY CAUSE & EFFECT

Re-read lines 13–21. What caused Allen Counter to become a proponent of Matthew Henson? What effect did Counter's work have?

_____
_____
_____
_____
_____

In a ceremony overlooking the Anacostia River in Washington, D.C., Arctic explorer Matthew Henson was posthumously awarded the National Geographic Society's highest honor—the Hubbard Medal.

National Geographic Society President John Fahey presented Matthew Henson's great-niece, Audrey Mebane, with the Hubbard Medal at the Matthew Henson Earth Conservation Center.

"The honor is long overdue," said Fahey at the November ceremony.

10   The medal recognized Henson's role in several Arctic expeditions with Robert E. Peary, including their historic 1909 trek to the North Pole.

"I had always been told by my grandmother that there was a black man [on the 1909 expedition]," said Allen Counter, director of Harvard University's Harvard Foundation, an organization that promotes intercultural understanding. "She took great pride in saying that."

Counter has become one of Henson's strongest proponents, researching Henson's polar treks and asking organizations,
20   including National Geographic, to properly recognize the African American explorer.

"National Geographic Society Honors Arctic Explorer" by Jennifer Mapes from *The National Geographic*, 2000. Copyright © 2000 by **The National Geographic Society.** Reproduced by permission of the publisher.

To the Pole

Henson's voyage into history began when he was hired as Peary's assistant in 1888. Already a seasoned seaman, Henson's keen navigational, linguistic, and hunting skills soon made him an indispensable companion to Peary.

In 1909, Peary, Henson, and four Inuit assistants reached the North Pole, making Peary and Henson the first Americans to stand at the Pole.

At that time, pointed out Counter, "Reaching the North Pole was tantamount to reaching the moon."

Upon their return, however, the road to equal recognition for Henson was often blocked by racial barriers of early-twentieth-century America.

Peary, meanwhile, received many honors, including the Hubbard Medal, and in 1920 he was buried in Arlington National Cemetery with full military honors.

Recognition at Last

Recent efforts to place Henson on equal footing with Peary are slowly meeting with success.

At Counter's urging, in 1988 Henson and his wife were reinterred at Arlington National Cemetery alongside his fellow explorer, Robert Peary.

In 1996, the U.S.N.S.° *Henson,* an oceanographic survey ship, was commissioned to honor the explorer.

The National Geographic Society's Hubbard Medal presentation, also initiated by Counter, came nearly a hundred years after Peary and one of his assistants had already received the medal.

"What surprised me," Counter said, "was that the National Geographic Society had given the Hubbard Medal to another member of the expedition who was white [but who] never made it to the North Pole."

° **U.S.N.S.:** United States Naval Ship.

> **IDENTIFY**
>
> State the **main idea** of the article.

"Henson got very little recognition," conceded Fahey, "[but] today we have an opportunity to change this."

Counter said that efforts by organizations such as National Geographic, albeit belated, were important to restoring honor to Henson as well as the award-givers.

"It sets the record straight," said Counter. "This is a great day for National Geographic as well as for Henson and the Henson family."

Matthew Henson

from Florida A&M University Web Site

"He (Matthew Henson) is a better dog driver and can handle a sledge better than any man living except some of the best Eskimo hunters. I couldn't get along without him."

—Explorer Robert Peary *from* Henson's autobiography, *A Negro Explorer at the North Pole*

Do you think Robert Peary discovered the North Pole alone? Peary was the only white man who reached that spot on April 6, 1909—with him were four Eskimos° and Matthew Henson, a multitalented black man without whom Peary could not have succeeded. Commander Donald B. MacMillan, one of the white men sent back to safer surroundings before the final push to the Pole, said that "Henson, the colored man, went with Peary because he was a better man than any of his white assistants."

Henson certainly came to the journey prepared. Born in Charles County, Maryland, in 1866, he went to sea at age thirteen as a cabin boy and became an able-bodied seaman and read widely during his six-year **sojourn.** Back ashore, he worked as a **stevedore,** a bellhop, a laborer, and a coachman before returning to Washington, D.C., where a store owner recommended Henson as a valet to accompany Peary when he surveyed a canal route through Nicaragua. Peary soon realized that Henson's ability to help chart a path through jungles and his experience as a seaman made him invaluable. Subsequently, Peary took Henson with him on seven of his eight trips to the Arctic, between 1891

° **Eskimos:** In 1977, the Inuit Circumpolar Conference officially adopted the name "Inuit," meaning "the people" as the term for the group of people known as Eskimos. Some Inuit, but not all, prefer that "Eskimo" not be used.

"Matthew Henson" from *Florida A&M University* website. Copyright © 2006 by **Florida A&M University.** Reproduced by permission of the publisher.

SYNTHESIZE SOURCES

Based on what you know about Peary from the other two articles you've read, does the introductory quotation surprise you? Why or why not?

_____
_____
_____
_____

CLARIFY

Re-read lines 9–21. Why did Henson's vast life experiences make him a good candidate to go on these expeditions?

_____
_____
_____
_____
_____

VOCABULARY

sojourn (sō′jurn) *n.:* period of time away from home.

stevedore (stē′və·dôr′) *n.:* one who loads and unloads ships.

SYNTHESIZE SOURCES

Pause at line 26. What new information do you learn about Henson and Peary's relationship in this paragraph?

_____
_____
_____
_____

DRAW CONCLUSIONS

What conclusions can you draw about Henson's quest for recognition based on the details in lines 27–32?

_____
_____
_____
_____
_____

IDENTIFY

In your own words, state the **main idea** of this selection.

_____
_____
_____
_____

20 and 1909, and was greatly aided by Henson's command of the Eskimo language.

However, Peary made Henson promise not to lecture about the historic final trip (a promise he kept until financial need forced him to break it twelve years later). And even after Henson disclosed his role, his contribution went largely unrecognized for many years—primarily because of his race.

But the Explorers Club made Henson a member in 1937; Congress awarded him one of the joint medals for the North Pole discovery in 1944; the Geographical Society of Chicago
30 gave him its Gold Medal in 1948; and Presidents Truman and Eisenhower saluted him in ceremonies in 1950 and 1954, the year before he died.

Matthew Henson and others who journeyed to the North Pole.
©The Granger Collection, New York

SKILLS PRACTICE

Matthew Henson's Polar Travails; National Geographic Society Honors Arctic Explorer; Matthew Henson

Synthesizing Sources In the chart below, list the main ideas and supporting details from the three articles you have just read. In the lines below the chart, synthesize the information from all three sources into one overall conclusion.

SKILLS FOCUS

Reading Skills Synthesize information from several sources on a single topic.

Source	Main Idea	Supporting Evidence
"Matthew Henson's Polar Travails"		
"National Geographic Society Honors Arctic Explorer"		
"Matthew Henson"		

Conclusion:
_____
_____
_____

Skills Review

Matthew Henson's Polar Travails; National Geographic Society Honors Arctic Explorer; Matthew Henson

VOCABULARY AND COMPREHENSION

Word Box
- indispensable
- abiding
- interred
- sojourn
- stevedore

A. Selection Vocabulary   Answer the following questions. Use a word map for each vocabulary word as a reference.

1. Which possessions of yours are considered *indispensable*?
   _____
   _____

2. What beliefs of yours are *abiding*? _____
   _____

3. In what kinds of places might you find someone *interred*?
   _____
   _____

4. To which places do you wish to take a lengthy *sojourn*?
   _____
   _____

5. What are the duties of a *stevedore*? _____
   _____

B. Reading Comprehension   Answer each question below.

1. Give two reasons why Henson was an important part of the North Pole expedition.
   _____
   _____

2. Why did Henson and Peary have a falling out?
   _____
   _____

SKILLS FOCUS

Vocabulary Skills
Use word maps to answer questions.

290   Part 2   Reading Informational Texts

Before You Read

Islam in America by Patricia Smith
Proud to Wear My Hijab
by Syeda Rezwana Nodi

Of the several million Muslims in America, many are high school students trying to balance devotion to their faith with the pressures of adolescence. In the selections you're about to read, you'll learn about Islam from a variety of perspectives, mostly those of American Muslim teenagers.

INFORMATIONAL FOCUS: PRIMARY AND SECONDARY SOURCES

When you do research on a subject, you collect information from a number of **sources.** Your sources may be interviews, magazines, newspaper articles, books, or information from the Internet. Sources can be divided into two types:

- **Primary sources** are firsthand accounts. They include autobiographies, eyewitness news reports, letters, diaries, photographs, and newsreels. In primary sources, writers present firsthand responses to and opinions about events they have taken part in or witnessed.
- **Secondary sources** are materials in which a writer summarizes, interprets, or analyzes events the writer did *not* take part in or witness. A writer may study primary sources and write articles or books based on information and ideas from these sources. The author may also express opinions about the information from the sources.

READING SKILLS: IDENTIFY AND ELABORATE ON MAIN IDEAS

When you read primary and secondary sources to collect information on a topic, you look for main ideas. The **main idea** is the most important point made in a paragraph or passage. The rest of the paragraph provides support (usually facts) for the main idea.

After you identify the main idea, you can **elaborate** on it. These are ways to elaborate on an idea:

- Connect the information to your own experience and knowledge.
- Ask questions about the ideas and information that are presented.
- Do further research, or develop your own opinions about the topic.

SKILLS FOCUS

Reading Skills
Understand primary and secondary sources. Identify and elaborate on main ideas.

Vocabulary Skills
Understand prefixes.

Islam in America; Proud to Wear My Hijab   291

VOCABULARY DEVELOPMENT

PREVIEW SELECTION VOCABULARY

Preview these vocabulary words before you begin to read.

affiliations (ə·fil′ē·ā′shənz) *n.*: associations.

> The U.S. census doesn't officially record people's religious **affiliations**.

coincided (kō′in·sīd′id) *v.*: happened at the same time.

> The Muslim holy month Ramadan **coincided** with football season.

transformative (trans·fôrm′ə·tiv) *adj.*: causing to change.

> Converting to Islam, as many African Americans have done, is a **transformative** experience.

misperceptions (mis′pər·sep′shənz) *n.*: incorrect ideas.

> Americans who haven't learned about Islam often hold **misperceptions** about the religion.

extracurricular (eks′trə·kə·rik′yōō·lər) *adj.*: referring to school activities that are not required.

> Rezwana joined **extracurricular** activities at school, such as the soccer and tennis teams.

PREFIXES

A **prefix** is a word part attached to the beginning of a word or root to change its meaning. Understanding the meaning of common prefixes can help you enlarge your vocabulary. The chart below gives several prefixes, their primary meanings, and examples of words containing each prefix.

Prefix	Meaning	Examples
ad– (*ac–*, *af–*, *ag–*, *al–*, *an–*, *ar–*, *as–*, *at–*)	to; toward; near	adjoin, affix, attend
com– (*col–*, *cor–*, *con–*, *co–*)	together; with	combine, conjunction, coexist
extra–	outside; beyond	extraterrestrial, extraordinary
mis–	wrong(ly); bad(ly)	mistake, misjudge
trans– (*tra–*)	across; over; through	transfer, trajectory

Islam in America

Patricia Smith

Like most American teenagers, seventeen-year-old Sana Haq enjoys hanging out with her friends and going to the movies. She just got her driver's license, and she's stressing over college applications. But Sana, a high school senior from Norwood, New Jersey, is an observant Muslim, and that makes her different from most of her friends.

She prays five times a day, as Islam requires. She wears only modest clothing—no shorts, no bathing suits, nothing too snug. Going to the mall for a pair of jeans can turn into a week-long quest because most are too tight or low-cut to meet her definition of "decent."

Islam, she says, affects every aspect of her life. "If you ask me to describe myself in one word, that one word would be Muslim," says Sana, who was born in the United States to Pakistani immigrants. "Not American, not Pakistani, not a teenager. Muslim. It's the most important thing to me."

Largely because of immigrant families like Sana's, Islam is one of the fastest-growing religions in the United States. Since the census doesn't track religious **affiliations,** the number of American Muslims is hard to pin down, but estimates range from 1.5 million to 9 million.

Whatever its size, the Muslim community in the United States is very diverse. According to a 2004 poll by Georgetown University and Zogby polling, South Asians (Indians, Pakistanis, Bangladeshis, etc.) are the largest group, followed by Arabs, and African-Americans. (Starting in the 1960s, a significant number of blacks in the United States converted to Islam.) Thirty-six percent

---

INFER
Read the title and the first paragraph of the text. What do you think the subject of the text will be?

IDENTIFY SOURCES
Pause at line 16. Underline the quotation from Sana Haq. Does the quotation lead you to believe that "Islam in America" is a **primary source** or a **secondary source**? Explain.

VOCABULARY
affiliations (ə·fil′ē·ā′shənz) n.: associations.

"Islam in America" by Patricia Smith from *The New York Times: Upfront,* January 9, 2006, vol. 138, no. 8. Copyright © 2006 by *Scholastic, Inc.* Reproduced by permission of the publisher.

TEXT FEATURES

Is any information in the graphs at right not mentioned in the text? Explain.

_____
_____
_____
_____

IDENTIFY & ELABORATE

Re-read lines 31–37. Circle the main idea of the paragraph. Then, briefly note how you would elaborate on this passage.

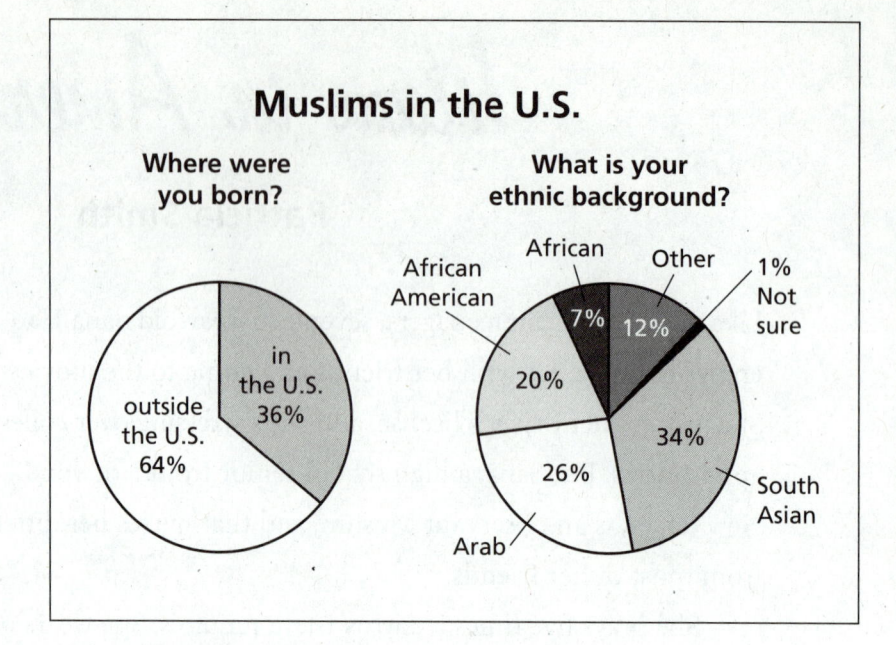

_____
_____
_____
_____
_____
_____
_____
_____
_____
_____
_____

Muslims in the U.S.

Where were you born?
- in the U.S. 36%
- outside the U.S. 64%

What is your ethnic background?
- African American 20%
- African 7%
- Other 12%
- Not sure 1%
- South Asian 34%
- Arab 26%

of American Muslims were born in the United States; the other 64 percent come from eighty different countries.
30 (See graphs above.)

Trying to carve an American Muslim identity out of this diversity is one of the challenges facing young Muslims. "They are creating traditions and a culture that is particular to them and not imported from another majority-Muslim country," says Tayyibah Taylor, editor of *Azzizah*, a Muslim women's magazine published in Atlanta. "Something that blends their American way of thinking and their American way of living with Islamic guidelines."

Contrast with Europe

As a group, American Muslims have a higher median income
40 than Americans as a whole, and they vote in higher numbers. In addition, they are increasingly contributing to American culture, forming Muslim comedy groups, rap groups, Scout troops, magazines, and other media.

294   Part 2   Reading Informational Texts

Their integration into American society and culture stands in contrast to Europe's Muslim communities, which have remained largely on the economic and political fringes. In November 2005, Muslims rioted in many French cities.

In parts of the United States with large Muslim populations, Islam mingles with American traditions. At Dearborn High School in Dearborn, Michigan, about one third of the students—and the football team—are Muslim. Because Ramadan (the Muslim holy month that requires dawn-to-dusk fasting) **coincided** with football season this year, Muslim players had to wake up at 4:30 for a predawn breakfast; go through their classes without eating or drinking; and start most Friday night games before darkness allowed them to break their fasts.

"When you start your day off fasting and you get to football at the end of the day, that's the challenge," says Hassan Cheaib, a seventeen-year-old senior. "You know you've worked hard. You know you've been faithful.... After fasting all day, you feel like a warrior."

Because some of Islam's social tenets—modesty and chastity, for example—are so different from American norms, they can present a challenge for young Muslims. For Sana, adherence to Islam means she doesn't date. "Dating means going out with someone and spending intimate time with them, and for me, that's not allowed," she explains. "But it's not that I don't talk to guys. I have guy friends."

Impact of 9/11

The terrorist attacks of September 11, 2001, were a **transformative** moment for Muslims in America. On the one hand, there has been an increase in anti-Muslim feeling, discrimination, and hate crimes. On the other hand, many Muslims have responded by taking more interest in their religion and reaching out more to non-Muslims.

COMPARE & CONTRAST

Re-read lines 39–47. The writer mentions two differences between American Muslims and Americans in general. Underline them. What difference between American Muslims and European Muslims does she observe?

VOCABULARY

coincided (kō′in·sīd′id) *v.*: happened at the same time.

WORD STUDY

The root of the word *adherence* (line 64), which contains the prefix *ad–*, is the Latin verb *haerere*, "to stick." What do you think *adherence* means?

VOCABULARY

transformative (trans·fôrm′ə·tiv) *adj.*: causing to change.

©Ed Kashi/CORBIS

IDENTIFY & ELABORATE

Underline the **main idea** in lines 70–81. Then, pose two questions about how September 11 affected Muslims in America.

_____

_____

_____

VOCABULARY

misperceptions
(mis′pər·sep′shənz) *n.*: incorrect ideas.

"September 11 exposed American Muslims for the first time to a large degree of hostility," says Ishan Bagby, a professor of Islamic Studies at the University of Kentucky. "So Muslims have come to the conclusion that isolation is a danger, because 80 if people don't know you it's easy for them to accept the worst stereotypes."

According to one 2003 poll, 63 percent of Americans say they do not have a good understanding of Islam as a religion. Indeed, many young Muslims spend a lot of time correcting common **misperceptions** about Islam: that it condones terrorism (it doesn't); and that it denies women equal rights (it doesn't, though many majority-Muslim cultures and countries do).

When Ibrahim Elshamy, eighteen, was growing up in Manchester, New Hampshire, Islam was a regular part of his life. Every Friday he left school at lunch to attend services at a mosque. Now a freshman at Dartmouth College in Hanover, New Hampshire, his religion remains important. Two days after his arrival on campus, he contacted the Muslim student group. And five times a day, he returns to his dorm room to say his prayers.

In college, Ibrahim has found for the first time a Muslim community in which he feels at home. The mosque he and his Egyptian father attended in Manchester attracted many Arab, Asian, and African immigrants. The problem with that, he says, was that people melded their cultural traditions with their practice of Islam. As an American-born Muslim, he found that frustrating.

"Here at Dartmouth, it was extremely refreshing," he says, "because I was finally around Muslims who were exactly like me in that respect."

Professor Bagby says many young Muslims want to distinguish between Islam's teachings and the cultural traditions often associated with Islam, particularly the role of women. Stressing that nothing in the Koran itself prohibits women's full participation (in religion or in life), American women are increasingly demanding not only equal participation but leadership roles in the mosque. "It's definitely rocking some boats," says Tayyibah Taylor of *Azzizah*.

"More American"

Samiyyah Ali, seventeen, grew up in Atlanta and describes herself as a practicing Muslim, rather than an observant one. She uses the principles of Islam to guide her but doesn't worry about following every last tenet. Like 20 percent of American Muslims, she is African-American. Her parents converted to Islam before she was born.

Other than her name, there's not much about Samiyyah that would tell a stranger she is Muslim. She's a senior at

FLUENCY

Read the boxed passage aloud quickly and smoothly, as if you were a newscaster.

IDENTIFY & ELABORATE

What questions do you have about the ideas in the paraphrased information from Professor Bagby (104–111)? Explain.

INFER

Pause at line 111. Why might American Muslim women's desire for leadership roles be "'rocking some boats'"?

Islam in America 297

IDENTIFY CAUSE & EFFECT

According to Samiyyah Ali, why is her family less strict about following every tenet of Islam?

_____
_____
_____
_____

IDENTIFY & ELABORATE

Underline the last sentence of the article. What do you think it means to be "'more American'"?

_____
_____
_____
_____
_____

IDENTIFY SOURCES

Is the text of the article a **primary source** or a **secondary source**? Explain.

_____
_____
_____
_____

Westminster Academy, a coed private school where she's a cheerleader, on the varsity track and field team, in the dance club, and on the school newspaper staff. And she does date.

She views the Koran as something that should not be followed literally, much like other historical documents that should be understood in context. "A lot of stuff is still applicable—honor and respect is always applicable," says Samiyyah. "But other things that are cultural—even ideas about sex—need to be taken in context. Back then people got married when they were fourteen.... Maybe because my family is a convert family, we're just not so orthodox."

The Muslim community in America is currently undergoing a generational shift. Most American mosques were founded by first-generation immigrants, and as their American-born children take over, the norms are changing.

"Islam in America will feel a lot different in the next forty years," Professor Bagby says. "It'll feel more American, that's for sure."

Proud to Wear My Hijab

Syeda Rezwana Nodi

"Hey, I wanted to ask you something for a long time. Are you Rezwana from tenth-grade English class?" Priya asked me as I was going to the French office after first period.

It was the second semester of my junior year and I hadn't seen Priya since summer. She was one of my closest friends in tenth grade when she sat beside me in English class.

"Of course it's me, Priya. I don't know how you forgot about me so easily but I still remember you," I smiled.

"Honestly, I didn't recognize you at all," she said laughing. "I guess it's because of that hijab. I swear you look really different."

Priya's not my only friend who didn't recognize me after I started wearing my hijab last summer when I turned sixteen.

To me, my hijab is not just a piece of cloth that covers my hair. It's the most visible symbol of being a Muslim. One of the reasons Muslim women wear the hijab is to protect them from unwanted attention from men.

And it was my choice to wear one.

It bothers me that people think I'm different, now that I wear a hijab. Yes, it changes my appearance a little and it covers my hair and makes me look like I'm twelve instead of seventeen.

But caring more about my appearance than my culture would disrespect the honor of wearing it. So when my friends didn't recognize me, and made absurd labels like "one of the hijabis," I really felt hurt.

For example, last December, my friends and I gathered around the sign-up sheet for an upcoming annual talent show in our community center. We usually did the performances together, but this time it was different.

IDENTIFY SOURCES

Pause at line 10. Do you think this article is a **primary source** or a **secondary source**? What clues tell you so?

IDENTIFY

Re-read lines 13–16. What is a hijab?

INFER

Pause at line 28. What do you think the writer is going to say about this talent show?

"Proud to Wear My Hijab" by Syeda Rezwana Nodi from *Tolerance.org*, December 15, 2004. Copyright © 2004 by Independent Media Institute. Reproduced by permission of **Wiretap**.

IDENTIFY & ELABORATE

Re-read lines 29–38. State the **main idea** of this passage in your own words. How does this passage **elaborate** on, or add information to, what came before it?

___

VOCABULARY

extracurricular
(eks′trə·kə·rik′yo͞o·lər) *adj.*: referring to school activities that are not required.

IDENTIFY CAUSE & EFFECT

Pause at line 60. What led the writer to be more comfortable and confident wearing her hijab? What resulted from her new attitude?

___

I was at the back of the line, and when my friends were nearly done signing up, a friend asked me, "Rez, you're not going to do any more performances right? 'Specially now that you're one of the hijabis."

A roar of laughter followed her comment. It was discouraging and disappointing, especially because I wanted to participate in the show.

Unfortunately, I care about what people say to me and I am a sensitive person. So I didn't perform because I didn't want to risk more comments like that.

People treated me differently after I started wearing my hijab, even though I was still friendly, fun loving, and enthusiastic. And I didn't understand the label of "one of the hijabis." What did it mean exactly?

Surprisingly my friend circle was narrowing down to only Muslims. I didn't have enough courage to participate in sports or **extracurricular** activities. I was afraid people would make more bizarre comments about me and I would feel left out.

Finally, I told my mom about my feelings.

She said I should try to see the positive in the situation. I should confront my friends and tell them their assumptions aren't true. "What's wrong with looking different?" she asked me.

"Don't you think you should have more confidence in yourself? Being a hijabi is something you should be proud of. If that's what some people want to call you, then let them. Try to be more optimistic. Take things lightly instead of getting offended."

She was right. She made me realize I shouldn't underestimate myself and I became more confident of my appearance.

I didn't need to confront anyone, but if anyone asked me about my hijab, I would explain why I wear it. Otherwise, I decided it was no big deal. In fact, seeing me wear the hijab with pride, inspired some of my friends to wear it, too.

When school sports started, I joined the soccer and tennis teams. My hijab didn't get in the way. A lot of Muslim people play on our soccer team and the players greet me happily. The

©Jeff Greenberg/PhotoEdit

tennis group showed me some helpful tricks and encouraged me all the way. The heavy tennis rackets gave me more trouble than anything else.

The best thing is no one calls me a hijabi anymore. It's a meaningless label that made me doubt my decision to wear the symbol of my faith and modesty.

70 Though it was hard sticking to my beliefs, the experience has proven to me that wearing my hijab and tuning out people's negativity made me feel dignified, and so I shall continue to wear it with pride.

> **COMPARE & CONTRAST**
>
> Do you think Rezwana, the writer of this article, is more similar to Sana Haq or to Samiyyah Ali (from "Islam in America") in terms of religious practices? Explain.

SKILLS PRACTICE

Islam in America; Proud to Wear My Hijab

SKILLS FOCUS

Reading Skills
Identify and elaborate on main ideas.

Elaboration Chart When you elaborate, you extend or expand on a topic by adding details, comments, and questions. Passages from "Islam in America" and "Proud to Wear My Hijab" appear in the left-hand column of the chart. Elaborate on those passages in the space provided.

Text Passage	My Elaboration
"Going to the mall for a pair of jeans can turn into a week-long quest because most are too tight or low-cut to meet her definition of 'decent.'" ("Islam in America," lines 9–11)	
"According to one 2003 poll, 63 percent of Americans say they do not have a good understanding of Islam as a religion." ("Islam in America," lines 82–83)	
"People treated me differently after I started wearing my hijab, even though I was still friendly, fun loving, and enthusiastic." ("Proud to Wear My Hijab," lines 39–41)	
"In fact, seeing me wear the hijab with pride, inspired some of my friends to wear it, too." ("Proud to Wear My Hijab," lines 59–60)	

Skills Review

Islam in America; Proud to Wear My Hijab

VOCABULARY AND COMPREHENSION

A. Prefixes   Match each word from the Word Box with the definition of its prefix by writing the letter of the definition on the line.

1. _____ transformative   a. to

2. _____ coincided   b. wrong

3. _____ extracurricular   c. across

4. _____ misperceptions   d. together

5. _____ affiliations   e. outside

Word Box
- affiliations
- coincided
- transformative
- misperceptions
- extracurricular

B. Reading Comprehension   Answer each question below.

1. How large is the Muslim community in the United States?
   _____
   _____

2. Why is playing on the football team during the Muslim holy month, Ramadan, challenging?
   _____
   _____

3. Why did Ibrahim Elshamy feel more at home in his Muslim community at college?
   _____
   _____

4. Why didn't Syeda Rezwana Nodi participate in the annual talent show?
   _____
   _____

SKILLS FOCUS

Vocabulary Skills
Identify prefixes.

Before You Read

Appearances Are Destructive
by Mark Mathabane

Mark Mathabane is the author of the bestselling autobiography *Kaffir Boy*. The book details his experiences and struggles in apartheid-era South Africa. In addition to his autobiographical pieces, Mathabane is well known for his journalism. In this article he offers his opinions on school dress codes.

INFORMATIONAL FOCUS: AUTHOR'S ARGUMENT

In some informational articles, authors offer a **claim,** or an opinion, on a subject. A claim can often be stated in a sentence—for example, "Human activities are causing dangerous climate changes." Claims are generally supported by an **argument**—evidence to persuade readers to accept the views.

There are two main types of arguments, also called **appeals.**
- **Logical appeals** use facts, examples, and opinions by experts on the subject.
- **Emotional appeals** are often just opinions—for example, "I know I can do the job." Emotional appeals include the use of loaded words, or words with strong emotional impact (such as *patriotism*), and anecdotes, or brief, true stories that may interest the reader and support the claim.

READING SKILLS: IDENTIFYING AUTHOR'S PURPOSE AND TONE

An author's **purpose** is his or her reason for writing (to convince, to alarm, to amuse, to inform, and so on). **Tone** is an author's attitude toward the topic of his or her writing. An author may convey a respectful tone, a serious tone, or a lighthearted tone, for example.

An author's purpose may be stated directly; sometimes, however, you have to examine the author's word choice to arrive at his or her purpose. To identify tone, examine an author's word choice and its effect on readers.

You may want to fill in a chart like the one below as you read "Appearances Are Destructive."

Passage	Purpose	Tone

SKILLS FOCUS

Reading Skills
Understand the elements of an author's argument. Identify an author's purpose and tone.

Vocabulary Skills
Use context clues.

VOCABULARY DEVELOPMENT

PREVIEW SELECTION VOCABULARY
Preview these vocabulary words before you begin to read.

preoccupied (prē·äk′yoo·pīd′) *adj.:* overly concerned about something; distracted.

*Many high school students are **preoccupied** with their appearance and don't pay enough attention to their studies.*

distraught (di·strôt′) *adj.:* extremely upset.

*The **distraught** girls cried about being teased at school.*

ogling (ō′gliŋ) *v.* used as *adj.:* staring at.

*Teenagers are obsessed with expensive clothes, **ogling** one another to check for the right brand labels.*

infringe (in·frinj′) *v.:* to restrict; encroach.

*Some people argue that school uniforms **infringe** upon students' freedoms.*

curtailment (kər·tāl′mənt) *n.:* shortening or reduction.

*A **curtailment** of students' rights to select what they wear may be necessary to improve our schools.*

CONTEXT CLUES
When you encounter a word you haven't seen before, its **context**—the words and sentences that surround it—may provide clues to its meaning. Follow these steps to try to figure out what an unfamiliar word means in context:
- Think of the word as a blank that needs filling in.
- Determine the word's part of speech.
- Re-read the whole sentence, looking for any other words or phrases that define or restate the word, give examples of it, or compare or contrast it with something. If there is nothing in the sentence, go back a couple of sentences and then forward one or two.
- Based on the clues you find, think of some words that might be synonyms of the mystery word. Try them to see if they make sense in the sentence.

APPEARANCES ARE DESTRUCTIVE

Mark Mathabane

As public schools reopen for the new year, strategies to curb school violence will once again be hotly debated. Installing metal detectors and hiring security guards will help, but the experience of my two sisters makes a compelling case for greater use of dress codes as a way to protect students and promote learning.

Shortly after my sisters arrived here from South Africa I enrolled them at the local public school. I had great expectations for their educational experience. Compared with black schools under apartheid, American schools are Shangri-Las,[1] with modern textbooks, school buses, computers, libraries, lunch programs and dedicated teachers.

But despite these benefits, which students in many parts of the world only dream about, my sisters' efforts at learning were almost derailed. They were constantly taunted for their homely outfits. A couple of times they came home in tears. In South Africa students were required to wear uniforms, so my sisters had never been **preoccupied** with clothes and jewelry.

They became so **distraught** that they insisted on transferring to different schools, despite my reassurances that there was nothing wrong with them because of what they wore.

I have visited enough public schools around the country to know that my sisters' experiences are not unique. In schools in many areas, Nike, Calvin Klein, Adidas, Reebok, and Gucci are more familiar names to students than Zora Neale Hurston, Shakespeare, and Faulkner.[2] Many students seem to pay more attention to what's on their bodies than in their minds.

---

1. **Shangri-Las:** imaginary places where life is nearly perfect.
2. **Zora Neale Hurston, Shakespeare, and Faulkner:** all great authors.

"Appearances Are Destructive" by Mark Mathabane from *The New York Times*, August 26, 1993. Copyright © 1993 by The New York Times Company. Reproduced by the **New York Times Syndication Sales.**

INFER

Pause at line 5. What do you think the author means by "dress codes"? What **claim** do you think the author will be arguing in support of?

IDENTIFY PURPOSE & TONE

Re-read lines 6–11. Underline the benefits of attending American schools. What **purpose** might the writer have for mentioning these benefits?

VOCABULARY

preoccupied (pre·äk′yoo·pīd′) *adj.:* overly concerned about something; distracted.

distraught (di·strôt′) *adj.:* extremely upset.

AUTHOR'S ARGUMENT

Re-read lines 21–26. How does this passage strengthen the author's position?

Teachers have shared their frustrations with me at being unable to teach those students willing to learn because classes are frequently disrupted by other students **ogling** themselves in mirrors, painting their fingernails, combing their hair, shining their gigantic shoes, or comparing designer labels on jackets, caps and jewelry.

The fiercest competition among students is often not over academic achievements, but over who dresses most expensively. And many students now measure parental love by how willing their mothers and fathers are to pamper them with money for the latest fads in clothes, sneakers, and jewelry.

Those parents without the money to waste on such meretricious[3] extravagances are considered uncaring and cruel. They often watch in dismay and helplessness as their children become involved with gangs and peddle drugs to raise the money.

---

3. **meretricious:** pretentious.

VOCABULARY

ogling (ō′glĭŋ) v. used as adj.: staring at.

Would the emotional impact of this sentence be different if *ogling* were replaced by *looking at*? Explain.

AUTHOR'S ARGUMENT

Pause at line 41. What does the author suggest leads to children selling drugs and joining gangs? Do you think he provides enough evidence of this connection? Explain.

IDENTIFY PURPOSE & TONE

Pause at line 47. Underline the **generalization** the author makes about why girls choose the clothing they do. How would you describe its **tone**?

_____
_____
_____
_____
_____

AUTHOR'S ARGUMENT

Pause at line 49. Underline the claim that the author attributes to civil libertarians. What fact does the author give in an effort to contradict the claim?

_____
_____
_____
_____
_____

VOCABULARY

infringe (in·frinj′) v.: to restrict; encroach.

curtailment (kər·tāl′mənt) n.: shortening or reduction.

When students are asked why they attach so much importance to clothing, they frequently reply that it's the cool thing to do, that it gives them status and earns them respect. And clothes are also used to send sexual messages, with girls thinking that the only things that make them attractive to boys are skimpy dresses and gaudy looks, rather than intelligence and academic excellence.

The argument by civil libertarians[4] that dress codes **infringe** on freedom of expression is misleading. We observe dress codes in nearly every aspect of our lives without any diminution[5] of our freedoms—as demonstrated by flight attendants, bus drivers, postal employees, high school bands, military personnel, sports teams, Girl and Boy Scouts, employees of fast-food chains, restaurants, and hotels.

In many countries where students outperform their American counterparts academically, school dress codes are observed as part of creating the proper learning environment. Their students tend to be neater, less disruptive in class and more disciplined, mainly because their minds are focused more on learning and less on materialism. It's time Americans realized that the benefits of safe and effective schools far outweigh any perceived **curtailment** of freedom of expression brought on by dress codes.

---

4. **civil libertarians:** supporters of freedom from government interference, especially concerning the Bill of Rights.
5. **diminution:** act of reducing or diminishing.

SKILLS PRACTICE

Appearances Are Destructive

Argument Chart The author of "Appearances Are Destructive" makes a case for stricter school dress codes. Use this chart to identify the types of details used in the author's argument. Fill in the right-hand column with passages from the article that are examples of each type of persuasive appeal.

SKILLS FOCUS

Reading Skills
Analyze the elements of an author's argument.

Type of Detail	Example Passage from Article
Claim	
Logical appeal	
Emotional appeal	
Generalization	
Opinion	

Appearances Are Destructive   309

Skills Review

Appearances Are Destructive

VOCABULARY AND COMPREHENSION

Word Box
- preoccupied
- distraught
- ogling
- infringe
- curtailment

A. Context Clues Write words from the Word Box to complete the paragraph. Use each word only once.

I was so (1) _____ when our principal announced that we'd have to start wearing uniforms to school. I was completely (2) _____ with thoughts of how I'd look in that drab polo shirt. For a moment I imagined all my friends would be (3) _____ my new clothes and laughing at me. Then I remembered that the (4) _____ of clothing choices applied to them too. The new dress code didn't just (5) _____ on my rights; it affected all of us students equally.

B. Reading Comprehension Answer each question below.

1. Why did other students taunt the author's sisters at their new school?

2. According to the article, over what do students compete fiercely?

3. Name four groups of people who wear uniforms, as mentioned in the article.

4. What characteristics of students in countries that have dress codes does the article cite?

SKILLS FOCUS
Vocabulary Skills
Use context clues.

Consumer, Workplace, and Public Documents

Academic Vocabulary

These are the terms you should know as you read and analyze the selections that follow.

Consumer documents Documents used in the selling and buying of products. Many consumer documents, such as warranties, protect the rights of the purchaser and the seller. Other consumer documents include advertisements, contracts, instruction manuals, and product information.

Public documents Documents that inform the public. Public documents are created by governmental, social, religious, or news-gathering organizations. They include safety information, government regulations, schedules of events, explanations of services, and newspaper items.

Workplace documents Documents used in offices, factories, and other work sites to communicate information. These include business letters, contracts, instruction manuals, memorandums, and safety information.

Technical documents Documents used to explain or establish procedures for using technology, such as mechanical, electronic, or digital products or systems. Technical documents include how-to instructions, installation instructions, and instructions on carrying out scientific procedures.

Functional documents Any documents prepared for a specific function, such as consumer, public, workplace, and technical documents.

Before You Read

WORKPLACE DOCUMENTS

The 411 on Your Job Rights; Youth@Work

Suppose you decide to look for a summer job. Before accepting a position, you should find out what sorts of rights you have as an employee. Workplace documents found on the Equal Employment Opportunity Commission (EEOC) Web site let you know what responsibilities your employer has and what responsibilities you have to maintain a fair workplace environment. The site also provides information on what the EEOC is doing to make sure your rights are maintained. There is a special area on the site with information specifically for young people, called Youth@Work.

INFORMATIONAL FOCUS: WORKPLACE DOCUMENT

Most workplace documents strive to present information as clearly and accurately as possible. The documents you are about to read fulfill that purpose. As with many workplace documents, they include features that will help you follow the text.

- **Headers,** which introduce the beginning of sections of a document
- **Boldface text,** which calls out important information
- A **bulleted list,** which organizes points in a clear way
- **Illustrations,** which enhance your understanding of the text

TERMS TO KNOW

Boldface—dark, heavy type.
Format—the design of a document.
Graphics—visual elements that enhance the text, such as art, photographs, and drawings.
Header—a label or heading that begins a section of a document.
Point-by-point sequence—a sequence that states each point as a separate item, in no particular order.
Step-by-step sequence—a sequence that tells you what to do first, second, third, and so on.

SKILLS FOCUS

Reading Skills Understand the purpose and structure of workplace documents.

The 411 on Your Job Rights

Real World . . . Real Rights . . . Real Responsibilities!

U.S. EQUAL EMPLOYMENT OPPORTUNITY COMMISSION
Ensuring the Freedom to Compete in America's Workplaces

Working in the summer or after school is a great way for you to learn important job and social skills, earn extra money and become more independent. Did you know that you have specific workplace rights and responsibilities under the laws enforced by EEOC?

Your Rights

As an employee or applicant, you have a right to

Work Free of Discrimination and Harassment because of your race, color, religion, sex, pregnancy, national origin, disability, or age (age 40 or older).

Complain About Job Discrimination without being punished, or treated differently, by your employer.

Request Workplace Changes because of your religious beliefs or a disability.

INFER
What does the number *411* mean in the title of this fact sheet?

TEXT FEATURES
How does the photograph give you a hint about the intended audience of this fact sheet?

FORMAT
Underline the parts of the text in **boldface** type in lines 8–17. Why are these phrases set in boldface?

TEXT FEATURES

Circle the header in line 18. Then, state in your own words the responsibilities of an employee, as described in lines 20–30.

_____
_____
_____
_____

TEXT FEATURES

A **step-by-step sequence** describes instructions or events in order of first, second, third, and so on. Re-read lines 31–36, which explain what happens when someone files a complaint. Rewrite these lines as a list in a step-by-step sequence.

_____
_____
_____
_____

PURPOSE

What is the purpose of lines 42–45?

_____
_____
_____
_____

Keep Your Medical Information Private. Your employer should not share or discuss your medical information with others, unless they have a need to know the information.

Your Responsibilities

As an employee, you have a responsibility to

20 **Report** any unfair or harassing treatment you experience to your company.

Respect others by acting professionally at work. Treat co-workers the way you want to be treated.

Request workplace changes for your religious beliefs or a disability by explaining what changes are needed and why.

You may have additional rights and responsibilities under state and/or local laws or your company's own policies.

If you manage employees, you have an even greater responsibility to act professionally since your employer could be legally responsible for things you say or do.

30

Need to File A Complaint?

If you think you have been the victim of illegal job discrimination or harassment, you can file a formal complaint, called a charge of discrimination, with EEOC. We will investigate your charge and take action to end any illegal discrimination.

We accept charges from all job applicants and full-time, part-time, seasonal and temporary employees, regardless of citizenship and work authorization status.

40 Charges may be filed by mail or in person. Our services are free.

Learn more about your employment rights and responsibilities by visiting our Web site at www.youth.eeoc.gov. You can also email us at info@ask.eeoc.gov or call us at 1-800-669-4000 (TTY: 1-800-669-6820).

---

314   Part 2   Reading Informational Texts

Youth@Work

from EEOC Web Site

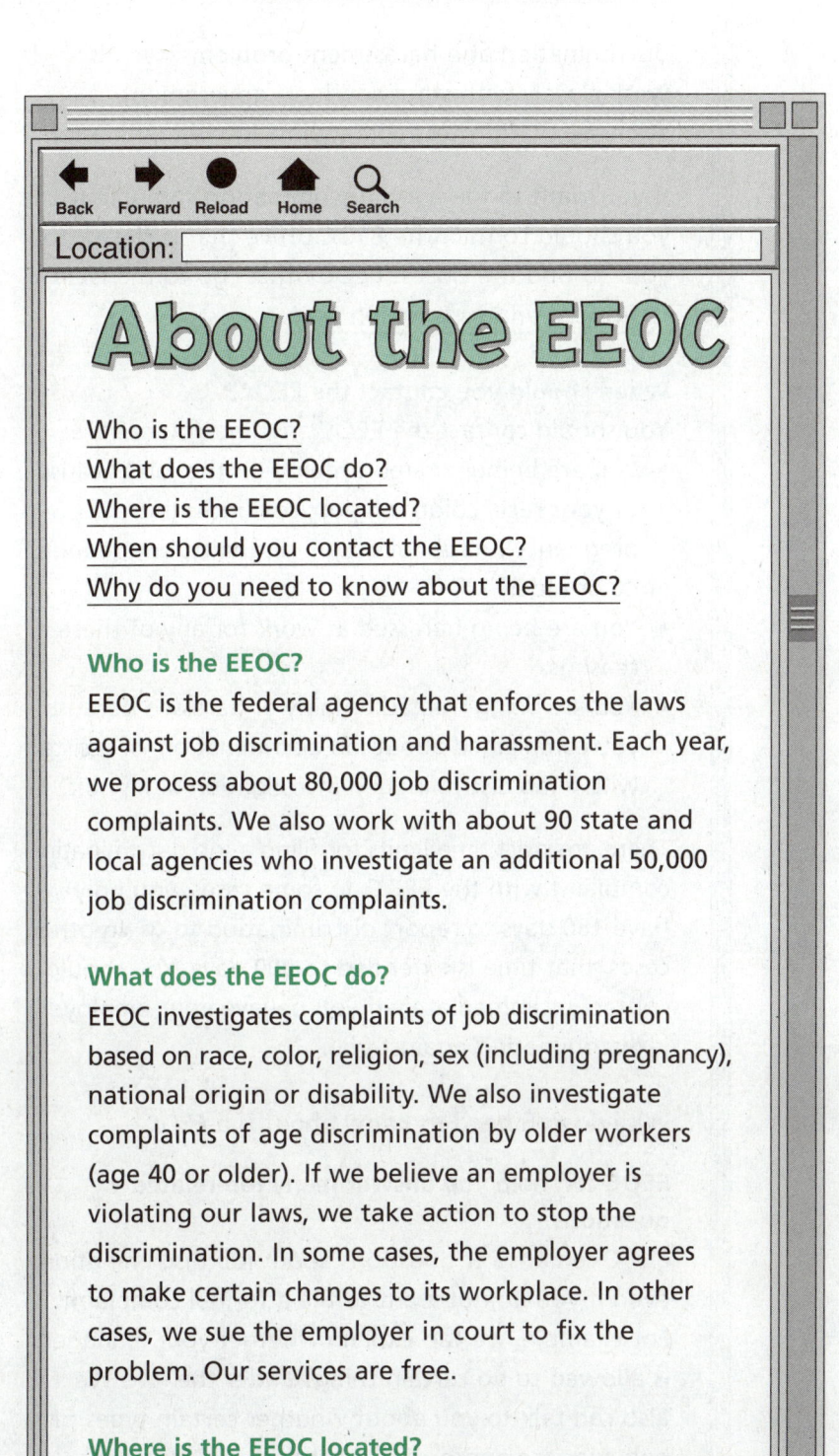

About the EEOC

<u>Who is the EEOC?</u>
<u>What does the EEOC do?</u>
<u>Where is the EEOC located?</u>
When should you contact the EEOC?
Why do you need to know about the EEOC?

Who is the EEOC?
EEOC is the federal agency that enforces the laws against job discrimination and harassment. Each year, we process about 80,000 job discrimination complaints. We also work with about 90 state and local agencies who investigate an additional 50,000 job discrimination complaints.

What does the EEOC do?
EEOC investigates complaints of job discrimination based on race, color, religion, sex (including pregnancy), national origin or disability. We also investigate complaints of age discrimination by older workers (age 40 or older). If we believe an employer is violating our laws, we take action to stop the discrimination. In some cases, the employer agrees to make certain changes to its workplace. In other cases, we sue the employer in court to fix the problem. Our services are free.

Where is the EEOC located?
Like many federal agencies, EEOC's main office is located in Washington, D.C. We have 51 field offices around the country that can help you solve job

---

TEXT FEATURES

Why is the text in lines 1–5 underlined?

IDENTIFY CAUSE & EFFECT

Re-read lines 14–23. What causes the EEOC to investigate an employer? What effects might this investigation have?

PURPOSE

Pause at line 34. Underline the sentence that tells you how to file a discrimination complaint.

TEXT FEATURES

Re-read lines 37–45. Why are these lines set in a bulleted list rather than a numbered list?

_____
_____
_____
_____
_____
_____

PURPOSE

Pause at line 51. How much time does someone have to report discrimination? How long should one wait before reporting it?

_____
_____
_____
_____
_____

---

discrimination and harassment problems. We also work closely with state and local government agencies that protect you against job discrimination.

If you want to file a job discrimination complaint, you should contact the EEOC office that is closest to you. To find the closest EEOC office, go to the **Field Office List and Jurisdiction Map**.

When should you contact the EEOC?

You should contact the EEOC anytime you believe:

- You are being treated unfairly on the job because of your race, color, religion, sex (including pregnancy), national origin, disability, or age (age 40 or older).
- You are being harassed at work for any of these reasons.
- You are being treated unfairly or harassed because you complained about job discrimination, or assisted with a job discrimination investigation or lawsuit.

There are strict time limits for filing a job discrimination complaint with the EEOC. In some cases, you only have 180 days to report discrimination to us. In other cases, that time is extended to 300 days. You should contact us immediately if you believe your employer is discriminating against you.

Why do you need to know about the EEOC?

EEOC can help you answer many job-related questions.

EEOC can answer questions about job discrimination even if you do not want to file a formal complaint. For example, we can explain whether your manager is allowed to do certain things under the law. We also can talk to you about whether certain types of behavior are appropriate in the workplace.

---

316 Part 2 Reading Informational Texts

EEOC can help you solve workplace problems.
Sometimes, your employer may not adequately address an issue that you raise with them. In other cases, you may be too scared to bring certain issues to your employer's attention. If you come to us, we can talk to your employer and try to solve the problem if it involves one of the laws we are responsible for enforcing. If we feel that the conduct you're complaining about is not illegal under our laws, we can put you in touch with other government agencies or organizations that may be able to help you.

EEOC can help you file a job discrimination lawsuit.
If we believe your employer is violating the law, we can sue in court to fix the problem. Even if we decide not to sue, we can give you the right to take your claim to court. You cannot file a job discrimination lawsuit against your employer without first coming to us.

EEOC can help you make the workplace better for everyone.
If you report illegal job discrimination to us, we will work to make sure that your employer does not do the same thing to you or someone else in the future. We can require employers to develop fairer job policies, train managers and other employees about discrimination, and obtain compensation for anyone who was treated unfairly. This makes the workplace a better place for you, your sisters and brothers, your friends, and your community.

PURPOSE

What is the purpose of lines 79–89?

SKILLS PRACTICE

The 411 on Your Job Rights; Youth@Work

SKILLS FOCUS

Reading Skills
Analyze the purpose and structure of workplace documents.

Workplace Documents Organizer Sometimes workplace documents can seem complicated. Most well-written workplace documents, however, allow their format and structure to make accessing the information predictable and easy. Re-read the fact sheet and Web site from the EEOC. Then, fill in the organizer below with the information the text features contain.

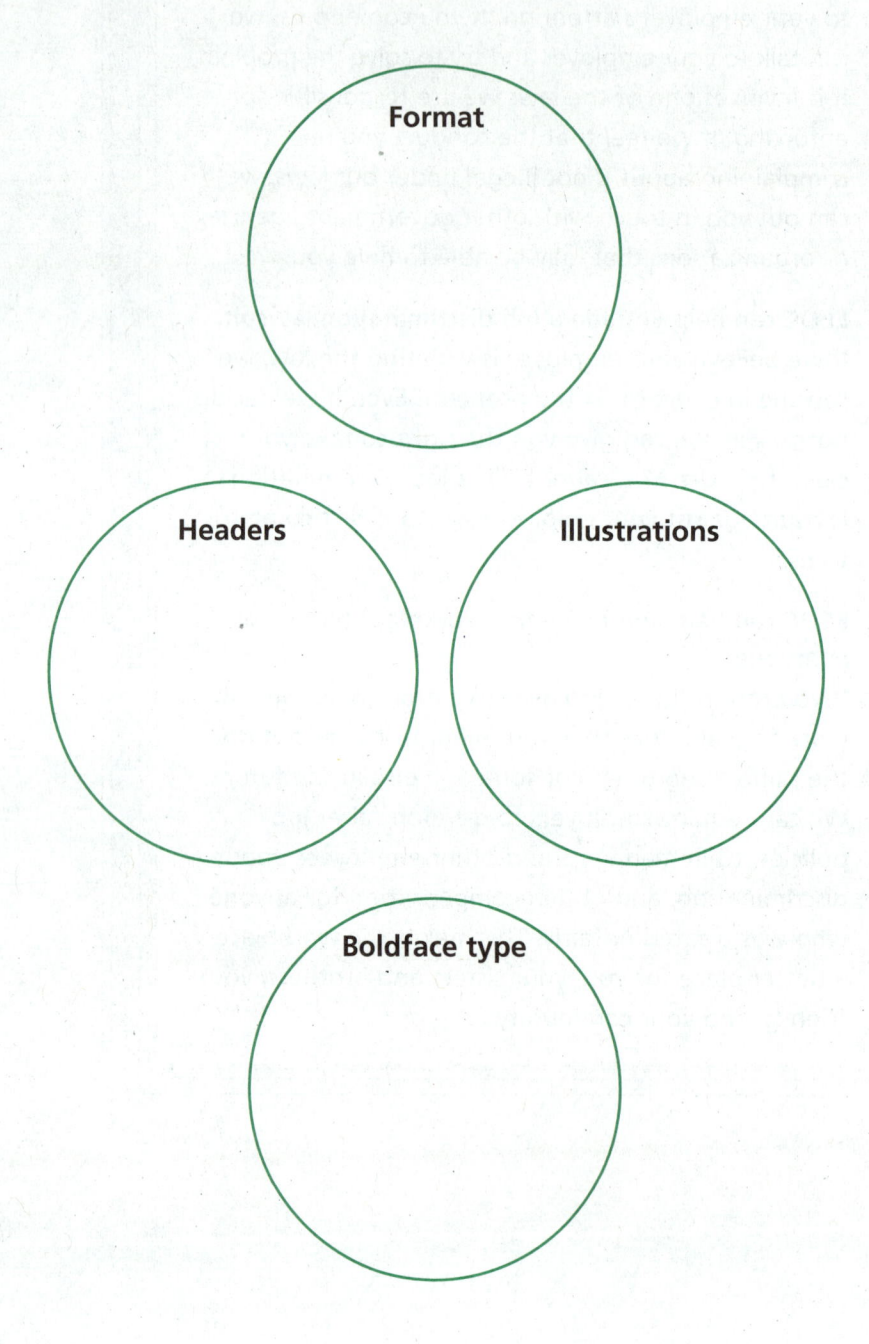

Format

Headers

Illustrations

Boldface type

Skills Review

The 411 on Your Job Rights; Youth@Work

COMPREHENSION

Reading Comprehension   Answer each question below.

1. According to the fact sheet, for what reasons could you ask for workplace changes?

2. What responsibilities do you have as an employee?

3. What does the EEOC investigate?

4. Why would you go to the Field Office List and Jurisdiction Map?

5. How can an employee make the workplace better for everyone?

Before You Read

TECHNICAL DOCUMENT

The Basics of Downloading a Podcast

Even if you're already a podcast pro, you probably have friends or relatives who aren't. Like Talib, whom you're about to meet, you'd have to supply them with information and instructions if you recommended a podcast to them. Of course, you may be unfamiliar with podcasts yourself. You won't be after reading Talib's helpful directions.

INFORMATIONAL FOCUS: TECHNICAL DOCUMENT

The following document contains directions for downloading a podcast. Look for these text features, which will help you find the information you need.

- **Main headings** clearly divide the document into logical sections.
- **Run-in subheadings** highlight podcast-downloading terminology and other important information.
- A **numbered list** presents directions in a step-by-step sequence.
- A **bulleted list** shows rules of thumb in a point-by-point sequence.

TERMS TO KNOW

Format—the design of a document.
Run-in subheading—a subheading followed by text on the same line.
Boldface—dark, heavy type.
Bullets—dots, diamonds, squares, or other shapes used to introduce lists in point-by-point sequence.
Point-by-point sequence—a sequence that lists items in no particular order.
Step-by-step sequence—a sequence that tells what to do first, second, third, and so on.

SKILLS FOCUS

Reading Skills Understand the purpose and structure of technical documents.

320 Part 2 Reading Informational Texts

The Basics of Downloading a Podcast

Talib has just discovered a great way to stay in touch with his family in India: podcasting. A podcast is an audio or video file available on the Internet that can be downloaded in the form of a computer file. Downloading a podcast is similar to recording a television show on a VCR; once you've downloaded a podcast, you can listen to or watch it whenever you want.

Talib is planning to record updates about his life in the United States for his family to listen to. Although downloading podcasts is not complicated, his family may not know all of the terms they'll need to do it.

Podcasting Terminology

Broadband Internet connection: Internet connection that allows a large amount of information to be transmitted at high speeds.
Download: transfer a file or program to your personal computer.
MP3: digital file containing audio data.
Podcast: audio or video file available on the Internet. The name *podcast* comes from the words "iPod" and "broadcast."
Podcasting subscription software: software that searches the Internet for the audio files you want, then downloads them to a portable player or a computer.
Portable digital music player: device that stores MP3 files and lets you listen to them at your convenience.

Now Talib is ready to give step-by-step instructions to his family on how to download his podcast:

How to Download

Step 1: The first thing you do is connect to the Internet. Since you have a broadband Internet connection, you shouldn't run into any complications.

PURPOSE

Pause at line 10. What is the purpose of the following section of the document?

_____
_____
_____
_____

FORMAT

In the podcasting terminology list, why are the terms in **boldface type**?

_____
_____
_____
_____

SEQUENCE

Beginning on line 26, numbered **run-in subheadings** introduce the steps for downloading a podcast. What type of sequence is used in these technical directions?

_____
_____
_____
_____

The Basics of Downloading a Podcast

FORMAT

Re-read lines 29–36. What kind of information is given in parentheses?

_____
_____
_____
_____
_____
_____
_____
_____

SEQUENCE

The rules of thumb for downloading a podcast are in a **point-by-point sequence**. Why is that type of sequence appropriate for this information?

_____
_____
_____
_____
_____
_____
_____
_____
_____
_____

Step 2: Next, download podcasting subscription software. (You'll need podcasting subscription software to browse the list of podcasts available.) There are many versions of subscription software available as free downloads. Look on the Web site of a radio station that offers podcasts for instructions on how to download its subscription software. (You can also use an Internet search engine to find podcasting subscription software.)

Step 3: Find the show you want (mine!). Search for "Talib's Weekly Update" in the directory of the subscription software.

Step 4: Click on the appropriate link to download my show. It will be saved in the form of an MP3 file, which most computers are able to play. You will probably want to save the file in a convenient place, such as a folder on your desktop.

Step 5: After you've downloaded and saved my show, click on the file to play it. You can listen to the show through speakers or headphones connected to the computer.

Talib hopes that his directions to his family are clear and concise. However, he knows some problems may arise. To make his family's experience as easy as possible, Talib also passes along some helpful tips:

Podcasting Rules of Thumb

- **Podcasts are free.** You can listen to my podcast free of charge. All the radio podcasts I listen to are free as well.
- **Taking my show with you.** You don't need a portable digital music player to listen to podcasts; it's just as easy to listen on a computer. But if you want to listen to my podcast on the bus or train, simply attach your portable music player to your computer and the podcast will be added to the portable music player automatically.

322   Part 2   Reading Informational Texts

- **Subscribing is easy.** Rather than downloading "Talib's Weekly Update" yourself every week, you can have it downloaded to your computer automatically by subscribing to the podcast. Simply click on a "subscribe" link on the podcast software's directory. Once you've subscribed, the podcast subscription software will search the Internet regularly and download each new show it finds.

- **I can't hear you!** One problem I've encountered with podcasts is that I'll subscribe to a show but when I try to listen to it, I don't hear anything. If this happens to you, verify that the correct audio file is downloaded to your computer. You may need to update the settings in your podcasting software to make sure it's capable of receiving subscriptions. After that, check that a new podcast has been posted.

CLARIFY

Re-read lines 60–66. What will happen after Talib's family subscribes to his podcast?

PURPOSE

What is the purpose of the information in the last bullet point?

SKILLS PRACTICE

The Basics of Downloading a Podcast

SKILLS FOCUS

Reading Skills
Analyze the purpose and structure of technical documents.

Structure and Format Chart Once you familiarize yourself with the structure and format of a technical document, you can locate information quickly and easily. Fill out this chart after reading "The Basics of Downloading a Podcast."

Main Headings (What are they?)	Run-in Subheadings (Give two examples from each section.)
Bulleted List (What information does it convey?)	Numbered List (What information does it convey?)

324 Part 2 Reading Informational Texts

Skills Review

The Basics of Downloading a Podcast

COMPREHENSION

Reading Comprehension   Answer each question below.

1. What is an MP3?

2. What two things must Talib's family do before finding "Talib's Weekly Update" in a podcast directory?

3. How can Talib's family play the podcast after downloading and saving it?

4. How much does Talib's podcast cost?

5. Where will Talib's family find a "subscribe" link to subscribe to his podcast?

Before You Read

FUNCTIONAL DOCUMENT

Audio Help

Have you ever needed help with a computer-related problem? Perhaps you called a tech support phone number for assistance. Many software companies and online services allow you to fill out a form and request help online instead of calling in. If you don't like waiting on hold for the next available technician, this option may be for you. Besides, sometimes it's the only one available. Talib had to use the following online form, which is meant to be easily understood and completed, to resolve a problem. Does the form seem clear and logical to you?

INFORMATIONAL FOCUS: FUNCTIONAL DOCUMENT

Forms such as this one are useful functional documents for people having trouble with online services.

- A variety of text features are used, such as boldface and italic type, drop-down lists, boxes to check, and clickable buttons and links, to make the document clear and accessible.
- Information is presented in the logical sequence most appropriate for clear understanding, such as **step-by-step** or **point-by-point sequence**.
- Form fields are labeled appropriately to indicate where information should be entered.

TERMS TO KNOW

Boldface—dark, heavy type.
Italics—type that slants to the right.
Drop-down list—a list of choices revealed by clicking an arrow button.
Form field—a place on a form where information is input.
Logical sequence—a sequence that makes sense.
Point-by-point sequence—a sequence that lists items in no particular order.
Step-by-step sequence—a sequence that tells what to do first, second, third, and so on.

SKILLS FOCUS

Reading Skills
Understand the purpose and structure of functional documents.

Audio Help

Talib became interested in podcasting after listening to a radio show made by one of his classmates and aired on a teen news radio station. When he couldn't hear a show he had subscribed to, he used the audio help form from the radio station's Web site to have his questions answered.

Audio Problem Report Form

If you have experienced difficulty with the station's podcasts and cannot find an answer to your problem on our <u>Audio Help pages</u>, please fill out the following form so that we may try to help you.

Fields marked with an asterisk (*) are required.

Which audio service is causing a problem?
* Audio type [--] ⬍

On which page did you try to play audio? (paste in a link from your browser)
* URL [   ]

* Type of problem (check all that apply)
  ☐ unable to connect
  ☐ connection fails
  ☐ poor quality
  ☐ broken link
  ☐ keeps buffering

When did this happen? [   ]

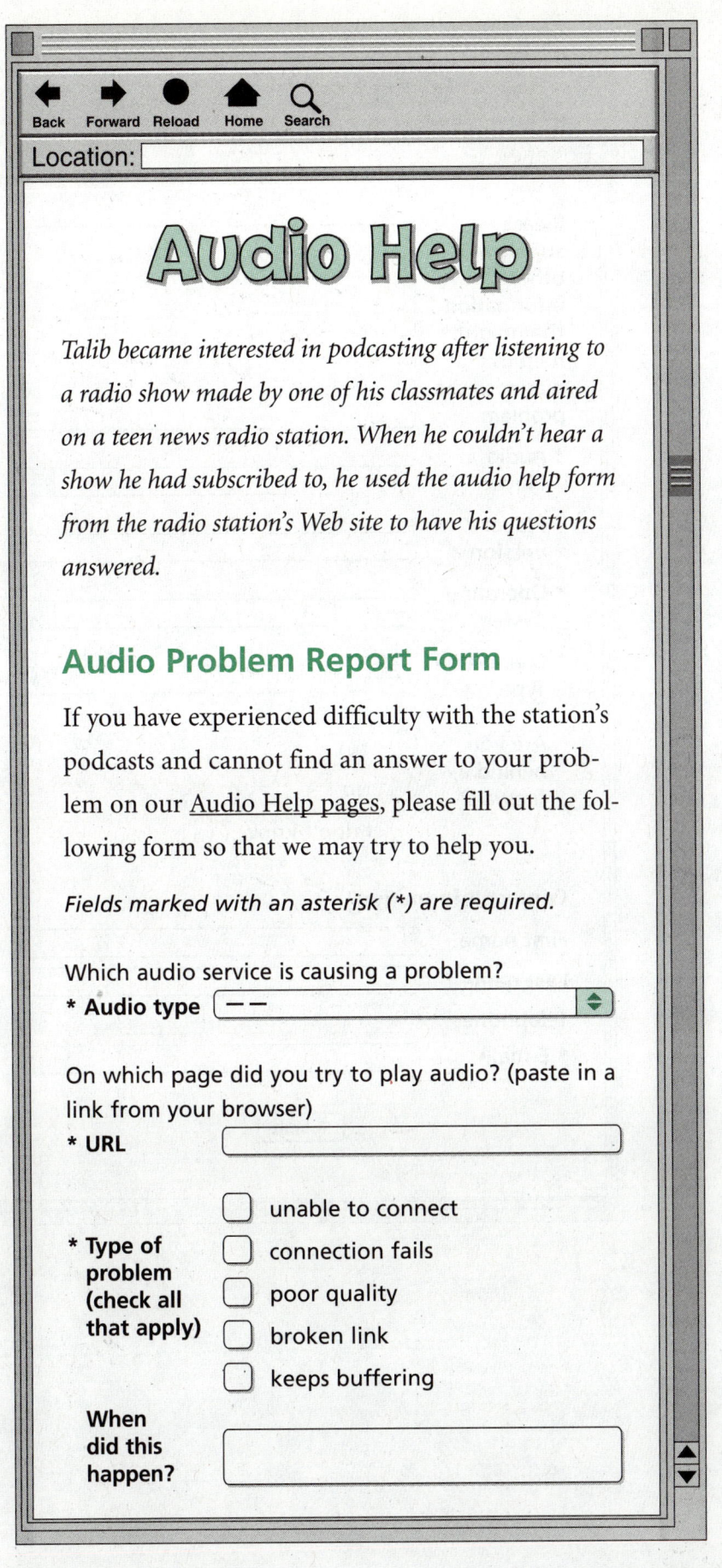

TEXT FEATURES

In the paragraph under "Audio Problem Report Form," why is the text "Audio Help pages" underlined?

PURPOSE

What are the up-and-down arrows to the far right of the "Audio type" field used for? Why don't the other fields on this page have them?

SEQUENCE

How do you know the items in the "Type of problem" checklist are in **point-by-point sequence**?

Audio Help 327

EVALUATE

Is the top of this page the most logical place for the "other information" field located there? Explain.

_____
_____
_____
_____

CLARIFY

How does Talib know which fields he *must* fill in? Why do you think certain fields are required?

_____
_____
_____
_____
_____

INFER

How did the radio station's staff *most probably* contact Talib after he filled out the form? Explain.

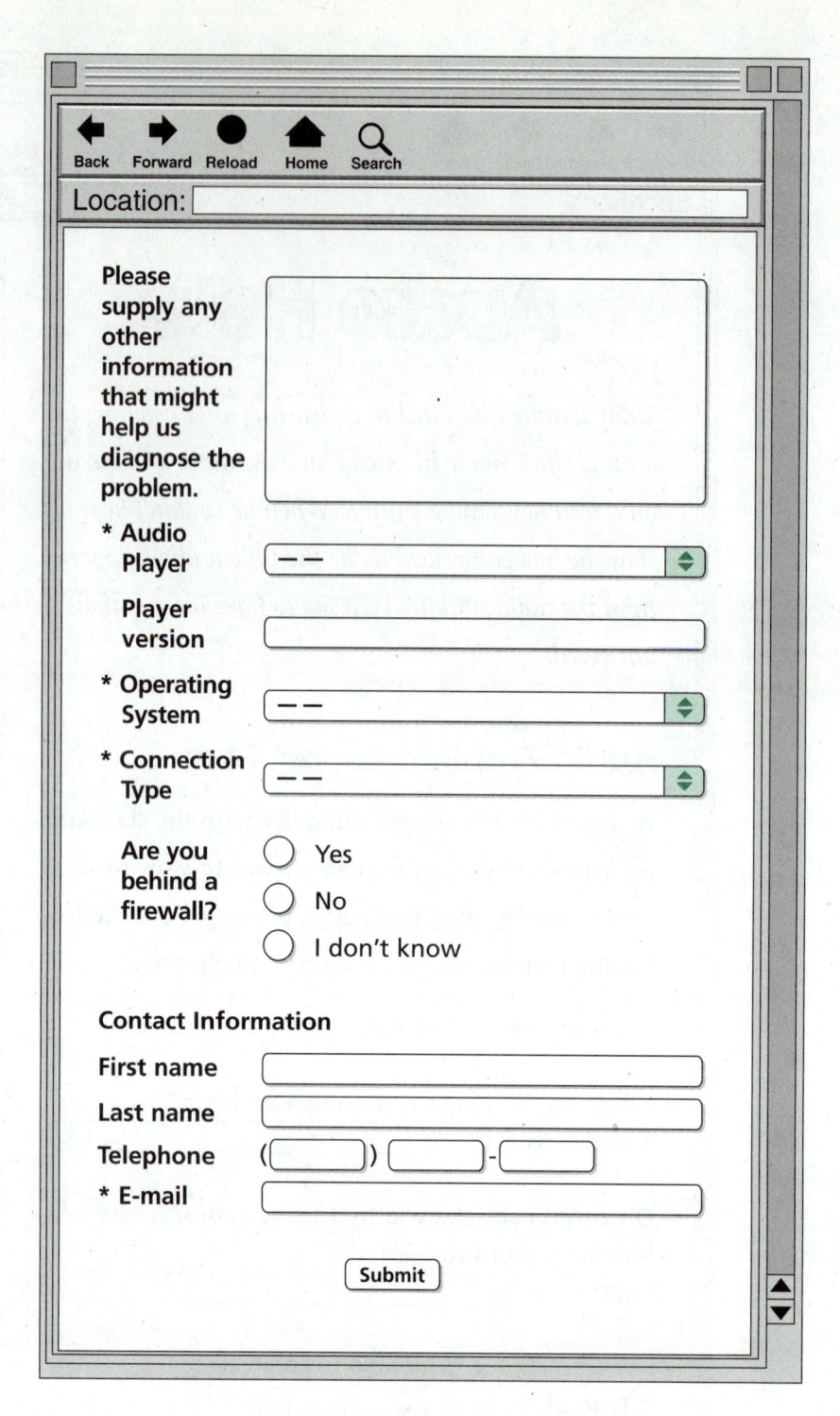

_____
_____
_____
_____
_____

Back Forward Reload Home Search

Location: _____

Please supply any other information that might help us diagnose the problem.

[text area]

* Audio Player   [-- ▼]

Player version   [_____]

* Operating System   [-- ▼]

* Connection Type   [-- ▼]

Are you behind a firewall?
○ Yes
○ No
○ I don't know

Contact Information

First name   [_____]
Last name   [_____]
Telephone   (___) ___-___
* E-mail   [_____]

[Submit]

---

328   Part 2   Reading Informational Texts

SKILLS PRACTICE

Audio Help

Form Fields Chart Filling out online forms is a fairly simple task, but you do need to be sure to fill in the required information (or you'll get an error message) and to place the information in the correct fields. In the chart below, give the most appropriate field labels for the given information, and then tell whether the information is required or not. The first one has been done for you.

SKILLS FOCUS

Reading Skills Understand the purpose and structure of functional documents.

Information	Where to Place It (Field Label)	Required?
Talib	"First name"	No
talib@talibspage.net		
podcast		
dial-up connection		
It happened this morning.		
Version 3.1		
I have been unable to hear my favorite show, "Talib's Weekly Update," and I've already checked that my podcast software settings are correct. Please help!		

Audio Help 329

Skills Review

Audio Help

COMPREHENSION

Reading Comprehension   Answer each question below.

1. How did Talib first become interested in podcasting?
   _____
   _____
   _____

2. What should be placed in the field labeled "URL"?
   _____
   _____
   _____

3. What is the purpose of the checklist?
   _____
   _____
   _____

4. What's displayed in the drop-down lists before a selection is made?
   _____
   _____
   _____

5. What four pieces of information can you enter in the "Contact Information" section?
   _____
   _____
   _____

Before You Read

BIBLIOGRAPHY

Citing Internet Sources: Podcasts

With the vast amount of information available on the Internet, researching topics is a lot easier than it used to be. You can use your school, library, or home computer to search the Internet for databases and Web sites. However, you do need to be extra careful that the sites you use for research are reputable. If you prepare a report on your research, you'll need to include a bibliography, or *Works Cited* list, like the following one that Talib put together. You'll notice that most of Talib's citations are several lines long. Citations for Internet sources generally require more information than citations for print sources.

INFORMATIONAL FOCUS: DOCUMENTATION

The following *Works Cited* is a listing of Internet resources on the topic of podcasting.

- The citations are listed alphabetically by author or title, following the style of the Modern Language Association.
- The electronic address (URL) is listed last in each citation.
- The date the Web site was accessed comes right before the URL.

TERMS TO KNOW

Bibliography—a list of sources of information on a subject, also called *Works Cited*.
Citation—an entry in a list of sources on information on a subject.
Source—a book, document, or person that provides information.
URL—Uniform Resource Locator; a site's Internet address.

SKILLS FOCUS

Reading Skills
Understand how to document sources in a *Works Cited* list.

Citing Internet Sources: Podcasts

As Talib continues to work with podcasting, he becomes more and more convinced that it is the future of broadcasting technology. When he is given an assignment to write about a topic of his choosing, he decides the subject of his report definitely will be podcasting. He focuses on students' and adults' listening to and watching podcasts to get information that they used to find through television, radio, and newspapers. Here is the *Works Cited* list from Talib's report.

Podcasts can be broadcast on portable music players like this one.
©Marianna Day Massey/ZUMA/CORBIS

Works Cited

"Catch Your Favorite Public Media." Pubcatcher. 2006. 13 Apr. 2006 <http://www.pubcatcher.org/>.

"Edinburgh CityGuide Podcast." Visitscotland.com. 2002–2006. 14 Apr. 2006 <http://www.visitscotland.com/sitewide/edinburghpodcast>.

LeMoult, Craig. "Podcasting Craze Spreads to Children's Programming." Columbia News Service. 28 Feb. 2006. 5 Apr. 2006 <http://jscms.jrn.columbia.edu/cns/2006-02-28/lemoult-kidpodcasts>.

Lieberman, David. "Papers Take a Leap Forward, Opening Up to New Ideas." USA Today. 30 Jan. 2006. 8 Apr. 2006 <http://www.usatoday.com/tech/news/techinnovations/2006-01-30-newspapers-change_x.htm>.

Natl. Public Radio. "NPR Podcast Directory." NPRonline. 2006. 12 Apr. 2006 <http://www.npr.org/rss/podcast/podcast_directory.php?type=help>.

New York Public Radio. "Podcasting @ WNYC." WNYC Online. 31 Mar. 2006. 25 Apr. 2006 <http://www.wnyc.org/podcasting/>.

Russell Educational Consultancy and Productions. "Home, School, and College Podcasts." Podcasts for Educators, Schools and Colleges. 31 Mar. 2006. 24 Apr. 2006 <http://recap.ltd.uk/podcasting/schools/schools.php>.

Skills Review

Citing Internet Sources: Podcasts

COMPREHENSION

Reading Comprehension Answer each question below.

1. In what order are the citations in a *Works Cited* list given?

2. Where does the title of the document go in a citation?

3. How is the URL indicated in a citation?

4. How can you tell where a new citation begins?

5. In the third citation, why is "Podcasting Craze Spreads to Children's Programming" in quotation marks?

Reading Skills
Analyze a *Works Cited* list.

Index of Authors and Titles

Alexie, Sherman 104, *109*
Alligator War, The 150
Appearances Are Destructive 306
Audio Help 327
Autobiography of Malcolm X, *from* The 96

Basics of Downloading a Podcast, The 321

Child of the Americas 177
Citing Internet Sources: Podcasts 332
Collier, Eugenia 56, *69*

Disappearances, The 226
Douglass, Frederick 86, *93*

Espada, Martín 5, *8*

For My Sister Molly Who in the Fifties 12
411 on Your Job Rights, The 313
Freeman, M. 274

Glancy, Diane 182, *183*
Golden Glass 74

Hansberry, Lorraine 244, *267*
How It Feels to Be Colored Me 232
Hughes, Langston 221, *223*
Hurston, Zora Neale 232, *237*

Islam in America 293

Kim, Derek Kirk 44, *48*

Lahiri, Jhumpa 211, *215*
Late-Night Chitlins with Momma 200
Learning to Read and Write 86
Legal Alien 175

Madgett, Naomi Long 187, *188*
Magic Island 170
Mapes, Jennifer 284
Mathabane, Mark 306
Matthew Henson 287
Matthew Henson's Polar Travails 282
Mora, Pat 175, *176*
Morales, Aurora Levins 177, *178*
Museum Indians 36
My Two Lives 211
My Wonder Horse 138

National Geographic Society
    Honors Arctic Explorer 284
Nodi, Syeda Rezwana 299

Offspring 187

Petty, Audrey 200, *206*
Power, Susan 36, *40*
Proud to Wear My Hijab 299

Quiroga, Horacio 150, *163*

Raisin in the Sun, *from* A 244
Real-Live Blond Cherokee and
    His Equally Annoyed Soul Mate, A 21
Reign of the Reader 274
Rosa, João Guimarães 124, *131*

Scliar, Moacyr 116, *119*
Seshadri, Vijay 226, *228*
Smith, Cynthia Leitich 21, *29*
Smith, Patricia 293
Song, Cathy 170, *172*
Superman and Me 104
Super Unleaded 44
Sweet Potato Pie 56

TallMountain, Mary 191, *193*
Theme for English B 221
There Is No Word for Goodbye 191
Third Bank of the River, The 124
Tony Went to the Bodega but
    He Didn't Buy Anything 5

Ulibarrí, Sabine R. 138, *145*

Van Gogh's Ear 116
Villanueva, Alma Luz 74, *79*

Walker, Alice 12, *16*
Without Title 182

X, Malcolm 96, *99*

Youth@Work 315

Vocabulary Development

Pronunciation guides, in parentheses, are provided for the vocabulary words in this book. The following key will help you use those pronunciation guides.

As a practice in using a pronunciation guide, sound out the words used as examples in the list that follows. See if you can hear the way the same vowel might be sounded in different words. For example, say "at" and "ate" aloud. Can you hear the difference in the way "a" sounds?

The symbol ə is called a **schwa**. A schwa is used by many dictionaries to indicate a sort of weak sound like the "a" in *ago*. Some people say that the schwa sounds like "eh." A vowel sounded like a schwa is never accented.

The vocabulary words in this book are also provided with a part-of-speech label. The parts of speech are *n.* (noun), *v.* (verb), *pro.* (pronoun), *adj.* (adjective), *adv.* (adverb), *prep.* (preposition), *conj.* (conjunction), and *interj.* (interjection).

To learn more about the vocabulary words, consult your dictionary. You will find that many of the words defined here have several other meanings.

---

at, āte, cär; ten, ēve; is, īce; gō, hôrn, look, tool; oil, out; up, fur, ə *for unstressed vowels, as* a *in* ago, u *in* focus; ' *as in* Latin (lat''n); chin; she; zh *as in* azure (azh'ər); thin, *the*; ŋ *as in* ring (riŋ)